SELF
EMPOWERMENT
AND YOUR
SUBCONSCIOUS
MIND

Lisa Novak

CARL LLEWELLYN WESCHCKE is Chairman of Llewellyn Worldwide Ltd., one of the oldest and largest publishers of New Age, Metaphysical, Self-Help, and Spirituality books in the world. He has a Bachelor of Science degree in Business Administration (Babson), studied Law (LaSalle Extension University), advanced academic work toward a doctorate in Philosophy (University of Minnesota), has a certificate in clinical hypnosis, and honorary recognitions in divinity and magical philosophy.

He is a life-long student of a broad range of Metaphysical, Spiritual, and Psychological subjects, and studied with the Rosicrucian Order and the Society of the Inner Light. After corresponding with Gerald Gardner and several of his associates in the late 1950s and early 1960s, he became known for holding the "Weschcke Documents" including a carbon copy of Gardner's own *Book of Shadows*.

He is a former Wiccan High Priest and played a leading role in the rise of Wicca and Neo-Paganism during the 1960s and 1970s. Author Donald Michael Kraig has referred to him as "the Father of the New Age" because of his early and aggressive public sponsorship of new understanding of old occult subjects. In the fall of 1973 Weschcke helped organize the Council of American Witches and became its chairperson. Weschcke rightfully prides himself on having drafted "The Thirteen Principles of Belief" Statement, one of the cornerstones of modern Wicca. This document went on to be incorporated into the U.S. Army's handbook for chaplains.

While no longer active in the Craft, he retains ties to the Wiccan and Neo-Pagan communities through Llewellyn. He was also, for a time, Grandmaster of Aurum Solis, an international magical order founded in Great Britain in 1897. He withdrew from the order in 1991, and is not actively affiliated with any group at the present time.

Warren H. McLemore

Joe H. Slate holds a Ph.D. from the University of Alabama, with post-doctoral studies at the University of California. Dr. Slate was appointed Professor Emeritus in 1992, after having served as Professor of Psychology, Head of the Division of Behavioral Sciences, and Director of Institutional Effectiveness at Athens State University in Alabama. He is an Honorary Professor at Montevallo University and former Adjunct Professor at Forest Institute of Professional Psychology. Dr. Slate is a licensed psychologist and member of the American Psychological Association. He is listed in the National Register of Health Service Providers in Psychology and the Prescribing Psychologist's Register.

As head of Athens State University Psychology Department and Director of Institutional Effectiveness, he established the University's parapsychology research laboratory and introduced experimental parapsychology, biofeedback, hypnosis, and self-hypnosis into the instructional and research programs into the curriculum. His research includes projects for the U.S. Army Missile Research and Development Command and the Parapsychology Foundation with funding from the U.S. Army, the Parapsychology Foundation of New York, and numerous private sources. He is founder of the Parapsychology Research Institute and Foundation (PRIF) (over 500 members) which has endowed scholarship programs in perpetuity at both Athens State University and the University of Alabama as well as undertaking research projects in dream work and mind/body health.

His official research topics included: Rejuvenation, health and fitness, the human aura, psychotherapy, reincarnation, precognition, retro-cognition, telepathy, clairvoyance, psychokinesis, objectology, numerology, astral projection, sand reading, crystal gazing, dowsing, dreams, the wrinkled sheet, table tipping, discarnate interactions, psychic vampires, hypnosis, self-hypnosis, age regression, past-life regression, the afterlife, pre-existence, the peak experience, natural resources, learning, problem solving, and the subconscious, to list but a few.

SELF EMPOWERMENT
AND YOUR
SUBCONSCIOUS MIND

Your Unlimited Resource for Health,
Success, Long Life & Spiritual Attainment

CARL LLEWELLYN WESCHCKE
JOE H. SLATE, PH.D.

Llewellyn Publications
Woodbury, Minnesota

First Edition
First Printing, 2010

Cover art © Digital Vision Ltd./SuperStock
Cover design by Lisa Novak
Editing by Connie Hill
Interior illustrations by the Llewellyn Art Department

Llewellyn is a registered trademark of Llewellyn Worldwide Ltd.

Library of Congress Cataloging-in-Publication Data

Weschcke, Carl Llewellyn, 1930–
  Self empowerment and your subconscious mind : your unlimited resource for health, success, long life, and spiritual attainment / by Carl Llewellyn Weschcke, Joe H. Slate. — 1st ed.
     p.   cm.
  Includes bibliographical references (p.   ) and index.
  ISBN 978-0-7387-2301-3
  1. Success—Psychic aspects. I. Slate, Joe H. II. Title.
  BF1045.S83W47 2010
  154.2—dc22   2010023648

Llewellyn Publications
A Division of Llewellyn Worldwide Ltd.
2143 Wooddale Drive
Woodbury, MN 55125-2989
www.llewellyn.com

Printed in the United States of America

Other Books by Joe H. Slate, Ph.D.

Aura Energy for Health, Healing & Balance
Beyond Reincarnation
Psychic Vampires
Rejuvenation
Connecting to the Power of Nature

Also by Carl L. Weschcke and Joe H. Slate, Ph.D.

Psychic Empowerment for Everyone
Self-Empowerment through Self-Hypnosis

Forthcoming by Carl L. Weschcke and
Joe H. Slate, Ph.D.

The Llewellyn Complete Book of Psychic Empowerment
Doors to Past Lives

Forthcoming by Carl L. Weschcke and
Louis Culling

Dream E.S.P.
The Pristine Yi King
The Manual of Sex Magick

CONTENTS

PREFACE: *Self-Empowerment—You Are the Captain of Your Own Ship* XIII

INTRODUCTION: *Subconscious Knowledge— Power and Challenge* 1

CHAPTER ONE: THE PERSONAL, CULTURAL, AND COLLECTIVE NATURE OF THE SUBCONSCIOUS 7

CHAPTER TWO: THE SUBCONSCIOUS: *A Storehouse of Personal Experience From Preexistence to the Present* 29

CHAPTER THREE: THE SUBCONSCIOUS: *A Repository of Dynamic Processes, Functions, and Mechanisms* 39

CHAPTER FOUR: INTERFACING CONSCIOUSNESS WITH THE SUBCONSCIOUS 47

CHAPTER FIVE: THE SUBCONSCIOUS MIND: *Your Resource for Problem Solving, Creativity, Mental and Physical Health, Rejuvenation, and Psychic Powers* 65

CHAPTER SIX: THE THERAPEUTIC POWER OF SUBCONSCIOUS KNOWLEDGE 87

CHAPTER SEVEN: SPIRITUAL RELEVANCE OF THE SUBCONSCIOUS: *A Doorway to Spiritual Realities and Interaction with the Spirit Realm* 99

CHAPTER EIGHT: DREAMS— GATEWAY TO THE SUBCONSCIOUS 111

CHAPTER NINE: THE EMPOWERMENT REWARDS OF
SUBCONSCIOUS KNOWLEDGE 125

CHAPTER TEN: THE SUPER-CONSCIOUS MIND 135

APPENDIX: *Self-Empowerment and Self-Hypnosis* 153

GLOSSARY AND SUGGESTED READINGS 161

INDEX 219

PREFACE
Self-Empowerment—
You Are the Captain of Your Own Ship!

Your Destiny is in Your Own Hands!

You can be in charge of your life. That's the way it is supposed to be. It may not seem that way because you started in life basically accepting what came your way. Your mother fed you and provided for your needs. Your father provided other of your needs. Life mostly continued to happen, even when you started school. Sure, you may have asserted yourself with various demands and wishes for this or that, but little if any of it was a truly original thought from your developing Conscious Mind. Essentially, things happened according to a pre-established script.

It wasn't accidental. At birth, you brought forward physical and psychological <u>karma</u> codes that *pre-onditioned* most of your childhood development, even on into much of your adult years.

Perhaps it seems almost unbelievable, but until you gain understanding of these codes and how they influence your life, and then learn techniques to change them, or to retract some of them and add new ones, you are going to basically follow a destiny pattern you brought with you that includes the genetic heritage from your parents (and their ancestors) and the psychological codes loaded into your Subconscious Mind reflecting the cultural patterns of your heritage as well as those of your birth culture, and the karmic instructions carried over from previous lives.

These physical and psychological codes are programs of information and instruction that act as the prime determinants of your developing life from birth onward. Yes, your parents' love and guidance, your education and environment, the influences from the Big World "outside" (everything from climate changes to political and economic developments), and even some influences from "inside" (from the Universal Consciousness through your Subconscious Mind) will bring change to your Destiny seemingly beyond your control—*until your learn differently!*

Why stay a <u>victim</u> of Fate when you can, and should, <u>be in command?</u> You should be the Captain of Your Own Ship. One of the primary goals of your life up to adulthood is training your Conscious Mind to <u>manage</u> the amazing powers and skills of your Subconscious Mind. Until you do that, you will remain unaware of those influences coming unbidden from your Subconsciousness.

ALL IS CONSCIOUSNESS

Everything has a beginning. Your beginning—the creation of the world, of life, and even of the Universe—had a starting point. And behind all that is manifest, we acknowledge the need for something else largely indefinable no matter that we call it: the Great Unmanifest, God or gods, the Force, Mother/Father Creator, the Ultimate Source, or the Will of God.

In the beginning is the Word: Consciousness. Through the act of Will—that which initiated the Beginning—consciousness is filled with information and instruction. Simultaneously, we have Energy and Matter. And with Consciousness, Energy, and Matter, we have Life!

Everything is Alive! From the beginning, there has been continuing growth; with growth there has been evolution; with evolution we see a Plan in manifestation. There is no place or condition where there is not life and consciousness and evolution. Even in dirt and sand, in stone and rock, in water and air and space, there is life, consciousness, and evolution. Think about a vein of gold, for example. *Did that happen at the moment of creation?* No, the gold grew because it has life and consciousness. It grew within stone, and the stone, also alive and conscious, welcomed the presence of living gold.

Nature is alive. Planet Earth is alive—and that includes the entire electromagnetic system that reaches out from the planet's core to the Moon and beyond. The Solar System is alive, and with it vast fields of energy connect from all planets and other solar bodies to the Moon and Earth, and the inhabitants of Earth. We are part of the Whole, and the Whole is within us.

Everything is alive, and everything is connected through energy and consciousness. Nothing is isolated. But the human person is unique in that we are intended to move from unconscious participation in the global life to individual self-conscious self-expression under the self-direction of our individual Conscious Mind. It is through Mind that we as individuals are intended to grow to become more than we are, to become Whole Persons developing all our innate powers and fulfilling the Super-Conscious Mind existing now only as potential. It is the Super-Conscious Mind, as Manager of the whole personal consciousness complex—reaching out as needed to the Subconsciousness and Universal Consciousness—that fully unites with the Conscious and Subconscious Minds to become the vehicle for the Soul.

Self-direction calls for acting with awareness of the consequences of our decisions. That means working with Intelligence, through Learning and Responsibility. We are created in God's image, with the power of individual Will. But the exercise of Will carries with it the responsibility to act with knowledge of the consequences and the obligation to work within the pattern of a Plan. Even that expression, "Not my Will, but Thine," reminds us to work with knowledge and understanding of the Plan.

THE SOURCE OF HUMAN KNOWLEDGE AND EXPERIENCE

With the obligation to act with intelligence and awareness of consequences comes the natural question of where to go for knowledge.

In our modern world, we have an ever growing resource of information available to the Conscious Mind—in education, in books and libraries, and even with an intelligent and wise use of the Internet. In addition, *we have the ability to <u>consciously</u> probe the Subconscious for the cumulative history, knowledge, and wisdom, of anything we need to know.*

The Subconscious Mind normally is an unconscious retainer of experience, repressed memories, and the accumulated lore and discoveries of all who have gone before, both human and nonhuman. Commonly, it is only in dreams and inspiration that the flow is reversed, bringing information up from the Subconscious into conscious awareness.

But, you—as Captain of your own ship—can and need to consciously use the great resource of the Subconscious Mind to answer all your needs.

That's what this book is about: to teach you what those resources are, and the many techniques and tools available to you to tap into those resources as easily as you can use a search engine to get particular information from the Internet. In fact, the Internet is a great analogy for understanding the Subconscious and, through it, the Collective Unconscious, and a search engine such as Google is an analogy for the Conscious Mind and its ability to probe for what it needs.

Through intelligent and conscious use of the great storehouse of knowledge contained within and available through the Subconscious Mind, you gain in Self-Empowerment. And it is this that gives the ultimate meaning to your life—that in fulfillment of the Great Plan pronounced in that Beginning Word you become not only fully empowered but a conscious co-creator with the Divine Source of life and purpose of this great planet that is our home.

This is the great and wonderful responsibility we all share, and the great adventure we live to experience: to become more than you are, to become the Whole Person that is your destiny, and to share in the Creative Process.

Carl Llewellyn Weschcke
June 21, 2009

Note: Recently we received the following in an e-mail attachment. No origin was indicated, no ownership or copyright asserted, so we can't give credit. Nevertheless, it makes some interesting points we think worth sharing.

INSTALLING LOVE

Service: Can you install Love?

Customer: I can do that. I'm not very technical, but I think I'm ready to install now. What do I do first?

Service: The first step is to open your Heart. Have you located your Heart?

Customer: Yes, I have, but there are several programs running right now. Is it okay to install while they are running?

Service: What programs are running?

Customer: Let me see, I have Pasthurt.exe, Lowesteem.exe, Grudge.exe, and Resentment.com running right now.

Service: No problem. Love will automatically erase Pasthurt.exe from your current operating system. It may remain in your permanent memory, but it will no longer disrupt other programs. Love will eventually overwrite Lowesteem.exe with a module of its own, called Highesteem.exe. However, you have to completely turn off Grudge.exe and Resentment.com. Those programs prevent Love from being properly installed. Can you turn those off?

Customer: I don't know how to turn them off. Can you tell me how?

Service: My pleasure. Go to your Start menu and invoke Forgiveness. exe. Do this as many times as necessary until Grudge.exe and Resentment.com have been completely erased.

Customer: Okay, I'm done. Love has started installing itself automatically. Is that normal?

Service: Yes it is. You should receive a message that says it will reinstall for the life of your Heart. Do you see that message?

Customer: Yes I do. Is it completely installed?

Service: Yes, but remember that you have only the base program. You need to begin connecting to other Hearts to get the upgrades.

Customer: Oops! I have an error message already. What should I do?

Service: What does the message say?

Customer: It says, "Error 412, Program not run on internal components." What does that mean?

Service: Don't worry, that's a common problem. It means that the Love program is set up to run on external Hearts but has not yet been running on your Heart. It is one of those complicated programming things, but in nontechnical terms it means that you have to love your own machine before it can love others.

Customer: So what should I do?

Service: Can you find the directory called Self-acceptance?

Customer: Yes, I have it.

Service: Excellent, you are getting good at this.

Customer: Thank you.

Service: You're welcome. Click on the following files and then copy them to the Myheart directory: Forgiveself.doc, Selfesteem.txt, Realizeworth.txt and Goodness.doc. The system will overwrite conflicting files and begin patching any faulty programming. Also, you need to delete Selfcriticize.exe from all directories, and then empty your recycle bin afterwards to make sure it is completely gone and never comes back.

Customer: Got it! Wow! My Heart is filling up with really neat files. Smile.mpg is playing on my monitor right now, and it shows that Warmth.com, Peace.exe, and Contentment.com are copying themselves all over my Heart!

Service: Then Love is installed and running. You should be able to handle it from here. One more thing before I go.

Customer: Yes?

Service: Love is freeware. Be sure to give it and its various modules to everybody you are meeting. They will in turn share it with other people, and they will return some really neat modules back to you.

Customer: I will. Thank you for your help.

Service: You're very welcome.

INTRODUCTION
Subconscious Knowledge—
Power and Challenge

You can't see it. You can't touch it. You can, however, feel it, and you can talk to it and you can listen to it.

Your Subconscious Mind is your best friend and a mighty resource. It's been with you since before you were even born, and . . . well, forever.

Consciousness itself is universal, timeless, and everywhere. It's often compared to a Great Ocean, a sea with no shores. And, then, each of us is a bit of that universal consciousness. We are separate, yet forever part of the whole.

Your Personal Consciousness that was once part of the Universal Consciousness remains forever connected to it.

Your Personal Consciousness is, at first, only what will later be your Subconscious Mind. "Above" it (but only figuratively) will arise your Conscious Mind and then your Super-Conscious Mind. These all pre-exist in a kind of matrix that becomes filled in with experience and development, and as their structure is completed they too—especially the Super-Conscious Mind—benefit from the continuous connection with the Universal Mind.

There are other elements to your Personal Consciousness that we will encounter later, but these three—sometimes also called *Lower,* *Middle,* and *Higher* Consciousness—concern our work in this book. And, again "above," but only figuratively, we have the Soul, which is not directly part of your Personal Consciousness in the same way, but it is your Immortal Soul that establishes basic guidelines for the structuring of the contents of your Personal Consciousness for each lifetime.

Part of your life goal is to build an interactive "bridge" between the Personal Consciousness and the Soul.

YOUR SUBCONSCIOUS MIND

Your Subconscious Mind remembers every event, every hurt, every joy, every fear, every trauma, every happiness, every fantasy, and every feeling that you've experienced from the moment of conception in this life. And, as you will discover, you have memories of previous lives and times between lives, all the way back to some beginning of which we have no understanding.

We will discuss these early memories through childhood later because some of them still can affect you negatively with stress, persistent but not understood fears, and even powerful fantasies born out of misunderstood observations.

What we want to establish in this introduction is just what a wonderful and powerful resource you have in your Subconscious Mind, its memories, and its continuous connection with Universal Conscious through what is called the *Collective Unconscious.*

THE COLLECTIVE UNCONSCIOUS

The Collective Unconscious is more than a repository of memories and a collection of knowledge sometimes referred to as the *Akashic Records.* Through the Subconscious Mind's connection to our Universal Consciousness, we each come into contact with collective cultural, racial, mythic, and even planetary memories, and more importantly, the world of Archetypes that form intimate parts of our *Psyche*—that function of the Personal Consciousness that <u>expresses</u> the *feeling* of inner selfhood.

Because of the importance of the Collective Unconscious as a resource, to which a search-engine like Google is a very inadequate comparison, I want to add a little more detail here.

Within the Collective Unconscious, we can access the memories of all of humanity, and perhaps of more than humans. The contents of the collective unconscious seem to progress from individual memories to universal memories as the person grows in his or her spiritual development and integration of the whole being. There is some suggestion that this progression also moves from individual memories through various groups or small collectives—family, tribe, race, and nation—so the character of each level is reflected in consciousness until the individual progresses to join in group consciousness with all humanity. This would seem to account for some of the variations of the universal archetypes each person encounters in life.

We will speak more of these memories and the functions of the archetypes later.

THE SUBCONSCIOUS MIND AND THE COLLECTIVE UNCONSCIOUS

It is through the relationship of the Subconscious Mind to the Collective Unconscious that many facets of the *Personality*—that portion of the Personal Consciousness that we feel to be our self, including the *Ego* and the *Psyche*—develop.

I don't want to burden our discussion with a lot of terminology, but there are many psychological terms you will encounter or have encountered that will sometimes seem different than our usage. What we really need to recognize is that many of these terms do not actually describe "things" so much as they do "functions." Just as a hand can be described as a *fist*, or an *open palm*, or a *light hand* or a *heavy hand*, and so forth—these describe functions of the hand. You don't have a fist, but you have a hand that can function as a fist.

So it is that a function of your Personality is described as the *Ego*—that which <u>confronts</u> the outer world. Another function is described as the *Psyche*—that which <u>expresses</u> the feeling of selfhood.

In this same regard, the Subconscious Mind is also called the *Unconscious,* and the *Personal Unconscious.* And, unfortunately, some writers have confusingly identified it as the *Soul.*

For our discussion, the Subconscious Mind is the *lower* part of the Personality containing forgotten and repressed feelings and memories; those feelings that make up the fundamental Belief or Operating System that filters Reality to our perceptions of the world; that collection of guilt feelings called the "Shadow"; the "Anima" or "Animus" collection of feelings representing our idealization or fear and sometimes even hatred of the opposite gender; and the various Archetypes and Mythic images formed through the history of human experience, all of which can operate as doorways or gates to the astral world and connect to the higher or super-consciousness. The Subconscious Mind is also home to our instincts and the autonomic system that cares for the body and its operation.

The Subconscious Mind is never asleep and is always aware, and while it normally functions below the threshold of consciousness it can be accessed by various techniques including meditation, hypnosis and self-hypnosis, prayer, ritual, automatic writing, forms of divination including the Tarot, and dreams and other contacts during sleep.

> *The subconscious is not only a content domain but a dynamic constellation of processes and powers. It recognizes that the wealth of our subconscious resources is complementary to consciousness rather than counteractive. It's a powerful component of who we are and how we function* (from Slate and Weschcke: *Psychic Self-Empowerment for Everyone,* Llewellyn, 2009).

THE DEVELOPMENTAL PROCESS

From even before birth, we grow into our *Psyche* just as we also grow into our *Psychic Potentials,* which we will also discuss later.

Our childhood experiences are the foundation of the Personality, but we live most of our lives as adults and not as children. As the Bible says, we have to put aside childish things (and even many perceptions of our young adulthood) and learn to see and think as an adult. But, to put our childish ways behind sometimes requires our conscious remembering and recognition of those childhood perceptions in order to see them freshly as an adult.

After all, you don't want to spend your adult life as a *Big Baby!* Yet, when you see news of barroom fights, child molestation, rape, road rage, mass shootings and suicides, sports violence and violent demonstrations, and more—not to even get into the matter of mass terrorism, piracy on the high seas, dictators who are responsible for mass murder and genocide, and demand for nuclear weapons—you realize the terrible consequences that can be associated with the adult child.

But, as an adult, you can relieve your *inner child* of those childish terrors, fears, and misperceptions that in those few cases have turned good people into monsters. You can recall those lost and repressed memories and relieve them of their fearful distortions, and regain the energies and the pure vision of the innocent child. And it is not just big and dangerous things that will benefit from your work, but even relatively innocent functions that never grew up that you can now reach and bring into adult consciousness.

Don't blame the Subconscious Mind for any of these bad things. It just does its job of remembering everything. It's up to the adult Conscious Mind to do its job and change childish conditioning into adult strength and wisdom. And, as a knowledgeable adult, it is your responsibility to do so.

THE GOOD BEYOND THE UGLY

Don't harbor any ideas that the Subconscious Mind is a *bad* place. Early psychologists first recognizing these units of Personal Consciousness often considered the Subconscious as a kind of garbage dump, and blamed it for a variety of emotional and physical illnesses—mostly female, since those early pioneers were all male.

The personal memories that fall into the Subconscious Mind are also all the beautiful experiences of love, of delight, of beauty, of personal discovery and adventure, of friendship, of success and reward, and your growing independence as you reached toward maturity.

More than personal memories are those universal memories that allow us to perceive not merely with our own eyes but those of generations past and even of the great philosophers, artists, scientists, and those who have attained spiritual enlightenment. The Subconscious Mind and the Collective Unconscious are the foundation of the greatness of Humanity, the glory of civilization, and the magnitude of our Spiritual future.

As you learn techniques to not merely access the Subconscious Mind but to work with it, you will be able to open doors and windows to the glory of human experience, the knowledge of Nature, and the wisdom of Universal Consciousness.

All this is available to you. You don't need to go to school for advanced degrees or sit at the feet of purported teachers and masters. You, yourself, have the ability to expand your consciousness and become great. There are no known limitations to the potentials of the human person, for we are made in the infinitude of our Creator's image. And it is this, the development of our potentials and their integration into our Whole Person, that is our ultimate purpose in life.

And the wonderful thing is that you need not put aside life and go into some retreat; you don't have to take vows of poverty and chastity, or anything else. It is through living life, through loving and giving, through daily work and aspiration, and the personal experience gained in working with the techniques shown in this book that will lead to your personal attainment.

It's a wonderful journey.

Bon Voyage,
Carl Llewellyn Weschcke

CHAPTER ONE

THE PERSONAL, CULTURAL, AND COLLECTIVE NATURE OF THE SUBCONSCIOUS

THE GREAT MYSTERIES

We have to start by asserting that the Subconscious Mind is a mystery—a very great mystery that has functioned to bring us religious and scientific inspiration, that has brought us great artistic and literary achievement, and that has driven us to explore new worlds of body, mind, spirit, and distant places.

At the same time, the Subconscious has inspired political and religious leaders and ordinary people to commit great horrors—often in the name of their God. The Subconscious Mind has no ethics or morals; it is your Conscious Mind that must make choices and impose order on chaos, develop distinct channels to reliable resources, and otherwise understand and learn that your Subconscious Mind is your key to the infinite resources of the Universe. Helping you to build the relationship between the Subconscious Mind and the Conscious Mind is the purpose of this book.

Consciousness itself is a mystery, and what we as psychologists, scientists, philosophers, metaphysicians, and spiritualists* believe is actually both speculative and pragmatic, and we do not yet have a firm unified theory with carefully established divisions, parts, and definitions.

---

* We are using this term not to identify persons interested in the practice or religion of Spiritualism but rather persons exploring the spirituality of the person, of humanity, and of the Cosmos itself.

But, really, all Life, all Existence, and the entire Cosmos are mysteries and all our science and probing are likewise speculative and pragmatic. If a theory seems supported by observation, experiment, application, and practical experience—*if it works!*—then we assume it to be correct. (Those of us old enough remember that some of yesterday's science is often today's folklore, and some things that were once fictional speculation are among today's science.)

Resolving these mysteries is not only the endless adventure of life, but for each of us it is a path to growth and development. Mysteries will always be with us, and will always challenge us—even when we think we've solved one, another will pop up. And even those previously solved will open up further mysterious dimensions. As the Cosmos is infinite, so are its mysteries, and so is the human drive to grow and understand.

Even physics—seemingly that hardest of sciences and among the oldest—is currently divided between Newtonian physics that seems to apply to big things and quantum theory that applies to sub-atomic things and energy. And within the sub-atomic range of things, there is an apparent split between phenomena that act as "particles" and the same phenomena acting as "waves." Then, there is the even *deeper mystery that indicates that it is the act of observation, and then even more spectacularly, the role of "intention" as in prayer, meditation, or ritual when the will to bring change is expressed, actually working at the most fundamental levels of Energy and Matter that can accomplish the intended change.*

Yes, it is true that the "Ancient Wisdom" and Sacred Literature still do provide answers and techniques to meet Humanity's evolving needs, but not always clearly and concisely enough for the modern user living a vastly more complex life than earlier times' simple subsistence farming, fishing, or hunting. Our vocabulary changes, the surrounding beliefs state things differently, education and experience call for different interpretations, and new science and current events call for contemporary approaches and broad applications rather than the limitations of elitist priesthoods guiding a blindly obedient populace through myth, symbol, and public drama.

Our interest in this book is specific to the Subconscious Mind, but it is important to remember that it is part of the overall Consciousness and there are no rigid demarcations between the levels of our Personal Consciousness that we term Subconscious, Conscious, and Super-Conscious. It is vital that we understand the power of the Subconscious and learn to use it wisely and with *conscious direction*.

THE ANATOMY OF THE BODY OF GOD

Many years ago, this writer had a vision while under hypnosis exploring a personal question. This vision, or experience, of the Great Pyramid may provide us with a good analogy to explore the entire structure of Personal Consciousness. This vision arose from my Subconscious Mind, just as the Pyramid appears to rise out of the Earth itself, and the Personal Consciousness rises out of the Subconscious and the Universal Unconsciousness. Using the Pyramid as an analogy, we will be able to show how the Subconscious Mind shapes answers to questions, and how it employs symbolism to convey its message.

In the vision, I was first standing at the northern base of the Pyramid and then rose part way up its face to the hidden entrance leading to the Grand Gallery. I entered, and moved up into the King's Chamber, lay in the granite coffer, and then floated up through the stone itself to the flat apex at the top. All the while a voice thundered, "And this shall be known as the Anatomy of the Body of God!"

We are told that we are made in God's image: "So God created man in his own image, in the image of God he created him; male and female he created them." (Genesis 1:26-27) Therefore we are to understand that the pattern of our Personal Consciousness was structured by Mother/Father/Creator/Source at the beginning of Existence itself.

We are not using biblical authority in support of this view of Consciousness, but rather to add to the symbolism involved in this analogous interpretation of my Pyramid vision.

Look at the Pyramid (see diagram, page 11) as the entirety of Personal Consciousness and think of this idea that it represents as the anatomy of the Body of God, *which is our own body of consciousness shaping our world of physical, emotional, mental, and spiritual experience.*

THE MYSTERIES OF THE GREAT PYRAMID

What we see today is not the historic Pyramid as originally constructed. There was an outer casing of polished stone about one hundred inches thick that reflected sunlight and even moon- and star-light like a beacon seen for many miles. It is believed that this reflected light could have been visible from the Moon. Unforgivably, this outer casing was pilfered in the fourteenth century by invading Muslims and used in the construction of mosques and other buildings in nearby Cairo.

The construction of the Pyramid remains an engineering wonder: the actual fitting of the stone blocks and the outer casing was near perfection and there still remains mystery about the movement and lifting of the blocks, which would be a challenge even with massive modern construction equipment.

The Great Pyramid is estimated to have 2,300,000 stone blocks weighing as much as 70 tons each. The base of the Pyramid covers 13.6 acres with each side greater than 5 acres in area. With so much stone mass, the interior temperature is a constant 68 degrees Fahrenheit, the same as the average temperature of the Earth itself. The Great Pyramid rises to a height equivalent to a fifty-story building, and has a volume equal to about thirty Empire State Buildings. The structure is perfectly aligned and is almost perfectly level, and probably was level at the time of its building. *How that was accomplished by primitive builders is a huge question.*

The height of the Great Pyramid is 5,449 inches, the same as the average height of the Earth's land mass above sea level. Assuming this was more than coincidence, *how did the ancient builders know that, and why was it important?*

The Great Pyramid lies at the center of all the land mass of the world, dividing it into approximately equal quarters. The north-south axis (31 degrees east of Greenwich) is the longest land meridian, and the east-west axis (30 degrees north) is the longest land parallel on the globe. There is only one place that these can cross, and it is at the Great Pyramid! How did the ancient builders know that? Why was it important to them?

The apparent star alignments related to the four air shafts of the King's and Queen's chambers suggest that the *upper part* of the Pyra-

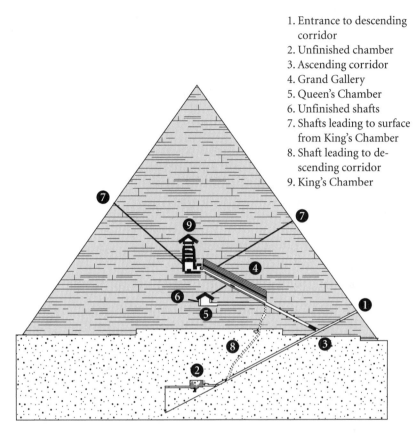

1. Entrance to descending corridor
2. Unfinished chamber
3. Ascending corridor
4. Grand Gallery
5. Queen's Chamber
6. Unfinished shafts
7. Shafts leading to surface from King's Chamber
8. Shaft leading to descending corridor
9. King's Chamber

Figure 1A: The Great Pyramid
Diagram of the interior structures of the Great Pyramid. The inner line indicates the pyramid's present profile, the outer line indicates the original profile.

mid was constructed around 2450 BC, whereas earlier parts may date to five thousand or more years earlier. It is interesting to speculate about the air shafts—if their only function was to bring in air, there would be no reason to precisely align them with particular stars. In fact, only those from the King's Chamber reach outside to bring in air. Those in the Queen's Chamber are blocked by small bronze doors two hundred feet up from the chamber. *Is there a stellar energy transfer? Was the Pyramid constructed over a period of many thousands of years on a consistent plan?*

Note also that the Great Pyramid is the only pyramid with ascending passages and rooms high above ground level. *Why this difference?*

It is important to note that no one was ever buried in the Great Pyramid despite the myth and fiction that it was built as a pharaoh's tomb. In fact, no human remains have been found within any of the seventy or so Egyptian pyramids. The Egyptians buried their dead in graves and underground tombs just like most other people do and have done. *What, then, is the function of these pyramids? Was the Great Pyramid the culmination of a long-range program, or experiment?*

The other major theory is that the Great Pyramid was (*and may still be on the inner planes*) an "initiatory temple." Another theory is that when the outer casing was intact, it served as a kind of giant piezoelectric generator of energies used in religion and magic. Other theories include the Great Pyramid being used as a record of the past and predictions of the future by means of complex calculations and symbolical assignments of events to parts of the different passageways.

There are ever new mysteries to be explored. Recently, employing high technology devices, a new chamber was discovered that had no entrance. Drilling into it, it was found to be filled with "singing sand" mined some five hundred miles away. Another large room has been detected underground between the Great Pyramid and the Great Sphinx, along with suggestions of passages throughout the Giza complex. There are many tunnels between the pyramids and beyond to the east and west. *What was their function? Were they and the above-ground structures part of a unified system or even a machine? Do they indicate a still earlier time for construction back several tens of thousands of years when the entire area had a wet climate?*

Note also the smallness of the entrance corridor that opens suddenly into the Grand Gallery, and from the Grand Gallery there is a small chamber before entering the King's Chamber. *Why such a small passage, and then such a grand one?* Note also the peculiar structures above both the Queen's and King's Chambers. Supposedly, these are some kind of stress relievers to prevent the collapse of the weight above into the chambers, *but considerable doubt about that has been raised.* These names for chambers and passages are not those given in Egyptian literature but the fanciful names given by the European archaeologists, and are purely speculative. *And what is behind those bronze doors in the airshafts of the Queen's Chamber? (The Egyptian authorities have refused to issue permits for their scientific exploration.)*

Perhaps the Great Pyramid's inner "anatomy" symbolizes the entrance to the afterlife—not as a "tomb" for the dead but as a map to afterlife choices. The Egyptian word for *pyramid* may also mean "an instrument or place of ascension." The entrance passage shows a descent to the afterlife encountering three choices: a continued descent to the Subterranean Chamber marking the fast path to reincarnation, the alternate choice to movement to the Queen's Chamber marking the slower path of staying on in the afterlife until a choice is forced between ascending to the King's Chamber or descending by the well shaft to the path of reincarnation. The choice of Ascension to and beyond the King's Chamber takes the self through the rich lessons of the Grand Gallery, the initiatory role of the granite coffer, and the ultimate place of transition through the stone to the apex and union with the Soul.

Amazingly, no one knows for sure what the Great Pyramid, the largest building ever constructed, was built for. Nor does anyone know for sure how it was built, or exactly when. It is believed to have been constructed in several levels, starting perhaps as early as circa 7,000 BC. Erosion studies indicate that the nearby Great Sphinx was built no later than 10,000 BC.

Everything about the Great Pyramid, and the Sphinx in particular, and the other evidences remaining of early Egyptian civilization are at the core of controversies between archeologists, geologists, astronomers, historians, nonacademic researchers, psychics, alternative theoreticians, and others about the age of mankind, the age and origins of civilization, the reality interpretations of myth and physical evidence, the teachings of the major and minor religious traditions centered about the Mediterranean, and what appears to be open-minded common sense. There is a nearsighted prejudice about the age of "modern man" and the beginning of civilization. Academics prefer to ignore any evidence that might alter "established" opinions, preferring to honor "scholars" with a fervor matched only by religious fundamentalists.

For a broad view of nontraditional research related to early Egyptian history, see *Before the Pharaohs: Egypt's Mysterious Prehistory* by Edward F. Malkowski (Bear & Co., 2006)

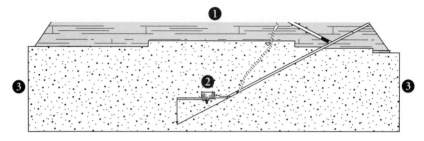

1. The area below the Queen's Chamber, including the "Unfinished Chamber" and the earth itself below the pyramid represents the Subconscious Mind.

2. The entire area from the base of the pyramid and through the earth itself represents the Collective Unconscious, accessible through the Subconscious Mind.

3. The Earth beyond the area of the pyramid, spreading in all directions represents the Collective Unconscious.

The area of the Queen's Chamber and above to just below the King's Chamber represents the Conscious Mind.

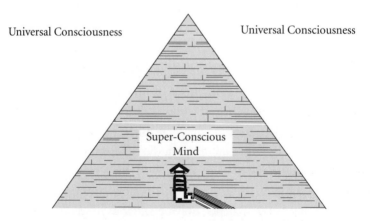

The area of the King's Chamber and above represents the Super-Conscious Mind.

Figure 2A: Sections of the Great Pyramid

The subterranean chamber is the largest and most unusual room of the Great Pyramid. It is located 100 feet below the base of the Great Pyramid and carved from the solid limestone bedrock of the plateau. This large room measures 27 feet from north to south and fifty-six feet east to west. The eastern half of the room is 11 to 13 feet in height, while the western half of the room is a 5'6" step or platform with a channel in the middle that starts at floor level and then tapers upward as it progresses toward the back, western wall. There are two "fins" on top of the platform that run from front to back, and a third "fin" that starts in the middle running to the back. All three fins reach up to near the ceiling.

On the main floor there is a pit set diagonally about five feet from the eastern wall. It starts 6 feet wide and then narrows to 4 feet. The depth drops about 5'6" to a step, and then drops to about eleven feet deep.

The entrance is near the floor at the northeast corner and in the southeastern corner is the entrance to a tunnel that measures 29 inches by 31 inches and runs for 57 feet due south to end at a vertical wall.

As we continue the analogy between the physical Pyramid and the body of consciousness, we must consider these various physical constructs in terms of <u>functions</u> of the body of consciousness.

The following is copied from Wanda Sue Parrot's as yet unpublished "Logos on Consciousness."

> Q. *Before closing this discussion, Logos, can you tell me more about why the Great Pyramid of Egypt can serve to illustrate this Dialogue?*
>
> A. *Within the Great Pyramid of Gizah is the geometrical depiction in stone of the Upper Triangle of the Body Beautiful. Contained within the pyramid are the Queen's Chamber and the King's Chamber, representative of the Pineal and Pituitary within the sacred space of the Body Beautiful.*

The Great Pyramid of Giza is a Book of Truth that inscribes man's history. It reveals where man was, where man is, and where man is going in his unending process of becoming conscious of consciousness.

The Pyramid itself rests on the surface of Earth, which in our analogy we will think of as the whole of Universal Unconscious. The Pyramid itself we will think of as our Personal Consciousness, rising from the surface of the Universal Unconscious. Even though they are not clearly marked as such, there are three levels within the Pyramid structure, just as there are three levels of our Personal Consciousness not precisely demarcated. Keep in mind that there is only one physical entry from the outside, and note the two ways to reach the Subterranean Chamber lying in the Earth itself beneath the Pyramid. There is the single access from outside that first descends toward the Subterranean Chamber, and then rises upward and divides to reach both the Queen's Chamber and the King's Chamber, which is entered through the Grand Gallery.

In addition to the three levels of the Pyramid, perceive that it rests solidly on Earth and reaches deep into the Earth with the Subterranean Chamber, and then, as in my vision when I rose upward through the Pyramid to the surface above it, we really have five levels, one above the other—two of which connect to universal dimensions: the Earth itself below, and the Heavens above.

Always remember that our Subconscious is awake and aware from before physical birth, and continues after physical death.

THE LESSONS OF THE GREAT PYRAMID

According to my vision, (1) the Great Pyramid is to be known as (2) the Anatomy of (3) the Body of God.

1. It is a lesson to us. We are being instructed about the anatomy of the body of God.

2. We are being instructed about the anatomy of our own Personal Consciousness.

3. This Personal Consciousness is made in the image of the body* of God.

In our analogy, the entire area of the Pyramid beneath the Queen's Chamber represents the Subconscious Mind; the Queen's Chamber and the area above it up to the King's Chamber is that of the Conscious Mind, and the King's Chamber and the area above it is the Super-Conscious Mind. Above the Pyramid is the area of the Soul, and the Subterranean Chamber beneath the Pyramid is that area of the Subconscious holding—among other things—repressed memories and feelings. If the analogy holds true, then this "function" of the Subconscious buried within the Universal Unconscious gives us a clue as to how childish (irrational) fears and fantasies can spread from one person to many.

However, it is equally important to recognize that just as the unfinished top of the Pyramid merges into the infinity and energies of the sky above, so the foundation of the Pyramid merges into the whole of the Earth and its energies. As "units" of Personal Consciousness, we are united with the Universal Unconscious at bottom and top, in our foundation and in our aspiration. From the Earth we receive (feminine) magnetic energies and from the Sky above we receive (masculine) electrical energies, and our physical bodies and our bodies of consciousness embrace both.

Considering the Subterranean Chamber as a particular unit of our Subconsciousness holding our repressions and lost memories, it is interesting to note the two passages accessing the Subterranean Chamber. One connects from the area of Middle Consciousness and one connects from the outside world. Some impressions and experiences of the repressions and lost memories sink down from the Conscious Mind and Feelings to the Subconscious, and others reach there directly from the outside as childish misperceptions of such things as sex between parents and fears generated by war and terror.

Remember, also, that this "stone" making up the seemingly solid structure of the Pyramid/Body is pervious: thus, in our analogy, memories and thoughts, strengthened by emotion, can move directly from one level to the next without having to use the open passages.

THE DEVELOPMENT OF THE CONSCIOUS MIND

Up to the age of six or so, the child's psyche is almost all in the area of the Subconscious. It is when the modern child enters school that he or she begins to rapidly build the Conscious Mind, but until he passes through the raging turmoil of puberty and the teen years, the Subconscious is raw and open, and the young adult is ruled mostly by emotion. Only as an adult can the Conscious Mind become dominant.

Whether it becomes dominant, and the extent to which it does, is largely determined by education, training, and development of the conscious Personality.

And it is as an adult that the Grand Gallery is open for the journey to the King's Chamber and then connecting to the Super-Conscious Mind. Note, however, that the route from Middle Consciousness to Higher Consciousness is not direct and it does bring with it contact from the outside world. Once this "ascension" required a priest, teacher, or guru, but now it can come through books and courses of self-study. *Rarely is one able to rise unaided directly from Middle to Higher Consciousness, and above* (symbolically), <u>*through all that stone!*</u> But that way has been traveled by others, and we learn of their techniques from the records they've left for us.

Note also that as we rise through the different levels, the consciousness becomes more and more focused—rising from the very broad base below the Queen's Chamber on through and above the King's Chamber. "Focus" means greater and greater self-control over the different functions of consciousness—from Ego and Psyche, on through the Etheric, Astral, Mental, and Spiritual Bodies. For more information on the psychic structure of the person, please see *Psychic Empowerment for Everybody*, by Slate and Weschcke.

THE FOUNDATION OF PERSONAL CONSCIOUSNESS

At the massive base, itself resting on solid earth, we have the dimension of subconsciousness. Part way up we have the only entrance to the pyramid itself, although we know that there are at least two other small ports from the King's Chamber to the outside.

---

* We need to state that we are not talking about the "physical" body of either man or God. "Body" means the whole of something. Here we are referring to the Body of Consciousness. It is important to understand that Consciousness precedes the Physical, not the other way around. Our physical body does not create consciousness; consciousness creates the physical body from the fertilized ovum.

The entrance opens to a small channel that goes downward a substantial distance beneath the Pyramid to reach the Subterranean Chamber, deep in the Earth itself. Part way down this channel, there is another channel leading upwards to encounter the Grand Gallery that leads to the King's Chamber. At the point where the Grand Gallery starts, there is another passage leading to the Queen's Chamber, which is located almost directly below the King's Chamber. At the same juncture, there is a strange descending passage that winds its way down to the Subterranean Chamber. It seems to have been constructed as an afterthought to the original design.

Now, for the moment, forget everything you think you know historically about the Great Pyramid other than its shape, its immensity (the largest structure on Earth prior to the twentieth-century dams), its age as one of the oldest structures, and its position not only at the center of one of the greatest prehistoric civilizations but at the geographic center of the Earth's surface.

Look once again at the drawing of the Great Pyramid and the breadth of the area beneath the Queen's Chamber that is the upper level of the Subconscious Mind, and then again note the Subterranean Chamber deep in the Earth beneath the Pyramid of Personal Consciousness and the two routes to it.

Also remember that the Earth represents the Universal Unconscious wherein we contact the Collective Unconscious. The contact is through the entire base of the Pyramid, and then also through the deeply buried Subterranean Chamber with its two passageways deviously connecting from the Conscious Mind. Repressed emotions and memories find their way to the Subterranean Chamber where they are held unless consciously released.

At this point it is desirable to assert that each person's Subconscious Mind is <u>permanent</u>. It is part of that which accompanies us from beginning to end, life after life. Within it are memories, not only of this life, but of previous lives and knowledge of the underlying pattern for future lives. Just as the Subterranean Chamber is carved from solid bedrock connecting to the entire planet, so the Subconscious Mind connects not just to the Universal Unconscious but it functions to open our awareness to the Collective Unconscious. More about this later.

There are several different theories about the Subterranean Chamber. It is actually the largest chamber and the most complex in the entire Pyramid. It is 100 feet below the base, and carved out of solid limestone. It is 27 feet wide and 56 feet long. Half the room averages over 11 feet in height, the other half steps up to only 5'6" feet in height. That step has a channel in the middle, and on top of the step are two "fins" that run from front to back, and a third fin starts half way back. Then there is a 6-foot square pit that is either 11 feet deep or 41 feet deep, depending on different researchers. In one corner a tunnel runs for 57 feet and ends at a wall. Everything about it remains a mystery.

What was the Chamber to become? Perhaps it was to be a burial chamber; perhaps it was to be used in an initiatory ritual. Others have suggested there were plans to connect that chamber to a secret chamber beneath the nearby Sphinx.

One of the most interesting theories is that it is <u>not</u>, as it has been called, an "Unfinished Chamber" at all but was actually a technologically sophisticated hydraulic ram pump used in a complex system to raise the stones of the Pyramid's construction, building from the inside out. In this scheme, water from an ancient Lake Moeris fed into a moat around the Pyramid, and from there down the descending passage into the Chamber to power the hydraulic ram.

Still another theory uses the same concept but turns the Subterranean Chamber into a sonic pump that sent sound pulses upward to resonate in the King's Chamber as part of the initiatory experience of the candidate lying within the granite coffer (also called a "sarcophagus"). It should also be noted that the coffer is of red granite, as are the walls of the King's Chamber, and that granite (a quartz mineral) has unusual electrical properties, and that the coffer itself, when struck, rings like a bell.

We are left with more questions than answers, with more mysteries than theories, and puzzle after puzzle.

We don't know the answers, but that doesn't change the symbolic value that the Great Pyramid contains for us. The Subterranean

Chamber, rather than being unfinished, is a sophisticated power center important to the entire Pyramid. In our analogy, this "heart" of the personal Subconscious powers Personal Consciousness. It is like the Serpent Power Kundalini rising from the base chakra of the human spine to sequentially open the other chakras and eventually empower the crown chakra to bring ultimate enlightenment.

The large base of the Pyramid symbolically shows us that the Subconscious Mind is far less focused than the higher levels of consciousness. The Subconscious is largely unorganized and hence its contents are less easily accessed except as we learn particular techniques for doing so. But, at the same time, *it is this huge foundation of the Subconscious that supports the whole edifice of Personal Consciousness.*

THE SUBCONSCIOUS CONNECTION TO UNIVERSAL UNCONSCIOUS

Not only does the base of the Pyramid, our Subconsciousness, rest solidly and precisely on the Earth itself—at the very crossroads of the Land Mass of the planet, evenly divided into quarters of East, West, North and South—but likewise, each of us stands at the center of a personal circle whose boundaries are infinite, while psychologically and metaphysically our personal circle is divided into quarters for East, West, North, and South. Metaphysically, these divisions are symbols that start us on the path of using our Subconscious powers in precise ways.

AS ABOVE, SO BELOW!

We have said we will see the Earth as the whole Universal Unconscious, but this is more than symbolic. The Earth is the source of our physical bodies—*"for dust thou art, and unto dust shalt thou return"* (Genesis 3:17–19 KJV)—but the Earth is also our home within which we have our being. We don't merely live on the surface but within the vast electromagnetic and spiritual field that reaches from the Earth's core to beyond the Moon. This is our Universal Field of Consciousness.

Yes, of course, planet Earth (or "Gaia") is also an intimate part of the Solar System of our Sun and all its planets, asteroids, and fluctuating energy system; and the Solar System is connected to the Galaxy as a whole, and our Galaxy to the Universe—but *it is the Earth that defines our place in the Universal Unconscious.*

Our Subconscious Mind rose out of the field of the Universal Unconscious and remains connected to it. Through those two connections: the Pyramid base resting on the Earth's surface and the Subterranean Chamber deep below the surface, the Subconscious Mind connects to the Universal Unconscious, but most particularly to what we call the "Collective Unconscious"—basically the human memories of everything that ever happened, human knowledge and myth, and those highly energized units of consciousness we know as Archetypes and Gods.

All the many gods we've worshiped and feared live still in the Unconscious, as do the Archetypes, those particular patterns of energized consciousness functioning very much like the images we see in the Major Arcana of the Tarot.

When we make connections with the archetypes or with the deific forms of the gods, we access their unique energies and knowledge. In the same way, we can access collections of knowledge and wisdom almost as if we were in a great library or hall of records. Indeed, metaphysicians refer to this aspect of the Unconscious as the "Akashic Records."

And, likewise, we can contact our own early memories of this current life and of lifetimes before this one.

Everything ever experienced by humans is there in the Collective Unconscious, and can be accessed or recalled by the Conscious Mind with varying difficulty or success through methods of meditation, hypnosis and self-hypnosis, ritual and altered states of consciousness, dreams, and conscious association.

Likewise, everything that exists or that has ever existed, human and nonhuman life, every thought, emotion, fear, and fantasy involves forms of etheric energy. While Good always overcomes Bad, it remains a challenge to distinguish True from False or to separate Fact from Fiction. The system of Kabbalistic correspondences allows us to test and verify our Subconscious perceptions.

Indeed, it is through *organization* of the Unconscious that we bring things of value into conscious awareness. Otherwise it is like an infinitely huge junk shop where no one has an idea where anything is.

THE PERSONAL NATURE OF SUBCONSCIOUSNESS
You were not born with a "clean slate."

Both your physical genes and your Subconsciousness carry codes— programs of information and instruction—that guide your physical and emotional development, and later your mental and spiritual development. Both your genetic and emotional codes reach back into the past to provide the matrix that will become your personality—of which your Subconscious Mind is the foundation.

Even as a baby, your Subconscious Mind establishes your unique personhood, as can be read in a personal horoscope. (I earnestly recommend using a horoscope as an initial step of self-understanding—essential for taking responsibility for your conscious growth and development.)

Day after day, year after year, the growing child adds conscious awareness, memories, and behavior patterns including rules of conduct established by parents, schools, and society. The Conscious Mind becomes dominant, but the Subconscious Mind is always there, always awake, always aware, and always available as a resource.

There is no real barrier between the Conscious Mind and the Subconscious Mind. In dreams, some Subconscious contents rise to the surface of consciousness—only to be quickly lost upon awakening with the Conscious Mind focused outwardly on daily life.

Look again at our Great Pyramid as a symbolic model of Personal Consciousness. Note the broad base of subconsciousness and its connection to the Collective Unconscious and the Universal Unconscious. But also note that as you move upward through the Conscious Mind and the Super-Conscious Mind, the Pyramid narrows and consciousness is more and more focused. The natural direction of that focused awareness is upward. Even the Subconscious is focused upward—its contents occasionally rising into conscious awareness.

Conscious memories fall downward out of awareness into the Subconscious, so it requires some action on our conscious awareness for anything to be recalled from the Subconscious. Something may happen to remind us of the repressed memory of the fantasized "monster in the closet" or the repressed memory of childhood abuse. Other times it is only with a deliberate act of concentration that we can recall lost or repressed memories, or make specific contact with the Collective Unconscious.

Why bother?

Because your Subconscious Mind, through its natural connections to the Collective Unconscious and Universal Unconscious, is the greatest resource you can have! But to use it, you have to reverse the normal upward focus of consciousness and learn techniques to concentrate downward to open select doors in the Subconsciousness. I say "select" because otherwise the contents could be overwhelming. Luckily, there is a natural equivalent to a computer network's "firewall" that normally prevents this blowback.

There are established procedures for accessing most of the personal and other human content of the Unconscious—the great "library" of knowledge and the even greater worlds of myth and the dominions of gods and goddess, past and present. We will be discussing these in other chapters.

It is with the Conscious Mind that we direct our way through these pathways to the resources of the Subconscious, and it is with the Conscious Mind that we develop our potentials and powers leading to the Super-Conscious Mind. Through our Conscious Mind we build on the work and discoveries of those who have gone before us, and continue the great adventure forward.

Truly, the Past is prologue to the ever more glorious future.

THE CULTURAL NATURE OF SUBCONSCIOUSNESS

One of the most wonderful and intriguing aspects of the Subconsciousness is its role in shaping us culturally as definitively as our genes define our body. You may be, for example, an African-American whose ancestors came from Kenya and Nigeria. Along with the physical genes that are reflected in body shape and structure, there are additional codes that reflect patterns in your emotional, mental, and spiritual makeup, and that give access to the ancestral and cultural heritage of your ancestors, right along with your American heritage.

It is this nonphysical transmission of cultural coding that may bring with it a love for the art and song of your compatriots back home, an intuitive understanding of who they are, and even a "feeling" for their history. It is in the Subconscious that we contact the "spirit" of a land and its people.

Isn't this really amazing? Look at how much richer we all are through this growing diversity of heritage. This alone further increases our ability to tap into proven paths in the Subconscious to access expanding lines of knowledge and resources of mind and spirit. Many people in the world are still isolated culturally—often because of rigid religious leadership that sees the outside world as "enemies" and prohibits secular education. Still others teach a prejudiced view of the outside world and deny contact with outside media, restricting education to their particular religious tradition.

We thrive on diversity! Humanity is unique among all mammals in its capacity to adapt to even the most hostile of environments and to eventually overcome cultural prejudices.

It is through the Subconscious Mind that we receive cultural inspiration for art, music, literature, and crafts. Interestingly, we can even use intuitive psychic skills, like psychic touch and psychic vision, to make contact with the cultural heritage and spirit behind an artifact, while participating in the culture through song, dance, drama, literature, etc. with open channels into cultural memories as deeply as you wish to go.

THE LAND SPEAKS

Such contacts are not limited to your ancestral heritage but are as true with the land of your domicile and even with the lands you may visit. The techniques are the same—using touch, participating in native celebrations, exploring the geography, etc. Your Subconscious Mind responds to your expressed interests and the more energy you put in your request, the more you will receive.

In many cases, you will attract exactly what you are looking for, sometimes in the form of clues, but other times more overtly through people expert in those matters.

Some writers refer to this phenomenon as "the law of attraction"—it's almost like entering a subject in an Internet search engine and seeing entry after entry for you to choose from. . . except that your Subconscious Mind, once you learn to use it, is of far greater power and reliability than the search engine.

Our goal is to teach you how to actively program the Subconscious Mind to respond to your direction.

THE COLLECTIVE NATURE
OF SUBCONSCIOUSNESS

We are using terms like the Subconscious and the Conscious Mind, the Collective Unconscious and the Universal Unconscious, and still others to give names to particular functions of our personal consciousness.

For the balance of this chapter we are going to switch to just two words: Conscious and Unconscious. I'll tell you why shortly.

Just think of the great ocean we've earlier referred to as Universal Consciousness, existing everywhere, the source for all that has ever manifested since the Big Bang of original creation. Out of this were birthed land and space, life and death, love and sorrow, and everything else.

But this Universal Consciousness is not "conscious" in the way we think. Being conscious is a "voluntary" function of Mind—which means that it takes time and energy to absorb and store new information, making it consciously available. It takes *conscious* effort, sometimes with concentrated attention, and methods to organize the material in useful ways.

Because each person is a holographic part of the infinite ocean of the Universal Unconscious, it is possible for the whole to be contained in the part.

But, we don't need to try to absorb the whole ocean when, as a holographic part, we can access anything we need from the whole. Instead we need to know what we want, organize our mind just as any other filing system, and develop channels of communication between the Unconscious and Conscious Mind.

A trained mind can access the powers of the universe! A trained mind can focus these powers to accomplish any goal, fulfill every wish. Of course, like anything else, there are strings attached that must be considered, a price that may have to be paid. But with knowledge comes understanding, and the price may gladly be paid in consideration of the reward.

Scientists estimate that we use only 10 percent of our mental capacity, and likewise it appears that 90 percent of the Universe is invisible to us. Could this serve as an analogy for what we can return to calling our Conscious Mind and our Subconscious Mind? The Subconscious is like the Dark Matter of the Universe from which we can make withdrawals to form stars and planets.

The point of all this is to impress upon you the immensity of the Unconscious and the resource to everything within through your personal Subconscious Mind. It is not that we want to absorb all of that immensity into the Conscious Mind, but to understand the nature of the resource and how to access whatever you need from it.

If you train to be a lawyer, you learn that there is an immensity of common law, statutory law, case law, opinions and dissenting opinions—any and all of which may be pertinent to your needs. You have to learn to find what you need. Thankfully, you are aided by commercial firms with services that constantly catalog and analyze the ever-increasing legal universe, and organize it for easier reference.

In the same way, there are systems to organize and make available to you in various ways and formats the hidden, lost, forgotten, secret, long-buried treasures of the Collective Unconscious through your Subconscious Mind. At the same time, as valuable and distinctively useful as these systems are, the most powerful of all is the concentrated force of our Conscious Mind.

Know what you need, and ask for its delivery to you. At the same time, be open to its arrival in the form of dreams, rediscovered memories, visions through meditation, insights arrived at with the help of Astrology or Tarot, the Kabbalah, the processes of ritual magic, or the concentrated focus of the entranced Mind. Many times, having asked for information from the Subconscious, it will "miraculously" appear in the next book you pick up, in casual conversation, in a documentary television program you happen to watch, and other synchronous phenomena.

Ask, and you will receive. Remember that your Personal Human Consciousness is modeled on the Body of God. The Powers of the Universe are yours to learn and earn.

CHAPTER TWO

THE SUBCONSCIOUS:
A Storehouse of Personal Experience From Preexistence to the Present

When does Time start? Well, at the Beginning, of course! Everything started at the Beginning. We don't know much about that except that we wouldn't be here if it hadn't happened.

But, we believe that at this beginning, whether called "the Big Bang" or "at the Beginning was the Word," it was the "Trinity" of Consciousness, Energy, and Matter that began the process that evolved into Life and the Universe we know today. Behind this Beginning Trinity there is, of course, an initiating factor that for convenience, at least, we can call "the Will of God," the "Creator," "Creative Force," or other name. I believe "Will of God" best expresses the concept that there is a Decisive Intelligence behind it all.

And, with Consciousness—which in this discussion we should start speaking of as "the Unconscious"—Time begins. When we speak of the Conscious Mind we will acknowledge that it rises out of the Unconscious.

THE BIAS OF OUR PHYSICAL PERCEPTION

Unfortunately, in their speculations, scientists, theologians, philosophers, and academics have tried to fit things together based on the world as we see it now. They ignore the more likely spiritual origins of life and the universe, and worse, we tend to believe that life arises from the physical universe, and that mind, emotion, and spirit are all products of the physical body.

The world's sacred literature, for the most part, says otherwise. Unfortunately for us in the West, our sacred literature has been censored to fit into a political agenda starting in 312 when the Roman Emperor Constantine issued the Edict of Milan, eliminating hundreds of books previously part of the new Christian religion but unacceptable to Roman policy. In 330, he further defined the new religion by combining it with established Pagan practices, declaring that—among other things—December 25, previously celebrated as the birthday of the Pagan Sun God, would instead be the birthday of Jesus.

Constantine's next step was to purge the new religion of its "Jewishness," and through a further series of councils and edicts still more formerly accepted biblical works were purged to completely make Christianity the uncompromising state religion of Rome.

Even within mainstream Christianity, there are conflicts. The official Catholic version of the Bible contains seventy-three books, while the Protestant King James version has only sixty-six books as approved by the Archbishop of Canterbury in 1885. The remaining five hundred or more books originally accepted as part of Christianity's sacred literature were officially banned, and known copies of some are under official lock and key.

Fortunately, some of these books cast aside by the Roman emperor and the British archbishop are still available and others have been recovered. It is with these mostly Gnostic texts that we perceive that the spiritual dimension of Christianity actually joins with other sacred literature as regards the "Beginning."

Creation moved "down" from the spiritual dimension, creating as it went what we call the Spiritual Plane, and then the Mental, the Astral, and then the Etheric and Physical Planes. In other words, Creation was downward from Spirit to Matter; Evolution is upward from Matter to Spirit.

It should be noted that these planes are not distinctly separate, but exist together. However, the physical and etheric bodies are uniquely joined together. More about that later.

Without time, nothing happens

Time is called the Fourth Dimension (after height, width, and length) and is associated with Space, as you can't have the one without the other.

Within Space/Time, consciousness coalesces into individual units formed "in God's image." Herein we have the *matrix* carrying forward the seeds of humanity. Those individual globes of nascent human conscious slowly gather about them subtle energy and matter as it appears in the cascade started with "God's word"—the idea that sparks Creation. Eventually, a spark of Divine Will, that is the Soul, is established within each globe. Associated with each soul, the "bodies" continue to develop and progressively move toward physical form.

This "involution" from the highest planes of Spirit creates the Spirit Body, the Mental Body, the Astral Body, and—eventually—the Etheric Body, which in turn forms the Etheric/Physical Body.

Please realize that this process I am describing is purely inspirational speculation. I've read what others have written. I've read how the myths and sacred books expressed these ideas many thousands of years ago. I've dreamt images of these globes of consciousness and meditated on them in order to describe the process as simply as possible to avoid debate about the "mechanics" involved. *From our present perspective, we have no way of knowing exactly the steps and stages that proceeded from the <u>Beginning</u> to the start of history. And, really, that doesn't matter. We live in the here and now, but I felt the need to provide a theoretical background to the practical applications we will discuss in the chapter.*

MEASUREMENT AND OBSERVATION: HOW TECHNOLOGY CONDITIONS OUR WORLD VIEW

When we speak of time, we realize we can only perceive it through some form of measurement. At first, presumably, the only measure was the alternations of Day and Night. Then, perhaps, as we became more sophisticated, we perceived the phases of the Moon, and then—perhaps—the declination of the Sun as the seasons progressed.

With these observations, the calendar was born—first as scratch marks on bone, and then more graphically as cave paintings, and then more artistically as wall paintings. And with the inventions of paper and the printing press, the modern calendar used by everybody was born. Time becomes a foundation of daily life.

The calendar is the early stage of technology. As time marches on, we will find more and more that we experience the world through our technology—the measurement of time, the weapons we use to defend ourselves and to hunt, the use of fire to warm ourselves and to prepare food, the use of animal skins to clothe ourselves and to ornament our homes, the invention of pots to collect water and to boil water, on and on to the domestication of animals, the invention of the wheel, the use of metals, and ever onward to greater power and complexity.

It was with the invention of the clock that the measurement of time became more precise and more minute, and our perception of time developed as a flow from the future through the present into the past.

THE RISE OF THE CONSCIOUS MIND

It is with this perception that memory became a major factor of human experience. With memory we have the birth of the Conscious Mind. It is with Conscious Memory that the division between the Conscious Mind and the Subconscious Mind becomes decisive.

Once again, our technology conditions our understanding.

Conscious Memory is mostly sequential. We remember things in the linear fashion in which events happen. We learn things as sequences of numbers, letters, and words. In school we memorize multiplication tables, word lists, spelling lists, history timelines, geographical names and places, science and mathematical equations, grammar rules, and foreign language vocabularies, and we follow logical rules to connect facts and principles.

The Unconscious and the Subconscious Mind remember everything, but without logical structure, without rules and lists.

With our modern technology, we can compare Conscious Memory to the "volatile" memory of your computer stored as RAM on your hard drive. It's only there as long as the computer is turned on—like Conscious Memory is only active while you are awake. "Nonvolatile" memory is always there, even when you turn the computer off. It is stored as ROM on chips, or solid-state storage, smart cards, etc. We can think of Conscious Memory as comparable to Disk Memory and Subconscious Memory as comparable to Solid-State Storage.

HOW DO WE ACCESS MEMORIES?

In the case of our Conscious Memory, we duplicate how we learn. First we put similar things in files that we name by the subject or name of the content, and then organize those files alphabetically into file cabinets and/or on our computer. We list forthcoming events and appointments by date in our date book or pocket planner and in a calendar program on our computer. We compile organized data into reports for analysis and file the results. We develop our analyses into bigger reports and books, and organize them by title. Even our artistic output is recorded, described, given names, and then organized and filed away.

As long as we work logically with established rules, we can access our memories and even find out where we will be on any particular future date and times. Our "disk" memory works with the Conscious Mind.

In the case of Subconscious memories, we have an entirely different situation. Rarely are those memories organized in any objective manner. Even though there are memories of events, an objective question as to what happened on a particular day and time is unlikely to recall the event. Nor do numerical or alphabetical sequences recall factual data.

What the Subconscious relates to is emotions and feelings, and things that may be associated with them. A question like: "*Do you remember what you felt when you fell off the barn roof?*" will almost certainly recall the event in full detail. "Yes, I needed twelve stitches and still carry the scar from landing on that darn pitchfork. And it happened right in front of that girl I was trying to impress. I never saw her again."

A different question, such as "*How many sour-tasting foods can you list?*" can call up a list, but it is because of the association with your emotional reaction to things that taste sour—like sour apples, sour milk, vinegar, lemon, lime, etc. It might not be a complete list of such foods because you will identify only those with which you've had personal experience.

Other questions like . . ..

> *Do you remember your first kiss?*
> *Do you remember the first time you went skiing?*
> *Do you remember the movie* Star Wars*?*
> *Do you remember* Star Trek, *the TV series?*
> *Do you remember being scared?*
> *Do you believe in God?*

will readily call up memories. And, for a time, they will become <u>conscious</u> memories, later to fall back into forgotten memories in the Subconscious.

Some memories will not be so easily recalled because they are too painful or disturbing, and you've unknowingly imposed a censor to keep them buried. Most traumatic childhood memories will heal themselves as you move into adulthood, while others may have so much repressed energy (feelings) holding them from recall that intervention may be required to allow you to fully experience those feelings as a healthy adult. Regression therapy employing hypnosis or self-hypnosis will release the childhood response when the event is reviewed from an adult perspective.

Regression therapy can be applied to traumas in past lives with equal benefit. Because memories of past lives continue in our Subconsciousness, a traumatic event of the past may have a harmful effect in the present life that can be released by recalling it and knowing that it is past and can't hurt you anymore. Sometimes it is necessary to relive the event to release all the muscular tensions and that may call for professional guidance.

Association is one technique for working with Subconscious memories, and sometimes those associations can reach beyond personal memories to bring forth more of the same. In our example of sour foods, you may be able to tap into all the memories of those foods in the Universal Unconscious. Deep meditation is a powerful tool in working in this fashion.

EVERY EVENT HAS MEANING

Unless you are able to go into deep meditation, or learn to make use of other techniques including Tarot, the Kabbalah, the Yi King, Runes, etc., the meaning of any particular event may remain a mystery.

Nevertheless, it remains mostly true that the meaning for you is determined by your reactions or your choices. A blizzard can be an exciting snowstorm for some and a terrifying and deadly event for others. A sell-off in the market can wipe out wealth for some people and create wealth for short-sellers. We're saddened to learn of the death of a beautiful polar bear, and then relieved when we learn it was shot just in time to save several children from its attack.

The problem is with the concept of meaning. Yes, an event of universal magnitude, such as the 9/11 attack on the World Trade Center in New York, affected millions of people, but in different degrees and ways. The firefighters and rescue units were intimately involved and deeply affected; immediate relatives of those who lost their lives were still more deeply affected; while those who saw the events unfold on the television news were affected but less grievously. But, nearly everyone on earth was affected. Some, of course, like Osama bin Laden, were happy to have been instrumental in causing so much death and pain.

"Meaning" at the level of the Subconscious is always personal, never abstract. The same event may bring pain to one person and joy to another; it may present exciting intellectual reactions to an American historian, and equally exciting but different reactions to an Arab historian. An unwitnessed event in a galaxy far, far away lacks meaning until some effect is perceived and then related to someone's personal experience.

While it is possible for a highly experienced meditator to move beyond personal reactions, it does require the ability to reach more deeply into the Unconscious than the personal Subconsciousness and this generally requires something as ancient as the Kabbalah to bypass emotional elements. We will explain more about this later, but it brings us to the next point: while it is emotions and feeling that energize the Subconsciousness, symbols are the common language of the Unconscious.

SYMBOLS ARE THE LANGUAGE OF THE UNCONSCIOUS

This is one of the deepest of mysteries. The careful use and interpretation of symbols in relation to questions and the pursuit of knowledge involves not only a study of interpretative programs like the Kabbalah, the Tarot, and the Yi King, but a particular "mindset" that is open and yet analytical—almost like that of a master detective, say Sherlock Holmes or Monsieur Hercule Poirot. While many symbols have established and readily recognized primary meanings, there is often a secondary one that fits another situation better. And like symbols showing up in a dream, they may be used differently to convey a reverse message or lead the dreamer toward a new adventure.

On the whole, symbols play a greater role the more you study them. When you master the language, you have a two-way interaction with the Unconscious that may provide you with serious opportunities for knowledge and even communications with spirits and non-human entities.

A symbol can also be like a computer icon, having a primary meaning but also opening whole new worlds of possibilities. An Apple can act like a Window to a new universe of previously unknown powers.

WHAT DO WE WANT, AND WHY?

So, the Subconscious has memories of everything that ever happened. *What does that really mean for us?* Memories are like hidden programs that drive our emotional reactions, our fears, our hungers, our ambitions and motivations. These programs can affect our health, can induce irrational behavior, and can lead us into harmful addictions and destructive actions.

We were not born with a "clean slate" but carry the memories from many previous lives, and through those memories we have a vast heritage of cultural and historic influences that may have dynamic effects in our current lifetime.

The trouble is that we don't know what is in this hidden programming. Mostly it doesn't matter because we live in the present. Sometimes, however, events in this life will trigger past memories to surface in surprising and uncontrollable ways. At times, there is reason to bring unconscious drives into present consciousness to come to terms with our hidden hungers, to discover why we do certain things, to enable us to impose rationality over irrationality.

MAKING THE UNCONSCIOUS CONSCIOUS

No, we can't bring everything of the past into the present. It would be overwhelming and self-defeating. You can't read every book held in the Library of Congress, and it would be meaningless to do so. Yet, when you know that certain books have information that would be constructive for you now, it becomes important to have access to that particular resource.

How do we discover what will be useful, and how do we access just that and not everything related to it? How do we enable the infinite resource of the Subconscious Mind to empower the Conscious Self? How can we focus the powers of the infinite to fulfill the matrix of potentials that are our destiny? How do we become more than we are and all that we should be?

That is the purpose of our study. Not all the answers are in this book, or in any book yet written. But the meaning of life is to be found in our journey of discovery, the book that each of us writes in the timeless records of Universal Consciousness. This is the adventure that you have chosen to undertake. It's the story of your future life, and lives.

CHAPTER THREE

THE SUBCONSCIOUS:
A Repository of Dynamic Processes, Functions and Mechanisms

There's more to the Subconscious than repressed and forgotten memories, and more than other memories of everything that has ever happened. Yes, and even more than the programming/matrix guiding the formation of our Personality and the Conscious Mind, the source for the Psychic and other Powers that will be developed into skills, and more than a source for the Archetypal influences underlying the development of the Personality.

Think about what we have learned so far:

1. The Subconscious is a kind of holding area for repressed and certain forgotten memories, childhood fears, and misperceptions. *Why?* So that, as may prove desirable, these can be reprocessed from an adult perspective.

2. The Subconscious is a memory bank for everything that has happened in your personal life. *Why?* Because those memories shape your Personality—the person you are. They are like the files of your Income and Expense, your Tax Returns, and all the data you find necessary in your financial life. They are the building blocks of your character, your dreams, your ideals, your desires, and more.

3. The Subconscious is a memory bank for everything from your previous lives and lives-between-lives. *Why?* Because this represents the raw materials for the lessons that are abstracted and

used in the development of the Soul. We are all here to learn and grow.

4. The Subconscious is an interactive psychological processor of certain contents of the Collective Unconscious, primarily the Archetypes that provide a structure for our perceptions of the major roles humans, including ourselves, assume in our lives. These are seen in the Major Arcana of the Tarot as Mother, Father, Warrior, Lover, etc. *Why?* These are part of the programming that gives an evolving structure to both the Subconscious and the Conscious Mind.

5. The Subconscious provides access to the Collective Unconscious and the Wisdom of the Human Race. Here are pantheons of gods and goddesses, each with their own special powers and knowledge; here also are the mythologies of heroic adventures and the stories of floods and disasters; here are all the attempts to make sense out of the world where we live, the inventions and theories of science, and the speculations of philosophers. Out of all the memories that are part of the Universal Unconscious, there are those that are collected into the highest aspirations of every culture. *Why?* We are evolving beings, not just as Souls, but as active participants in the whole of Universal Consciousness/Unconsciousness. We build on the bones, and all the experiences of our ancestors, human and nonhuman, and contribute our own bones and experiences so that others may also benefit. The image that is Man is a matrix into which all the past is poured according to certain established rules that were set at the Beginning—of which we still only speculate.

6. As evolving beings, it is now our role, through our Conscious Mind, to accelerate our processing of the Past into the Future. We learn to draw from the Subconscious what we need to become more than we are as we grow into Whole Persons. *Why?* Because we are, literally, Co-Creators of the ever-evolving universe and Gods in the making. Even though we are still largely unconscious of our function as Co-Creators, and working

without understanding of the Great Plan, it is because of this that our evolution is now accelerating.

The Subconscious is all of this and more. Through the Subconscious we have access to the Universal Consciousness out of which everything was and is created, has evolved, and which continues to create and lead toward further evolution.

But the major message we want to give you is that the Subconscious Mind is an unlimited resource, not only of memories and information but also of powers and skills. It is the foundation and matrix to all we are and all that we will become. Our unit of consciousness is part of the Universal Consciousness so we have unlimited potential and have yet to discover any limits to our capacity or ability to use that potential. Our goal is to become *adept* at calling these powers and resources to match our needs and interests, and to keep "pushing the envelope" toward yet greater capacity and ability.

THE CONSCIOUS MIND AS MANAGER
"It's a dirty job, but someone has to do it!"

In a way, that's true, except it's not really a dirty job but the best job in the world—one worthy of a grand corner office with the best view in town, and a huge communications console and command center from which you, with your Conscious Mind, take charge of the great resource of the Subconscious Mind. Information is constantly coming in, more than you can take full cognizance of, and so much of it is automatically diverted to the Subconscious Mind.

The Subconscious Mind is more than a passive collection of memories. Remember that the Subconscious Mind is your personal connection to the Universal Consciousness containing all that is from the very Beginning. Within this are all the potentials for all that you may become. This includes what we call "powers"—generally thought of as *psychic* powers. But before these powers are fully meaningful, they must be developed to become consciously directed <u>skills.</u>

But wait, as they say in television commercials, *there's more!* All that is the Conscious Mind—with its magnificent potentials for rational thinking, for creative development, for abstract analysis, for organization, for the use of imagination, for planning, and for all those skills that make it possible for the human being to manage the resources of the natural world—rose out of the Subconscious Mind. Note: we did not say that humanity has always done a good job at managing the resources of the natural world, but that we do have the ability and such stewardship, or partnership, is part of the job we've been assigned.

Outwardly, that's what we do; inwardly, we manage Consciousness, because that is what we are. In particular, the job of the Conscious Mind is to manage the Subconsciousness and develop its innate powers into skills that we can then deploy consciously with awareness and intention to work with the Great Plan. In another sense, it is to make Conscious the Unconscious through careful management of its resources.

MANAGEMENT DOES NOT MEAN TO SUBVERT!
This is important!

Good management means to use talent as well as skills wisely. There is much that the Subconscious does better than the Conscious Mind can ever do, but the Conscious Mind can assign those works and open the way for the Subconscious to play its role more effectively.

Music, Song, Dance, Art, Instinct, Inspiration, Feeling, and more. All these functions of the Subconscious express themselves truly when openly called upon, as so often may be the case with Psychic Powers and even magnified physical powers. We've all heard the old story of the mother able to lift an automobile in order to save her child from harm. Whether we can authenticate an actual instance like this or not, the fact remains that the Subconscious Mind can mobilize extreme physical resources in extreme circumstances.

The Subconscious Mind is not in a separate basement room. Even in the model shown in the Great Pyramid it was emphasized that the stone of the pyramid is pervious, and much of the Personal Unconscious is actually above ground and easily and often spontaneously accessed by the Conscious Mind, or it will bypass the Conscious Mind when needed.

All levels of the Personal Consciousness are able to interact and react, but as the Conscious Mind gains understanding of these other levels, it is able to more efficiently deploy these resources to the greater benefit of the Whole Person. It's worth remembering that the Unconscious is the home of the Old, and not so old, Gods who are still capable of manifesting with all their powers when correctly called upon. Remember, too, that Nature can show the ways to knowledge and understanding of her secret powers when you learn to listen. The Sun, the Moon, and the Planets, too, have powers to share with Man in his wholeness.

As Manager, it is your job to know, understand, and direct all these resources. It's the most exciting, most gratifying, most rewarding, and grandest job you will ever have, and it's one that is yours forever! You can't be fired, nor can you abdicate.

WHAT ARE THE DYNAMIC PROCESSES, FUNCTIONS, AND MECHANISMS OF THE SUBCONSCIOUS MIND THAT EMPOWER US?

Becoming self-empowered and thus fulfilling our Co-Creative responsibility depends largely on our ability to experience and use the powers of the subconscious mind.

The Subconscious mind is far more than a dormant storehouse of past experiences or extraneous baggage. It's an ongoing phenomenon that includes a myriad of dynamic processes, interactive functions, and empowering mechanisms, all of which are developmental and growth related. The Subconscious is like the "back office" always at work, always ready with everything that is needed, always renewing its abilities and expanding its capacities.

The *dynamic processes* of the subconscious include its capacity to integrate our present experiences into a life-history pattern that is forever evolving, life after life and in between. Through such programs as past-life regression, we can experience that integrative process and discover the subconscious insights related to our present-life strivings. At some point you will know that you have many lives, *but also know that you have only one life with many, many chapters.* With increasing knowledge and understanding, you will become more and more the conscious author of this book of your life.

Another program provides access to the "Akashic Records," that seemingly totally comprehensive library of information, historical fact, and memories. Being able to call up infinite information and integrate it into your present life needs is of enormous benefit—similar to but beyond the capacity of any present-day Internet Search Engine.

Dreams, the most familiar gateway to the subconscious, are still among the most underutilized and underdeveloped of techniques.

There is also the function of the Subconscious as a doorway to spiritual realities and interaction with the spirit realm, including non-human entities such as angels, elves, gnomes, and other elemental and stellar intelligences. The Conscious Mind, working with these other intelligences, can benefit enormously from their knowledge and ability to manipulate natural energies.

Aside from the integrative process, there's evidence suggesting that the subconscious can literally generate new potentials and growth energies independent of our conscious interactions through processes not yet fully understood, possibly through the synergistic or holistic results of the integrative process alone. What we need to understand is that the Subconscious Mind is <u>not </u>a passive bystander, but always aware and always active. As you grow in consciousness and integrate more of your psychic and other powers into your Whole Person, the Subconscious Mind grows and contributes more to the Whole Person you are becoming.

Understanding these creative processes of the subconscious mind is among our greatest challenges, with potential for enormous benefit. The point here, as elsewhere, is always that the greater our understanding, the greater the benefit, *but even as we face the continual challenges, the very attempt at understanding stimulates positive developments.*

The *interactive functions* of the subconscious mind include its readiness to embrace our probes of its powers and direct them toward accelerating our growth and achieving our personal goals. Resolving conflicts, solving personal problems, and overcoming fear are among the possibilities when we experience the powers of the subconscious mind.

Subconscious *empowering mechanisms* include such enlightenment channels as dreams, intuition, and psychical insight. Among the most common empowering mechanisms is subconscious motivation that, even though unrecognized, can give us a winning edge in our goal-related strivings. Examples include the subconscious need to help others that motivates us to succeed in a helping profession, or at another level, the subconscious need for acceptance or recognition that motivates us to accomplish a challenging goal that wins public applause.

Empowerment rewards of subconscious knowledge include: a) overcoming growth blockages,(b) resolving conflict, (c) self-enlightenment, d) happiness and success. The major undeveloped Potentials include Problem Solving, Creativity, Mental and Physical Health, Rejuvenation, and the Therapeutic power of subconscious knowledge. In addition, of course, we have the entire range of Psychic Powers: ESP, OBEs, and PK.

The most familiar Interfacing Programs include those that connect consciousness with the subconscious: Meditation, Interacting with Nature, Hypnosis, Dream Analysis, Kabbalistic Pathworking and other Guided Meditation techniques, and Astral and Mental Travel.

Becoming aware of all this potential and using the established techniques for access and development is the most positive road to Emotional and Mental self-development and the most dynamic path to Spiritual Growth and Attainment.

The subconscious thus becomes not just a source of content and potential, but an active empowerment partner.

CHAPTER FOUR

INTERFACING CONSCIOUSNESS WITH THE SUBCONSCIOUS

Contrary to some views, the subconscious is "the essential you," the essence of your being as an evolving soul. Without the subconscious, you would not exist at all. It's the vast totality of your existence: the *old you* of the past, the *dynamic you* of the present and the *infinite you* of the future. It's the vital combination of empowering resources and undeveloped potentials, along with vibrant processes, functions, and mechanisms. As a collective force, it embodies the inexhaustible wisdom of the ages and energizes your destiny for greatness. It sustains the essential foundation for your success, happiness, and never-ending growth.

When you take deliberate charge of the subconscious, your life takes on a new dimension of both meaning and power. Rather than a risky existential leap into a dark cavern of the unknown, your probe of the subconscious is an "inward leap of power" that clarifies the nature of your existence and reaffirms your destiny for greatness and meaning. It's a leap of progress that not only accelerates your growth, but guides you toward greater happiness and fulfillment as well.

The subconscious is energized by the life force that sustains your existence and ensures your survival as a unique spiritual being. It is the center of your spiritual genotype, that counterpart of your biological makeup. While your biological characteristics change with each lifetime, your spiritual genotype is forever fixed, yet without borders. It's within that spiritual makeup up that you evolve as an

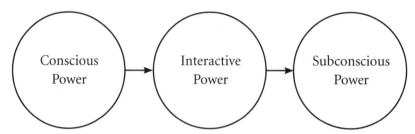

Figure 4A: Three-Dimensional Concept of Personal Power. This concept emphasizes interactive power as the essential link between conscious and subconscious resources. The Subconscious Check-In Program, which is based on this concept, is designed to activate an empowered state of attunement and readiness that targets subconscious resources and focuses them on designated goals.

endless soul being. Central to that spiritual framework is the subconscious mind with its vast reserve of experiences, potentials, processes, and mechanisms.

Within the totality of your past are experiences that are at present beyond your conscious awareness. Although embodied within the subconscious, they are laden with growth possibilities. They remain with you as ultimate growth resources. They beckon your awareness as a doorway to success and happiness. Fortunately, they are now available to you through a host of self-empowerment programs designed not only to retrieve them but to activate their empowerment potentials. You can at last uncover the subconscious sources of phobias and extinguish their disempowering effects. Given past-life enlightenment, you can dissolve blockages to your growth resulting from unresolved past-life trauma. You can extinguish the disempowering effects of past-life failures and disappointments. You can retrieve past-life accomplishments and use them to build a success orientation that cannot fail. These are only a few of the possibilities when you connect to the powers of the subconscious.

Aside from its wealth of past experiences, the subconscious mind houses a wide range of dynamic processes and functions. Its mechanisms, all empowerment charged, include dreams with their hidden messages, intuitive impressions, and various psychic channels as sources of enlightenment. Included are telepathy, precognition, psychokinesis, and out-of-body experiences, along with interactions with the spirit realm, including communicating with not only the deceased but spirit guides as well.

Undeveloped potentials and suppressed skills existing in the subconscious function as foundations for your continued growth and development. Through appropriate interfacing programs, you can facilitate your development and energize the dormant skills that exist as foundations for your continued growth. Accelerating learning, stimulating your creative powers, improving your memory, and acquiring totally new skills, often instantly, are all within the scope of your subconscious powers.

Aside from these, you can dissolve all blockages that inhibit your growth. You can become liberated from the residual effects of past-life conflicts and trauma as well as the shackles of painful present-life experiences. The result is triumphant self-empowerment over disabling self-defeat.

Incredible as it may at first seem, totally new skills, such as instant mastery of a new language or a complex body of scientific skills, have been known to spontaneously emerge through programs that probe the subconscious. There are numerous reports of this phenomenon having occurred during hypnosis. A full-blown skill emerging spontaneously in that context is typically called *hypnoproduction.* This phenomenon can, however, occur under a variety of other conditions, including meditation and other states of concentrated awareness.

Through the programs presented in this chapter, you will discover how to uncover your subconscious powers and interact with them. You will discover how to achieve your personal goals and actualize your highest potentials for growth and self-discovery. You will find ways of effectively solving personal problems, improving your mental and physical health, and overcoming the fears and uncertainties that threaten your well-being. You will master new ways of enriching your social relationships, achieving career success, and dissolving all blockages to your growth. In a word, you will become SELF-EMPOWERED.

THE SUBCONSCIOUS CHECK-IN PROGRAM

Basic to the structure of the subconscious are a host of specific power centers. They exist as holding areas or storehouses of power as well as dynamic generators of new power upon demand. They are receptive to our recognition of them through the *Subconscious Check-in Program*, which can be used daily or as often as needed to meet our empowerment demands. Through this program, you not only check into the centers, you become connected and attuned to them. In that state we call *subconscious readiness*, your subconscious powers are placed in a state of spontaneous alertness and receptivity. They become constantly poised to yield their powers and instantly intervene into any life situation, including important decision making or other potentially stressful life situations such as important job interviews, public presentations, and unanticipated emergencies. Protracted life situations requiring adjustment or adaptation related to stressful transitions involving relationships and career decisions are especially receptive to the Check-in Program. Requiring only a few minutes in a quiet, comfortable setting—possibly upon awakening in the morning— this program is an excellent way to start your day.

THE CHECK-IN PROGRAM, STEP-BY-STEP

Step 1. Clearing. Begin by simply clearing your mind of active thought. In that passive state, allow relaxing images, preferably related to Nature, to spontaneously emerge.

Step 2. Focusing. As the images flow through your mind, select a particularly peaceful image, perhaps a fluffy cloud, a bird in flight, or a tree in a meadow, and focus your full attention upon it. Think of that image as your gateway to your subconscious mind.

Step 3. Attunement. Allow the peaceful image to gently fade away, making a signal that the gateway to the subconscious is now open and you are an integral part of it. There exists, in this state, no separation between the energies of the conscious and subconscious. Take plenty of time to linger in this attuned state as you sense the powers of your subconscious permeating your total being. It's in this state that important insights related to your past-life experiences and present-life situation will spontaneously unfold. Awareness of an enlightened guiding presence will often accompany this step.

Step 4. Affirmation. Affirm in your own words your state of oneness with your subconscious and your attunement to its powers.

Step 5. Conclusion. Allow the relaxing image you experienced in Step 1 to again gently emerge. Focus your full attention on the image and affirm that by simply recalling the image, you will become instantly connected to all the subconscious powers within. Use this concluding step as often as needed throughout the day.

Although the Check-in Program is recommended as an early morning exercise, it can be used at other times if needed. A pre-med student reported that he used the program regularly upon awakening as a way to clear his mind and improve his academic performance. Another student used the program immediately before an important job interview to build her self-confidence and increase her interactive skills. She's convinced that the Check-in Program gave her the winning edge that resulted in her being selected for the highly competitive position.

Aside from specific goal-related applications, this program is among the most effective stress-management approaches known. College students have found it to be especially effective in reducing test anxiety when used immediately prior to course exams. In the competitive sports setting, athletes who used it before a competitive event consistently experienced a powerful increase in self-confidence as well as improved performance, particularly for skills requiring a high level of coordination.

You'll find that, with practice, this program becomes even more effective. Among subjects who've used hypnosis to explore their past lives, the Subconscious Check-in Program often becomes the program of choice. During the attuned state in Step 3, the conscious often unites with the subconscious, not only to uncover past-life experiences but to identify their present-life relevance. Examples include the discovery of past-life sources of phobias, compulsions, and conflicts. A pre-law student who was hounded by feelings of inferiority, along with fear of knives, discovered through this program that he was orphaned as a child in a recent past life and rejected by the family that took him in. During his late teens in that past life, he became homeless, and was eventually stabbed to death as he slept on a city-park bench. Given that insight, he successfully resolved his fear of knives and overcame his feelings of inferiority. He is today a highly successful university administrator.

In another instance, a college student discovered through this program that her fear of rejection was the result of having been abandoned as a child in a past life. Given that insight, she successfully resolved the fear that had limited her life for years. Enlightenment, including that related to past-life experience, is one of the most powerful therapeutic forces known, and the Subconscious Check-in Program is one of the best programs available for discovering that force. Unlike certain other past-life regression programs, this approach requires no specialist other than the one existing within yourself.

THE CENTERS OF POWER PROGRAM—
A TWO-WAY EMPOWERMENT EXERCISE

This program is based on the premise that the subconscious, rather than being simply an intermingled collection of energies and powers, is an organized constellation of power centers, each with its unique functions and mechanisms. Each center, according to this program, is characterized by a particular color frequency that represents its power. The program uses color imagery to connect consciousness to a particular subconscious energy center. The results are twofold: first, a mental, physical, or spiritual infusion of that center's amazing power; and second, an exercising of the center in ways that actually increase its power. The Centers of Power Program thus becomes a two-way exercise that empowers both the conscious and subconscious.

The relevance of colors associated with the subconscious centers of power is consistent with the significance of colors found in the human aura, the system of energy enveloping the physical body. For instance, the color indigo is associated with spirituality, whereas the color pink is associated with affinity. Blue is associated with tranquility; green is associated with health and fitness; and yellow is associated with intelligence. The color black is found neither in the human aura nor among the subconscious centers of power.

Here are a few examples of subconscious centers of power and the colors related to them:

The Center of Intellectual Power. The color <u>yellow</u> signifies this center, which is associated with intellectual power including reasoning, abstract thinking, problem solving, and decision making, to list but a few.

The Center of Healing Power. This center is characterized by the color <u>green</u> and is associated with building the immune system, managing pain, and promoting wellness. Unlike other centers of power, connecting to the healing center of power can result in the transfer of health-related energy to others. Psychic healers are typically highly attuned to their inner center of healing power.

The Center of Rejuvenating Power. This center is characterized by <u>iridescent emerald green</u>. It's found in proximity to the healing center and, like that center, is also associated with health and fitness. Longevity as well as miraculous healings are believed to be manifestations of this powerful center.

The Center of Spiritual Power. This center is typically characterized by the color <u>indigo</u>. It's almost always found in the central region of the subconscious where it radiates its power throughout the subconscious. Connecting to that realm promotes spiritual growth and enlightenment, as well as greater access to other subconscious energy centers. Gifted psychics and spiritual mediums are typically highly attuned to their inner center of spiritual power.

The Action Center of Power. The color <u>red</u> characterizes the action center of power. It signals the power of decisive action in achieving difficult goals. Interacting with this center can provide the extra measure of determination required for both immediate and long-term achievement, including successful performance such as in competitive sports, as well as long-term success in achieving such goals as career success and financial independence. By connecting to this center, you can jump-start the skills required to overcome even the most adverse situation. As a college honor student put it during his commencement address: "When you interact with the action center within you, all things are possible."

The Center for Higher Good. The color <u>violet</u> is associated with the subconscious center for the higher good. Connecting to this center is an excellent individual or group activity for building commitment and promoting success in giving back to the world and contributing to the common good. In its effort to establish a student scholarship program, the International Parapsychology Research Foundation used the Center of Power Program as detailed later to connect the group to the Subconscious Center for Higher Good. In record time, the group established a scholarship program at Athens State University. A second scholarship program using the same approach was established at the University of Alabama, again in record time. Both scholarships are awarded annually.

The Center of Multiple Powers. Certain centers of power are characterized by <u>multiple colors</u>, typically pastel in nature. They suggest the possibility of multiple enrichment and overall improvement in the quality of one's life. Connecting to the Center of Multiple Powers can dramatically increase your ability to cope with complex relationships, find solutions to difficult problems, and overcome barriers to your success. Financial gain, happiness, and success are all associated with this center.

The research subjects, many of them college students, who participated in our study of the subconscious centers of power began early on to identify the typically spherical shape of each center and its location in relationship to other centers. Somewhat to our surprise, the pattern that eventually emerged was strikingly similar for all subjects. The Center of Spiritual Power characterized by the color indigo was, as earlier noted, typically found at the central region of the subconscious, a possible indication of the spiritual nature of our existence. The brightness of this center and the extent of its radiation among other centers, however, varied widely among the individuals participating in our studies. Could the degree of radiated energy be a pos-

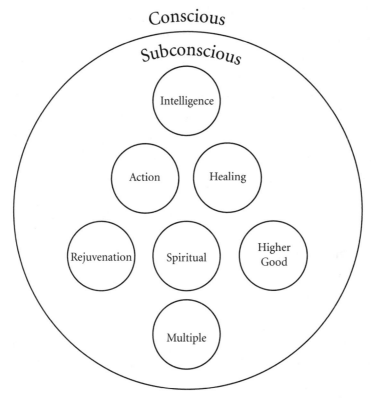

Figure 4B: Subconscious Centers of Power. This concept recognizes the subconscious as an organized, circular arrangement of power centers with each center receptive to conscious intervention.

sible indication of a given center's development and its significance in relation to other centers? Our findings, though tentative at this stage, strongly suggest that possibility.

With indigo usually located in the central region of the subconscious, the remaining centers typically formed an outer circular pattern, with the size and brightness of each center suggesting that center's degree of development and influence in its association with other centers. For instance, an extensive radiant green center of power was typically characteristic of students preparing for careers in the health fields; whereas a center of glowing red was often characteristic of students who were highly active in sports and such activities as body-building and karate.

The color violet was typically the least intense and less frequently noted center of power among the subjects of our studies, a finding suggesting the possible absence of a strong commitment to the higher good. Fortunately, our interactions with even the most neglected center of subconscious power not only connect us to its powers, they promote the development of the center itself. It follows that by connecting to the Center for Higher Good, we can literally increase the center's brightness and the extent of its influence over other subconscious centers of power. Perhaps not surprisingly, nothing is more personally empowering and rewarding than actively contributing to the higher good.

THE CENTERS OF POWER PROGRAM: STEP-BY-STEP

The Centers of Power Program—like the Check-in Program—requires only a few minutes in a quiet, comfortable setting free of distractions. Here's the program.

Step 1. Goal Statement. Begin by settling back and clearing your mind of all clutter. Take a few moments to formulate your goal and state your intent to connect to a subconscious center of power related to it.

Step 2. Color Visualization. Having formulated your goal, visualize a color that's relevant to your stated goal. For instance, if your goal is rejuvenation, visualize iridescent emerald green. If your goal, on the other hand, relates to spiritual enlightenment, visualize indigo.

Step 3. Focusing. Focus on the subconscious energy center with color properties consistent with your stated goal. Sense the merging of the colors and the infusion of power related to your goal. Allow plenty of time for the merging of energies to run its course.

Step 4. Conclusion. Conclude by affirming in your own words the empowering effects of this program on your total being, both conscious and subconscious. Further affirm that by simply visualizing the color related to your goal, you will instantly engage the subconscious center of energy required to achieve it.

INTERFACING THE POWER OF NATURE

On a very grand and magnificent scale, *the subconscious is your connection to the universe and the life force that sustains it.* When you become attuned to the universe, you are attuned to the powers within yourself. Through your interactions with Nature, you can experience the power that underlies not only the natural world, but your own existence as well.

As a source of unparalleled power and enlightenment, the subconscious is our most advanced teacher, healer, and therapist. Although the subconscious may give us glimpses of its powers through dreams, impressions, and fleeting moments of profound enlightenment, the subconscious never imposes its powers upon us. The subconscious knows that *self-discovery is our best teacher.* Although the solutions to life's most complex problems may exist in the subconscious, we value them more when we discover them for ourselves.

The subconscious knows that imposing solutions upon consciousness could meet with resistance and possibly rejection. Nevertheless, the subconscious often uses the natural world as a channel for spontaneous personal empowerment, to include enlightenment and healing. A magnificent sunset, for instance, can become a profound conduit for empowerment. A college student, whose hospitalized fiancé had been in a coma for over two weeks following a serious boating accident, experienced his unmistakable presence as she viewed a glowing sunset following a visit with him at a hospital. By her report, she actually heard him saying, "I'm here." She immediately returned to the hospital where, upon entering his room, he greeted her with the same words, "I'm here." As they embraced, she knew that his recovery would be rapid and complete. It was the sunset, by her report, that not only connected her to his presence, but to the healing powers of the universe as well.

LISTENING TO NATURE
THROUGH SELF-HYPNOSIS

Nature speaks to us, but unfortunately, we're not always good listeners. As we separate ourselves more and more from nature, we become increasingly alienated and unaware of its messages. In an interesting experimental study in our labs at Athens State University, we used self-hypnosis to increase the ability of our subjects to see and hear the language of Nature. The audio CD used to induce the trance state is described in the book, *Self-empowerment through Self-hypnosis* (Weschcke and Slate, 2010) and is available from the publisher. The CD was used exactly as presented with one minor modification—once in the successful trance state, the subject added the auto-suggestion: "I am now attuned to Nature and receptive to its powers."

The results were dramatic. An art student discovered a totally new creative side of Nature that she incorporated into her paintings. Her instructor took note of the dramatic change in her work and suggested to her that she was ready for her first exhibition. An exhibit was arranged and, as expected, she received rave reviews and critical acclaim.

In a similar instance, a creative writing student began listening to Nature for ideas to incorporate into his writings. He listened to birds, trees, and streams. He even listened to clover, which guided him to a four-leaf specimen. For the final examination, he wrote a short story that the instructor suggested he read to the class. The instructor commented, "Why have you not been doing work of this quality all along?" She considered his work sufficient to merit a final grade of "A" for the course. As a footnote, he framed the four-leaf clover, which now hangs in his private office.

EXPERIENCING THE TOOLS OF NATURE

In a laboratory effort to investigate our capacity to connect to the power of Nature, a total of twenty rocks and minerals were used as possible tools for activating certain subconscious mental faculties. The study was based on the twofold premise that Nature's material

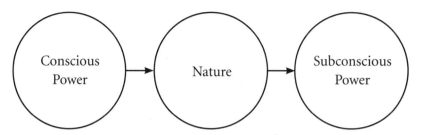

Figure 4C: The Conscious/Subconscious Continuum. The conscious and subconscious domains of power exist on a continuum in which nature becomes the connecting force.

substances including rocks, minerals, and gems possess their own unique structural characteristics and energy frequencies; and second, by interacting with them, if only through physical touch alone, we can access their powers and focus them on desired goals. If physical touch is effective in initiating the empowering possibilities of rocks, we could further assume that programs beyond physical touch could be developed to further increase nature's receptiveness to our interactions, not only with rocks, minerals, and gems, but with other objects of nature as well, including plants. There exists strong evidence supportive of that possibility.

In Phase I of the study, twenty-five volunteer subjects, all college students, held each of the small samples, one by one, while engaging in various tasks using ESP cards. Of the twenty rocks and minerals studied, quartz crystal was highest in its capacity to promote all three ESP faculties. The second highest in promoting precognition was the rose quartz; and the second highest in promoting telepathy was the siderite. Azurite and olivine tied for second place in promoting clairvoyance.

In Phase II of the study, the rocks and minerals were studied to determine their capacity to facilitate learning and memory. In this phase, the same twenty-five volunteer subjects held each of the small samples while engaged in certain learning and memory tasks. Analysis of results showed quartz crystal to be the most effective in increasing the rate of learning as well as promoting memory. The bornite was the second highest in promoting learning and the beryl was the second highest in promoting memory.

Here are the other rocks and minerals used for this study: fluorite, spodumene, rhodochrosite, barite, feldspar, obsidian, calcite, lepidolite, travertine, kyanite, wollastonite, jasper, and garnet.

This study raises an intriguing question: Could simply holding a stones actually connect us to the powers of Nature in ways that promote academic success, and by extension, professional performance? For the most part, the subjects of our study were convinced that the stone did just that. They began using the quartz crystal to promote academic success, including their performance on course examinations. To enhance the crystal's effectiveness, several of the students applied certain programming techniques in which they first rinsed the crystal with warm water and allowed it to air dry. They then stroked the crystal while addressing it as an academic enhancement resource or partner. A pre-law student who participated in our research and is now a highly successful practicing attorney continues to carry a small programmed crystal in his pocket. By his report, the crystal is a valued companion that empowers him to more effectively meet the demands of his profession. He attributes in large measure his outstanding success as an attorney to the crystal, which he calls a valued companion rather than simply a tool of nature. (For step-by-step programming procedures for crystals, see page 133, *Connecting to the Power of Nature* by Joe H. Slate, Llewellyn, 2009.)

The results of this study clearly suggest that by connecting to nature through its rocks and minerals, we can become empowered to interface consciousness with the subconscious in ways that activate our highest faculties.

THE LEAF OF PROGRESS

As Earth's oldest and biggest living things, trees are Earth's antennae to the universe. Just as our hands are the antennae for the body, leaves are the antennae for the tree. It requires no quantum leap to imagine that by bringing the two together, we could become connected to the powers within ourselves as well as the universe at large. The Leaf of Progress is a step-by-step program specifically designed to achieve that goal.

Step 1. Formulate a personal goal and state clearly your intent to achieve it.

Step 2. Select a tree that appeals to you and remove a leaf from it. Think of the leaf as the tree's antennae and manifestation of the tree's contact to the powers of the universe.

Step 3. With the leaf resting in either hand, view the leaf for a moment, studying each of its features to include its shape and color. Stroke the leaf gently and note its texture and energy.

Step 4. As the leaf continues to rest in your hand, think of your hands as the antennae to your body.

Step 5. Bring your hands together in a praying hands position with the leaf resting between your palms. Sense the leaf with its unique features, including shape, texture, and energy. Visualize the leaf and affirm in your own words your connection to it.

Step 6. With the leaf resting between your palms, think of your right hand as the antennae for the conscious and your left hand as the antennae for the subconscious. Think of the leaf as your connection to the powers within as well as the universe beyond.

Step 7. Clear your mind and allow relevant impressions and images to emerge. Sense the infusion of powerful energy accompanying this step, and remind yourself that you are empowered with all the resources required to achieve your personal goal as earlier stated. Use visualization of yourself having successfully achieved your goal as you affirm your complete success.

Step 8. Either return the leaf to the earth or place it at a convenient place, perhaps between the pages of this book, for future reference. Tell yourself that by either viewing the leaf or simply visualizing it, you will at once activate the full effects of this program.

This is an excellent program for such self-development goals as quitting smoking, losing weight, building self-confidence, and managing stress, to name but a few of the possibilities. A psychology doctoral student who had been a heavy smoker since a very early age used the Leaf of Progress to instantly quit smoking. His motive, aside from health concerns, was, "As a psychologist, how can I help others quit smoking if I cannot help myself?" He is today a practicing, nonsmoking psychologist who regularly uses the program with both individuals and groups. By his account, the program is far superior to other quit-smoking approaches.

The Leaf of Progress has shown special effectiveness for career-related goals. It can be used routinely to promote productive performance or solve career-related problems. It's especially effective as a preparatory approach prior to important conferences or public presentations. The simple leaf, if we could call it simple, is ready to work for you, and its powers appear to be unlimited.

The Leaf of Progress can be readily adapted for use in couples counseling. It can bridge the gap in relationships and motivate couples to find solutions to problems and conflicts in their relationship. Here's the adapted program for use by couples.

Step 1. Together with your partner, select a tree that appeals to you both and remove a leaf from it. While viewing the leaf with its unique features, think of it as your connection to the tree as Earth's antennae to the universe.

Step 2. While comfortably seated or standing and facing each other, join your hand with the hand of your partner and place the leaf between them. As partners, think of the leaf resting between your joined hands as your connection, not only to the tree, but to each other and the subconscious powers within.

Step 3. With the leaf resting in the palms of your joined hands, take a few moments for mutual eye gazing. As partners gazing into each other's eyes, let thoughts, feelings, and impressions, including those from deep within your subconscious, emerge.

Step 4. Once the gazing process runs its course, and with the leaf remaining between the palms of your joined hands, close your eyes and sense your attunement, both within yourself and with each other.

Step 5. Conclude by placing the leaf aside and mentally affirming together: "We are now empowered, both individually and as a couple. We are destined for fulfillment, empowerment, and success."

This program is applicable to a wide range of problems in couples' relationships. It has been highly effective when used by couples to bring new meaning and satisfaction into the relationship. The program has been especially useful in situations involving sexual dysfunctions, including erectile insufficiency. Even when the relationship seems to have lost its viability, the program can be used to bring forth new vitality and fulfillment. While recognizing that some relationships simply run their course, this program has been highly effective in bringing forth a workable resolution.

Nature is communicating with you right now. Learn to listen to her messages and your life will be enriched. You will become empowered to reach your highest goals. Once connected to nature and attuned to the universe, nothing is impossible for you.

CHAPTER FIVE

THE SUBCONSCIOUS MIND:
Your Resource for Problem Solving, Creativity, Mental and Physical Health, Rejuvenation, and Psychic Powers

We may be undergoing a substantial change in our conscious relationship with the Subconscious Mind, and of the role of the Subconscious Mind in our lives.

There was a time when humans functioned primarily in their subconsciousness, and more as part of a clan unity than as individuals. As time marched on and we continued to evolve in response to environmental changes and the inner drive of our initial programming, we became less a "clan-animal" and more conscious of our individual identities. The Conscious Mind rose out of the Subconscious and became more dominant while the clan consciousness functioned in the background to later take on the role we now call "the Collective Unconscious."

As we became more aware of ourselves as individuals and operated more in the Conscious Mind, developing personal memory, rationality, and new ways of thinking, we perceived ourselves in relationship to the natural world rather than as part of it. We learned to store knowledge in our memory rather than having immediate "feeling" access to it. Rather than relating internally to the rhythms of the Sun, Moon, and Planets, we saw them externally and developed sciences of astronomy, astrology, and agriculture. And we became aware of linear time.

Human Consciousness, like the human brain, was split, and instinct, intuition, and empathetic perceptions were layered "beneath" the Conscious Mind, along with repressed feelings and forgotten memories in the Subconscious Mind.

While the Subconscious remained connected to the Universal Consciousness (also known as the "Unconscious") through what we subsequently termed the "Collective Unconscious," the connection was mostly a one-way spontaneous eruption of content from the subconscious into the conscious mind in the form of unconscious drives and emotion-driven behavior, dreams and nightmares, myths of gods and goddesses, and feeling-driven physical movement.

The emerging Conscious Mind learned to plan activities for the days and seasons ahead, and to do so based on rational analysis of needs and opportunities, and experience in the form of memories. Humanity learned to consider the needs of the future, and to plan to provide for their food needs by planned movement following the seasonal migration of animals, and later learned to harvest and preserve their food so they could remain in stable locations. And from this, culture and civilization developed. Much of this historic culture lives in the subconscious while civilization is more a product of the conscious mind, sometimes hindered by "clan" feelings and emotion erupting from the subconscious.

As the conscious mind grew in prominence more and more, the subconscious mind was seemingly "driven underground" and forgotten. Early mind scientists thought of it as a "garbage dump" of repression, childish fears of fantastic monsters, misunderstood perceptions of their parents' sexual relations, fears generated by adult stories of the hunt and attacks by neighboring tribes, and so on. And as the conscious mind became more dominant, unconscious drives, fears, and irrational behavior were deemed unacceptable and either criminalized or termed "hysterical" and "demonic."

THE NEW CONSCIOUSNESS

In just the last few decades, there has been a whole new perception of the subconscious mind as a resource of considerable power, and a realization that "consciousness" itself is bigger, older, and more fundamental than previously perceived.

Consciousness is even more elemental than Energy and Matter, and extends throughout Time and Space. Modern science, and in particular quantum physics and what we now dare to call "new age psychology" along with paranormal studies, have restored balance to our cosmology. We see Life and Consciousness as universal and limitless.

We are evolving into a new relationship between different levels of personal and extended consciousness with the conscious mind as manager, able to call upon the resources of the extended range of consciousness to tap into memories, knowledge, and perceptions. The new relationship is a two-way communication with the conscious mind, calling up specified content from the subconscious, the collective unconscious, and the greater universal consciousness, and using nearly forgotten psychic powers to expand awareness beyond the limitations of the physical senses.

The divisions between the conscious mind and the subconscious mind are becoming less substantial and are merging toward Wholeness, with the conscious mind functioning more like a Managing Director and the subconscious as a Director of Resources. While the conscious mind is still the functional director, the relationship to the subconscious is becoming more one of interactive teamwork than previously.

Evolution for humanity is continuing and accelerating. It is driven by purpose and meaning, and not only by chance and Darwinian natural selection. Evolution is not founded in biology but in consciousness, and continues to build upon a long-ago "programming" for which no end is in sight.

THE CHICKEN OR THE EGG—
WHICH CAME FIRST?

The answer is, of course, "neither, or both" because they're really the same—you can't have one without the other. And both are of the physical "body," conceived and developed in consciousness.

Which came first, the brain or consciousness? Modern science makes the mistake of "thinking" that consciousness is a product of the brain, whereas the obvious truth is that the brain—along with the rest of the body—is a product of consciousness. Nevertheless, just as mind and body function as an integral unit, so do consciousness and the brain function together to produce what we experience as mind.

Mind, and memory, exist outside the brain, but may be activated through that area of the brain known as the "right temporal lobe." (See *Where God Lives: The Science of the Paranormal and How our Brains are Linked to the Universe*, by Melvin Morse, M.D., HarperCollins, 2000, for some very interesting research.)

Understanding the primary role of consciousness better enables us to understand the potentials of the subconscious mind as our director of resources and the source point for our psychic powers. Even though areas of the physical brain as well as the chakra system are involved in both spontaneous psychic phenomena and in developed psychic skills, their source is in the subconscious mind. The "doorway" to the psychic world is through the subconscious, and the conscious mind must work through the subconscious to use these psychic powers in a controlled manner.

PSYCHIC SKILLS AND PARANORMAL PHENOMENA

It is important to distinguish between *involuntary* paranormal phenomena and *voluntary* psychic skills, even though both have their origin in the subconsciousness. It is further important to understand that through the subconscious mind we can, <u>potentially</u>, access not only vast knowledge and perceptions but unlimited life energy.

Many paranormal phenomena involve spontaneous eruptions of energy in response to emotions, repressed memories, and—sometimes—contacts with nonphysical entities and "thought forms." While interesting, the discussion of paranormal phenomena doesn't serve the purposeful values of developed and trained psychic skills. Don't confuse "seeing a ghost" with the magical skill involved in creating a psychic entity to act, for example, as a household guardian spirit. While wonderful and a resource for study, spontaneous "miraculous" healing isn't the same as intentional psychic healing by a skilled healer. And dreaming of an airplane disaster doesn't compare with the ability to accurately foresee the potential problem that could lead to saving hundreds of lives.

The psychic (or some people would prefer the word "spiritual") dimension of the subconscious/extended consciousness reaches to the extremes of space and time, and taps into the source of primitive energy. It is this that allows for all forms of paranormal phenomena, and—more importantly in this book—natural psychic powers and developed and trained psychic skills.

The conscious mind, working through the subconscious mind, is able to <u>manage</u> these abilities that include clairvoyance, mind-to-mind telepathy, spiritual healing, automatic writing, psychokinesis, spirit communication, dowsing, astral projection, precognition, remote viewing, past-life regression, personal rejuvenation, psychic defense, and more. Our goal is to intentionally make use of psychic skills for our practical benefit—*and in developing these psychic powers into skills we are fulfilling the potential of the Whole Person and developing the Super-Conscious Mind.*

Think again of our Great Pyramid model of Personal Consciousness presented in chapter one, where we described the entire area below the Queen's Chamber with its foundation upon the Earth and its connection to the Subterranean Chamber in the earth as the subconscious mind, the Queen's Chamber and the area immediately above as the conscious mind, and then the King's Chamber and the area above as the super-conscious mind. And above the Pyramid itself we have the subtle connection to the Soul.

That area above the King's Chamber may appear to be solid stone, but it is pervious and it is our job to make it home to the Super-Conscious Mind to fulfill the Whole Person that completes the matrix of our Personal Consciousness. Ultimately, the whole of the Unconscious is open to the Conscious Mind, just as the whole of the Internet is available to the competent computer operator. And in the same fashion, for the contents of the Internet do not overwhelm the operator but are accessed at his command, and the more defined is his command the more precise the results of an Internet search.

And like the computer keyboard, there are "tools" that we can use to interface with the Unconscious, although—in truth—we don't need them. Still, a dowsing rod is convenient and adds to our sense and accuracy of control as we search for the particular energy patterns given off by seams of water or particular minerals that we seek. A deck of Tarot Cards establishes a matrix for our reading and the cards themselves tune to the archetypes and symbols that act as keys to particular areas of the Unconscious to facilitate our "reading."

Whether a crystal ball, a deck of cards, a collection of shells, yarrow sticks, or a horoscope, these all are tools for extending our minds into chosen areas of the Unconscious to provide information by which we complete a creative process to accomplish the intent of our operation.

OUR RESOURCE FOR PROBLEM SOLVING

Whether we use any of these tools or enter directly into the Subconscious through Meditation, Dreams, Self-Hypnosis, or shamanic methods of Altering Consciousness, we are essentially asking questions and "channeling" answers that most likely require some degree of interpretation by the Conscious Mind to be meaningful. And this art and science of interpretation can be learned as well as intuited. *Practice—as with any endeavor—leads to greater success.*

Understanding that our resources are limited only by our determination and ability to imagine, we learn new ways for presenting our problems and asking our questions.

We gain confidence by looking to the recent past with its scientific and political breakthroughs, and wonder at all the new physical, medical, biological, psychological, and social technology that has developed in just the last half century. Look past the economic and financial challenges of 2008–2009 brought about by uncontained greed and misguided (mostly lack of) regulation, and perceive the actual progress made in providing new solutions to old problems—even where the vision was narrow and contaminated by greed and ideology—and perceive the increasing power of creative problem solving.

Only a few years ago, two of the world's largest nations, India and China, were mired in poverty and misery and are now economic powerhouses and leaders in industry, commerce, and technology. Despite dire predictions that the world was running low on fossil energy, we are now on the edge of achieving clean and pollution-free energy independence. While threats to world peace still remain, new political vision is replacing old ideologies of conflict and repression. A new world order is synchronous with a new age of expanding consciousness.

While challenges still remain, human life span has advanced and health concerns are being increasingly resolved. Education is reaching more and more young people, girls in particular, and moving them out of the shadows of ignorance and repression. The rule of law, with its concept of individual freedom within an understandable and evenly balanced playing field, is replacing tribal law often administered for the personal benefit (and even entertainment) of tribal leadership. Micro-loans and inexpensive tools of craft and trade are bringing new opportunities for financial development and independence to impoverished rural areas even as government sponsored training and aid is enabling the transformation of primitive farming into sustainable agriculture.

We've gone to the Moon and back, we're exploring our solar system, and sending robot ships beyond to gain greater knowledge and understanding of cosmic forces. We've penetrated the atom and discovered quantum forces that have changed our fundamental understanding of matter and energy and the role of consciousness at the sub-atomic level.

Every bit of this is the result of the new partnership between the Conscious Mind and the Subconscious, utilizing available tools to tap into their deep resources. Scientists have <u>dreamed</u> images leading to new discoveries of biological and physical structures. Medicine has learned the benefits of meditation, and its practice has led to advancements in health and new understanding of alternative therapies. Expanding awareness and practice of techniques of altered consciousness has led to new insights in human perception, while the breaking of barriers between academic disciplines has changed the exposition of history, our understanding of evolutionary dynamics, and the meaning behind myth and sacred literature.

MASTER THE PROCESS

You should now have confidence in the potential to bring the infinite resources available through the Subconscious Mind into conscious objectivity. The next step is for each of us to master the process by which the Conscious Mind is empowered to answer any challenge.

The essential process is in four parts:

1. "Composing" the Question or stating the Problem in the Conscious Mind.
2. "Transmitting" it to the Subconscious Mind.
3. "Channeling" the Answer from the Subconscious Mind.
4. "Interpreting" the Answer in the Conscious Mind.

However, as with any "esoteric technology," there are two approaches:

A. Direct experience.
B. The use of various tools and aids.

In both approaches, we can benefit from the cumulative experience of many thousands of practitioners recorded in studies, journals, folklore, and expositions of theory, practice, and application. With either approach, we need to open the Conscious Mind to the Subconscious and experience the unity of consciousness as indeed there truly is.

Within that unity, just as there is in the ocean everywhere on Planet Earth with its layers, currents, variations in temperature, etc., there will often be practical barriers preventing the free flow of information from the one to the other. Through our disciplines we must do the same kind of thing as wireless communications technology: establish a channel of our own that is "interference free." We calm the mind through ritual, breath control, meditation, and routine. We isolate our channel from the noise of others and direct it toward known sources.

No matter which approach we adopt, it is what the practitioner does that powers up the actual process, and this is done with defined intention to establish the *channel* and then to clear it of all interference. The "channel" may be the various tools, or the tools may only use the mentally created channel. Again, it is the practitioner's intention that matters.

The conscious mind can create the channel as an act of creative imagination in which a gate, door, natural stream, road of light, tunnel, etc., can serve as an "information highway," or it can just feel the intention itself, or your own journal will itself serve as a channel (as in dream processing and automatic writing). Find what has the strongest appeal to you, something that satisfies your sense of drama or propriety.

Clearing the channel of interference is commonly accomplished by keeping the whole operation secret, or revealed only to a group of supporters so that no expression of amusement, criticism, contrary images, or doubts interferes with your own sense of correctness.

The choice of either direct experience or a divinatory or communication tool will, to some degree, shape the remaining elements of composition, transmittal, receiving, and interpretation.

The first and most important step is to compose the question or problem, and establish that you need the response quickly or by a set time. Make it as simple and concise as possible without limiting or preconditioning the answer. This should always precede any operation. The question can be in the shape of a rhyme, a petition, a prayer, a formula, or whatever appeals to you in heart and mind. Familiarize yourself with the style of possible answers, but without unconsciously specifying anything. *Remember you wouldn't be asking the question if you knew the answer, so develop a sense of humility as you undertake the operation. Equally, you have to remove any self-imposed limitations, <u>and let the imagination run wild</u>.* The time for practicality comes later when you have choices to make.

The Tarot, Horary Astrology, Casting of Runes, and other tools each have their own methodology that shapes both question and answer.

The second step is the transmittal, or consultation. *Before the transmittal it is important to "make the call,"* just as it is necessary to dial a telephone number. You can do this in the form of a simple ritual, a prayer to deity, a chanted mantra, a moment of silence to calm the mind, or a more involved meditation that visualizes the question in some manner.

If you are using the Tarot, transmittal is the laying out of the cards; if Horary Astrology, it is the casting of the horoscope; it could be writing the question in your journal or on a piece of paper that you will burn or simply turn over. In the case of Dreaming, write the intent in your Dream Journal. Do what seems right to move the question from the world of the Conscious Mind to that of the Subconscious with its mysterious inhabitants and strange powers.

It is important to develop this feeling of respect or even of awe toward the Subconscious in this work.

The third step is to complete the transmittal and channel the answer. With the Tarot, finishing the laying out of the cards and seeing the whole pattern develop as you turn over hidden cards may commence the channeling as you speak out the meanings. Record your dream following the statement of intent mentioned in step two. Do the same with a journal for automatic writing.

Learn to listen impersonally to voices; pay attention to happenings that seem to stand out from the background. Do not pre-judge the answers or the form in which they may arrive. Honor the mysteriousness of the Subconscious.

In the fourth step of interpretation, you are bringing the language of the unconscious to the conscious—even when the message seems, at first, to be absolutely clear. As you continue your work, you may find it desirable to develop your own personal dictionary of symbols, unusual words, names, and expressions that have proven meaningful in the past. While the great unconscious, or universal consciousness, is indeed universal, the Conscious Mind is unique and personal, and its needs are specific. You may need to learn patience as well as tolerance as the interpretation proceeds.

PROBLEM SOLVING

As outlined above, you must compose the question or state the problem in as concise a manner as possible. It is just like using a search engine on the Internet—unless you are specific, you will get thousands and even hundreds of thousands of results in a meaningless milieu, but in this case you are more likely to get nothing.

Mostly, when you state a problem you need to ask a question to provide a direction for the solution. "I am overweight; how can I lose weight?" "I am a compulsive gambler; how can I stop?" "We must develop a new marketing program; what direction should we take?" "I have a mental block in my novel; what should be the next step?"

In framing the problem and the related question, think about the way the answer might be presented. It may not be obvious, but may come obliquely. You will need to recognize it. You are not dealing with a rational, conscious mind but the Subconscious Mind that works more often with symbols, mythic elements, images, secondary references, associated words, and so forth.

If you have the unusual ability to frame your problem in symbol form, it may bring you a more direct, but symbolic, answer. And it is for this reason that the various tools mentioned—the Tarot, Astrology, Runes, etc., along with the Kabbalah—work so well.

All in all, working with the Subconscious Mind is a lifelong learning program.

Problem solving will be further explored in the following section on creativity, with the understanding that creativity is intrinsic to problem solving, answering questions, and seeking information.

CREATIVITY

Everybody, it seems, wants to be thought of as "creative." It's a sought-after characteristic on your resumé—especially in the fields of advertising, art, music, dance, writing, marketing, and also in science, technology, and even in mathematics. It is also desirable in fashion and your social style. It is recognized as valuable in every kind of problem solving.

But what is it?

Our standard response largely relates creativity to the capacity to have new ideas and to create unique expressions. It's innovation and inventiveness—to look at a problem and come up with a new way to solve it; to take an old concept and come up with a new model; to take an old look and come up with a new one. But creativity must also be applicable to a situation. Generally, at some point, it needs to be practical and attainable.

Commonly we associate the creative process with the solitary thinker or with group "brainstorming." Either works.

What is the process?

Once again there is the need to define the problem and relate it in the form of one or more questions. At the same time, we want to see those questions as seeds for many answers rather than one, and then proceed to balance the many with the few that are most practical and applicable to the situation—which needs to be recognized in the definition of the problem.

To illustrate, let's take one of the most complex challenges in the fashion industry: to create a <u>new</u> fashion dress shoe for young women. Not being an expert on the subject, we are only making intelligent guesses for illustrative purposes.

What factors must be considered?

Marketing Position: Are we leaders or followers? Does our brand limit us in any way? What specifics in terms of style, materials, colors, etc. are predetermined because of manufacturing or other requirements?

Target Market: Fashion-conscious young women, ages twenty-four to forty-eight, college educated, mostly single, living and working in an urban environment, white collar to executive level. *Why will she choose this particular shoe, and for what occasion?*

Retail Price Range: $75 to $200.

Style: Slender high heel. As a date shoe, height should be three to four inches. Choices: Open toe, sling back; closed toe, pump. Alternative: ankle strap.

Look: Sexy, *avant-garde,* modest, or conservative.

Material: Calf or Patent Leather.

Color: Red or Black only.

Other Elements: Classic, Conservative, Dancing, Dinner Date, Fantasy, Fetish, Goth, etc.

Comfort: Important, of minor importance, of little concern, etc.

Having defined the factors to be considered, we are ready for brainstorming. Presumably, this would involve a group including one or two women from the target market, others representing knowledge of influences and trends from the entertainment world, the retail shoe industry, shoe manufacturing so that design remains practical, certainly someone active in shoe merchandising, and someone responsible for advertising and promotion.

Brainstorming

Once the important factors are known—a function of the Conscious Mind—it is time to bring in the Subconscious and have some fun! Brainstorming should evoke wild ideas, whether we're talking about fashion or quantum physics. It's the time for fantasy and heresy. Some ideas may appear to be too extreme when first presented, and then later turn mundane as the concept of the target market itself shifts. If "sexy" is chosen over "modest," then new questions arise that may position the shoe for "dancing" or for a "fetish look," and each answer opens up other ideas.

Brainstorming is not a time for restraint, but genuine unrestrained creativity. But then comes a time when we return to practicality and feasibility. Let's assume something wild in design is developed, then some creativity may still be necessary when it comes to practical issues involving manufacturing, pricing, and marketing. Creativity is not just for "those crazy people in design." It should always hover in the background, ready to come front and center to help solve new challenges.

How do we involve the Subconscious in brainstorming? We start, as described, by defining the problem and outlining the factors to be considered. While we start by asking what our target customer's personal goal actually may be, we have also to consider what your personal goal is in calling this meeting: *Is this purely a business matter, or is it a personal matter? Are you seeking recognition in your job for an outstanding design, or a successful new product, or something you'd want to wear?* The <u>personal goal</u> is vital to your Subconscious Mind. And relating that goal to <u>personal fantasy</u>—seeing yourself receive an imaginary award or a professional award, or receiving admiring glances when wearing the shoe or being complimented for your good taste, etc.—invokes your inner creativity.

Once the problem, factors to be considered, and the personal goal are established, then we confront the question of brainstorming techniques and the alternate questions of utilizing the various divinatory tools we've already outlined. Both can be combined. At this point, the Tarot—for example—can become an "engine" of creativity, as can almost any divinatory tool. The more familiar you are with their use, the more effective they will be. Their use is amply covered in many recommended books.

The need for creativity is part of every job, every activity, whether personal or social, in relationships, parenting, household management, gardening, cooking, etc. Creativity enriches your life and could be said to solve every problem.

MENTAL& PHYSICAL HEALTH

The Subconscious Mind is more than a simple *resource* for information on Mental and Physical Health. It can also be a *source,* as is well established through our growing understanding of the <u>Mind-Body connection</u>. Specific programs of Hatha Yoga, Martial Arts, Physical Movement, as well as Meditation, Prayer, Visualization, and Nutritional discipline work in connection with Conscious Planning, Self-Hypnosis, Prayer, "Art Therapy," and Dream Work.

In health matters we generally face one of two problems:

1. What to do about a known condition?
2. What to do when you don't know what's wrong, but you know that something is?

With a known condition, whether being treated with conventional medicine or not, we will benefit by employing the Conscious Mind in personal study and research to better understand the condition and the treatment options and to coordinate planning and personal discipline to optimize our return to full health. In addition, we should employ the Subconscious Mind to reinforce our image of full health now. Here we utilize techniques of prayer, visualization, and self-hypnosis to establish our target goal, and we make that image of perfect health as strong as possible.

With an undiagnosed condition, we know the symptoms but we don't know their cause—and we have to be unwilling to merely accept our "fate," or "God's will." *Neither Fate nor God make you sick!* Sometimes outside factors make you sick; other times, it's "you" who make you sick! That's hard to believe, but self-analysis will often show you that it is true for various motives.

How do you make this kind of self-discovery? The phrase "self-analysis" sounds challenging, but it need not be. Essentially, we are looking at a health problem and we need to employ the same basic creative process to find the answer as we've previously described.

Regardless of who has a health problem—you or another—it sometimes helps to objectify the matter by pretending it is another person who is neither you nor anyone close to you. Give the person a different but common name, like John or Mary (so long as that name does not belong to either yourself or anyone close to you) or Mr. X or Ms. Y. Then you can employ any divinatory technique with which you are familiar, or you can use meditation or prayer to transmit the problem to the Subconscious just as described earlier.

However, in most cases, the closer you are to the person with the health problem—including yourself—the more oblique will be the likely answer. You may have to let your imagination explore symbols and images or stories given in your divination or in dreams and through meditation and prayer. And likewise in order to receive inner guidance for the solution or cure.

None of this, of course, is intended to replace professional medical diagnosis or treatment, but to mobilize your inner resources to complement it. Health is a precious resource and needs your full attention, inwardly and outwardly.

PAIN MANAGEMENT

Whether our health problem has been diagnosed satisfactorily or not, we often face the problem of pain control. While modern drugs, prescription and over-the-counter, can be very effective in pain management, there can be hazards to their long-term usage.

Are there alternatives? Yes, of course there usually are—except in the case of terminal illness. Sometimes the basic approach that may have better results than expected is simply to "grin and bear it," and get busy with your life. The older we get, the more often we seem to develop pains from both known and unknown causes. In many cases, time will heal the cause of the pain and you will suddenly realize that you don't hurt any longer.

But there are other times when you will have severe pains with no known cause. Your doctor may do tests and take x-rays and such, and report back that everything looks all right. Then, *why the pain?*

By communicating with your all-knowing Subconscious Mind, you may get an answer. Always, the first step is to state the question as specifically as you can: "Why do I have such severe pain in my upper left arm when it clearly is not a shoulder injury or bone problem?" Next you may choose to use any divinatory tool or technique that you favor, and hopefully you will find an answer as to the cause or source of the pain. Or, you may choose to dream on the question, to meditate on it, or to directly address your subconscious mind through self-hypnosis.

Your answers may need interpretation, and so you have to be open to looking at them from many angles. By word association you may discover an answer that works or you may have to think in terms of symbols. And you may just have to keep asking the question.

Maybe you don't get a quick answer and need to do something about the pain beyond more and more medication. Assuming your familiarity with the technique of self-hypnosis, you may address the subconscious directly in the following manner: "I invoke the powers of my Subconscious Mind to heal the source of my pain," and repeat your invocation several times. Then, follow that with a condensed version that you perceive as an "echo" of the main invocation, such as: "Healing the source of my pain," and letting that repeat several times like an echo. Repeat several times daily when you can.

It may bring relief, or at least partial relief. The Mind-Body connection is powerful, and even if the source of your pain has a still-unidentified physical cause, your invocation may help.

See also the "Dream Works Program: Interactions with the Spirit Realm" in chapter eight.

REJUVENATION

Rejuvenation! We can see this as a health matter or as a life matter, by which we mean thinking and living youthfully.

Dr. Slate has written *Rejuvenation: Strategies for Living Younger, Longer & Better* (Llewellyn, 2001), in which he says:

As human beings, we are designed to grow, not deteriorate. The physical body seeks youth and health. It is always responsive to our efforts to stay young and undo aging. Rejuvenation is a natural process of renewal and growth. We have the built-in potential to repair, re-create, and rejuvenate ourselves. By developing that potential, we could conceivably live and grow indefinitely while, at the same time, improving the quality of our existence.

And then, he continues:

But all too often, we reject the sources of rejuvenation within ourselves and our surroundings. As a result, our biological systems deteriorate, and our bodies finally wear out—all within an artificially fixed life span that we accept as absolute and immutable. Because we expect to age and die, we eventually self-destruct. We fail to discover the limitless possibilities for continued growth and fulfillment.

The book then provides fourteen simple rules and forty-five basic strategies to counter this negative pattern of self-destruction and activate your "internal fountain of youth." That's right, it's right there in each of us within the purview of the Subconscious Mind.

As with any shift of ingrained habits and expectations, it takes time and effort and real self-discipline to turn off the old programming and start something new. Dr. Slate's approach is through education and self-hypnosis using "strategies that defy aging by protecting and fortifying the self's innermost energy system." He writes that in this book

We will examine new ways of actively decelerating aging and, in some instances, literally reversing its effects. We will conclude by offering a seven-day plan designed to initiate an upward growth spiral that counteracts aging and promotes continuous renewal of the mind, body, and spirit. Always, our emphasis is on workable strategies that facilitate not only rejuvenation and longevity, but quality of life as well.

It's beyond the capacity and purpose of this book to cover the whole subject of Rejuvenation, but one more excerpt from the book describes both method and principle, and further shows the power of the Subconscious Mind to function as a "full partner" with the Conscious Mind in meeting the challenges and opening the opportunities for a more complete life.

Our conscious powers represent only a small fraction of our total potentials. Like the distant reaches of space, the subconscious mind is a vast region of exciting possibilities awaiting our probes. It consists not only of our past experiences not presently available to conscious awareness; it is also an intricate maze of potentially empowering mechanisms. Some of our subconscious mechanisms are only marginally active, whereas others are totally dormant. Through self-hypnosis, we can uncover that vast store of possibilities and use them to achieve our highest potential goals, including rejuvenation, while dramatically increasing the richness of our lives. Fortunately, the subconscious with its wealth of resources is always a willing partner in our rejuvenation efforts.

Despite conventional assumptions that aging is largely an uncontrollable physiological phenomenon which is determined largely by genetics, new emerging perspectives recognize the complex mental, spiritual, and physical interactions underlying aging as well as our capacity to deliberately influence them. Through self-hypnosis, we can eliminate subconscious age accelerants and introduce new age-defying interactions. We can uproot the aging influences of negative self-perceptions and replace them with positive self-awareness. We can identify the corrosive effects of aging on the mind and body, and replace them with youthful vitality. We can introduce totally new mechanisms that arrest aging, revive worn organs and stressed systems, and reverse the negative processes that energize aging. The result is a longer, richer, and healthier life.

More and more we realize that *life is what we make of it,* and the more fulfilling life each of us makes, the still greater opportunities for all of us as the individual contributes to the evolving potential for all.

PSYCHIC POWERS

Unlike the Conscious Mind functioning within an energy field connected to the human brain, the Subconscious Mind has the whole universe serving as its brain. Understanding these differences is important to our perception of the opportunities each creates. The Conscious Mind, involved with but not a product of the brain, has learned to use the brain for intentional action in the physical world, in particular for speech and communication.

The Subconscious Mind relates to the universal consciousness (also known as the "unconscious") that pervades the whole universe but most closely relates to each Conscious Mind with which it is associated. In its association with the Conscious Mind, the Subconscious can actually use particular areas of the human brain for communication and expression, but is not limited to the physical world. Instead, *it opens the realm of the psychic world to the Conscious Mind.*

It almost seems as if this is a critical time in history requiring humanity to have new areas of the Unconscious accessible to the Conscious Mind in the form of expanded awareness and the development of innate psychic powers into reliable psychic skills.

Psychic Powers are extensions of familiar senses so that physical sight and hearing may be augmented as clairvoyance and clairaudience, so that physical touch enlarges to include psychic touch, so that mental telepathy becomes reliable and intuition becomes familiar and dependable. *Can we expect astral projection and spirit communication to likewise become familiar, everyday occurrences? Can we expect to be able to walk on hot coals and levitate at will? And what about precognition?*

There are degrees of psychic success, just as in all other powers and skills. Almost anyone can draw a crude map, but skilled cartography takes training and practice. Even if you suddenly find yourself levitating you will, no doubt, have to learn how to balance yourself, just as you would when first working with a trampoline.

Yes, we will discuss actual psychic skills and their benefits, but the most important point is that global psychic skills are increasing. just as are global temperatures. It is a change that is happening as inevitably as the increase in extreme weather phenomena and the rise in sea levels.

We've always had the Unconscious (Subconscious Mind), while full Consciousness is a recent experience during which the Subconscious Mind was largely repressed, ignored, and forgotten. Now we have to learn to blend the two together under willful control. As we formerly functioned in "clan consciousness"—which became tribal and then national and perhaps even ethnic and (as some anthropologists claimed) racial—we recently (over a few thousand years) developed the personal Conscious Mind.

We need both Conscious and Subconscious, and we need the unique and positive powers of both: we need rationality and irrationality, we need logic and we need intuition, we need practical skills and artistic skills, we need to go step-by-step and we need to be able to "leap over tall buildings." Our vision will extend from the microscopic to telescopic, from sub-atomic to cosmic, from the study of past causality to a realization that the future is calling—and that we can have a hand in shaping it.

One caveat: Much of our increase in psychic skills is really an extension and expansion of awareness leading to changes of perspective beyond the familiar limitations of time and space. Unlike the United States' use of remote viewing to spy on the old Soviet missile sites or bioweapon factories, new clairvoyant visions will bring colorful perceptions of emotions and energies, auras, thought forms, and non-human entities.

Here's the realization: we have all along been unconscious co-creators, and now we have the growing realization that we must be <u>conscious</u> co-creators, broadly aware of our own transgressions of natural law, or else the human experiment will end in failure.

CALL IT MAGICK

Call it Magick because that is exactly what creativity is. It's the ability to cause change in accordance with WILL. We have to make decisions about the future we want based on rational analysis and intuitive awareness of present and future situations.

Yes, we have other names for it too. Psychic and Spiritual Healing, Reading the Past and Seeing the Future, Psychometry and Psychokinesis, Out-of-Body Experience and Remote Viewing, and so on—all really amounting to Extrasensory Perception and Action Beyond the Body, with responsible choices.

Do we really need to describe what this means? Your creative imagination will provide the answers. The vital need is for each of us to accept a vastly increased need for perception of the interrelationships among all creatures, big and small, visible and previously invisible, and of our increased responsibility to act for the benefit of all and the planet as a whole.

The greater our field of resources becomes, the greater becomes our obligation to act with intelligence and spiritual awareness. We need to think big and leave a small imprint.

CHAPTER SIX

THE THERAPEUTIC POWER OF SUBCONSCIOUS KNOWLEDGE

THE SELF-EMPOWERMENT PERSPECTIVE

Your best therapist, like your best hypnotist and healer, exists within yourself as a functional, advanced part of your subconscious. It is your direct link to the resources required to advance your growth and enrich the quality of your life. As a fundamental part of your being, it recognizes your basic nature as a person of dignity and incomparable worth.

Through your interactions with that inner therapist, you have direct access to the subconscious knowledge required to solve even your most difficult problems. You will discover new and more effective ways of enriching your life and dissolving all blockages to your growth. When connected to the therapist within, nothing is beyond your reach. You will become empowered to achieve your highest goals while helping others to do the same. Whether simply extinguishing an unwanted habit, overcoming a debilitating fear, or resolving a haunting past-life trauma, all the therapeutic powers of the subconscious are available to you at any moment.

Aside from these, the therapist within can become your link to the abundant powers beyond, to include the spirit world. As your link to the beyond, your subconscious can connect you to protective spirit guides, therapeutic counselors, and advanced growth specialists from the spirit realm who will become empowerment companions with the power to enrich your life with abundance, happiness, and success.

The subconscious is, in fact, in continuous interaction with the higher realms of power to meet your empowerment needs, including protection in times of danger, comfort in times of grief, and hope in times of despair. Through your connection to the spirit realm, you will experience the full beauty and power of your existence— past, present, and future—as an evolving soul.

Admittedly, we do not know all there is to know about the subconscious and the complex dynamics associated with it. We do know, however, that the subconscious is a vast reservoir of power that is available to us at any moment. It is essential to our continued existence—without it, we would not exist in the first place.

Like the many other functions of the subconscious, its therapeutic role can be explained from a variety of perspectives, including the psychoanalytic theories developed first by Sigmund Freud and then continued by others. Unlike other approaches, however, the self-empowerment perspective focuses on your capacity alone to experience the subconscious, activate its powers, and focus them on self-designed goals. That's what self-empowerment is all about!

The self-empowerment perspective recognizes the subconscious as an interactive phenomenon in which various subconscious processes work in concert with each other to promote our personal empowerment. That interaction among functions can be illustrated by a recurrent dream that depicts past-life trauma and then activates therapeutic functions related to it. A dream, for instance, of falling to your death in a past-life can provide therapeutic awareness of the source of a present-life fear of heights. There's a mountain of evidence that enlightenment about the past-life origin of a persistent fear can instantly extinguish it. Along a different line, our subconscious interactions with a personal spirit guide can promote increased feelings of personal worth and well-being. Once the guiding presence becomes known to conscious awareness, the effects can be worth hours of conventional psychotherapy. Invariably, self-enlightenment is self-empowering. Enlightenment of subconscious origin is one of the most powerful therapeutic agents known.

The self-empowerment view recognizes the developmental nature of both the conscious and subconscious. Differences in rates of development for both are seen, not as imperfections, but expressions of individuality. Both conscious and subconscious perfection, from this perspective, are best defined as an endless growth process rather than a finished product. Fortunately, the therapist within can facilitate that developmental process by activating the subconscious faculties related to it.

It follows that our personal empowerment depends largely on our capacity to interact with the subconscious. Therapeutic techniques based on this view include hypnosis, dream analysis, free association, and various forms of meditation that focus on specific subconscious processes. The therapeutic value of the resultant interaction between the conscious and subconscious seems to have no limits. Even interactions characterized by symbolism and disguise, as in dreams, can be therapeutic. Rather than limiting and problematic, they command our attention and motivate us to discover their hidden significance.

The self-empowerment perspective recognizes the capacity of multiple subconscious elements to function as a collective force that is far more powerful than the sum of its independent parts. Like an orchestra, each subconscious element functions in concert to create a symphony of power. It obviously follows that attunement and balance become critical in perfecting the combined effects of the multiple functions.

The self-empowerment perspective recognizes the conscious and subconscious as existing on a continuum with no clear line of separation between them. All behaviors, including our thoughts, actions, interests, emotions, orientations, predispositions, decisions, and drives, have both conscious and subconscious elements. They each can be seen as strings existing between the conscious and subconscious. Becoming self-empowered depends largely on our capacity to bring the strings of subconscious power into an interconnected state of oneness with consciousness, and then focusing them on specific objectives. Specific therapeutic programs based on this perspective emphasize certain essentials, as we'll later see, designed to generate a state of integrated wholeness that builds positive expectations of success and personal fulfillment. Personal empowerment programs are formulated by the individual to generate positive, goal-oriented interactions. Goals that are multidimensional in nature, such as stress management, rejuvenation, career success, personal well-being, and quality of life, are especially receptive to empowerment programs based on the concept of interconnected strings and integrated wholeness. The results can be both immediate and powerful.

The self-empowerment perspective recognizes the diversity of subconscious faculties and their capacity to interact with each other in promoting our personal growth and empowerment. When viewed through the prism of diversity, the highly divergent faculties of the subconscious are considered critical in that they mirror in many ways the mental, physical, and spiritual complexities of our existence. Awareness of the diverse functions of the subconscious can increase our understanding of the world. Given a clearer understanding of the subconscious, we begin to see the differences among cultures as strengths, not weakness. Similarly, diversity within cultures is seen as increasingly important to cultural advancement and the evolvement of the globe. At a personal level, recognizing our individuality with our own personal characteristics, including personal identity, abilities, motives, and preferences, can promote our feelings of self-worth and add quality to our existence. The different sides of the self become balanced and attuned. The private self becomes empowered to interact more effectively with the social self. The result is higher self-esteem and more rewarding social relationships. Our masculine and feminine sides become empowered to interact in ways that enhance not only our understanding of ourselves but the other sex as well. Once in touch with the different sides of the self, we become empowered to integrate them and experience the full joys of self expression.

According to the self-empowerment perspective, the subconscious never sleeps—it is in continuous interaction with consciousness. It embraces the physical, spiritual, and psychical nature of our existence. Awareness of future events, telepathic communications, and clairvoyant insight are all among its powers. The subconscious welcomes our probes and challenges us to use its powers.

The self-empowerment view recognizes the subconscious as a storehouse of knowledge not yet manifest to conscious awareness. As we dive deeper into the subconscious, the more we learn about ourselves and the more empowered and balanced we become. Amazing though it may seem, complex bodies of new knowledge have been accessed and transferred to conscious awareness through appropriate empowerment programs, including hypnosis. Among the striking examples are fluency in a new language and competency of important technical skills, a phenomenon called hypnoproduction. While explanations of this phenomenon vary, a common view holds that our past achievements (including those of past-life origin) are integrated into our being and thus never lost—they remain forever a part of our evolvement. Although they may exist in the subconscious, they influence consciousness and are receptive to our efforts to retrieve and reactivate them.

The self-empowerment view recognizes the subconscious as a powerful motivator that actively communicates with consciousness, often in inventive and challenging ways that suggest new approaches to solving problems and achieving personal goals. Examples include déjà vu, intuitive awareness, symbolic dreams, spontaneous ESP, and a wide range of spiritual interactions. These spontaneous messages of subconscious origin can literally change the direction of our lives. Among the striking examples is the sudden flash of insight associated with past-life trauma that instantly extinguished a lifelong fear. This remarkable phenomenon was illustrated by a teenager whose lifelong fear of crowds instantly vanished when she discovered through a vivid dream that she had been stoned to death in a distant past life. In a similar instance, a college student experienced during self-hypnosis a brief past-life image of himself as a World War I soldier being stabbed during combat. The insight extinguished, once and for all, his fear of knives, a phobia that had persisted since early childhood.

The self-empowerment view recognizes the subconscious as an empowering force that often reaches beyond physical reality to become an important link to the spirit world. It recognizes the therapeutic power of interacting with the departed along with spiritual guides and other growth specialists. A psychologist reported that among his most vivid memories was the touch of a hand on his shoulder as he received his Ph.D. degree in clinical psychology. Accompanying the touch was the clear message, "There's more than this." The experience inspired him to study the paranormal and integrate nonconventional concepts into his practice as a highly successful clinician.

The subconscious often turns to nature as an effective therapeutic messenger. Trees, streams, flowers, and animals, to mention but a few, can become messengers of healing and growth. A student participating in our laboratory research of brainwave patterns experienced upon reaching the alpha state a clear image of her recently deceased twin brother against a bright sunrise in the distance. As she lingered in the altered state, her brother smiled broadly and reached forward with the simple message, "Love you." Comforted by the assurance of her brother's safe transition, her grief instantly vanished. In our research, a magical sunset, moonlit snowscape, still lake, and regal tree have all been comforting emissaries of subconscious healing power. Even a gentle breeze has been known to whisper comforting messages from a guiding presence. On the day of her wedding, a former student upon entering the sanctuary experienced a sudden stirring of the air and the loving embrace of her deceased father. In her own words, "It was a moment of splendor I will never forget." A few years later when she received an award for her services to her community, she again experienced during the ceremony the unmistakable presence of her father through a gentle breeze.

Animals are often comforting messengers that connect us to the therapeutic powers of the subconscious as well as the spirit realm. A psychology professor reported that a butterfly was all it took to lift the weight of grief following her father's recent death. As the butterfly lingered briefly upon her hand, she felt the warm and loving presence of her father. When the butterfly took flight, she felt a complete lifting of her grief. It was for her a peak moment of healing power. She is today a therapist whose specialty is the treatment of depression and grief.

THERAPEUTIC APPLICATIONS

The self-empowerment perspective embraces therapeutic diversity and the importance of multiple techniques, including innovative approaches not yet integrated into conventional empowerment programs. The energy massage, out-of-body interactions, connecting to the power of nature, discarnate communications, self-hypnosis, meditation, and the relevance of spiritual planes of power—to list but a few—are all included in this approach. It's an eclectic, experiential approach that focuses on *what works*. It's based on the premise that the best evidence of subconscious therapeutic power is personal experience. If a specific technique is found to be effective, it is accepted and utilized. If it is found to be of questionable value, it is either discarded or set aside and reexamined. As a therapeutic approach, the self-empowerment perspective recognizes your capacity to set your own personal goals and to develop your own approach for achieving them.

The self-empowerment perspective recognizes certain therapeutic essentials and your capacity to apply them. Given these essentials, you can design your own self-empowerment programs to achieve your personal goals and enrich your life with happiness and success. Here are the essentials.

1. Positive Goal Statement

Self-empowerment depends largely on your effectiveness in formulating your personal goals. The two essential elements of effective goal formulation are: (1) a clear statement of your goal in positive terms, and (2) a positive statement of your intent to achieve it. The simple statement, "I am empowered to achieve this goal" is one of the most powerful affirmations known. It builds an expectancy effect that programs you, both consciously and subconsciously, for complete success. You can increase the empowering effect of your stated goal by writing it down in a journal and referring to it from time to time.

2. Positive Inner-dialogue

Go to your bosom; Knock there and ask your heart what it doth know.
(William Shakespeare, *Measure for Measure*)

Positive inner-dialogue is self-empowerment at its peak. It can be defined simply as *the empowering messages you send to yourself.* Once you've formulated your personal goals, innerdialogue can activate the resources required to achieve them. Think of your dialogue as personal affirmations of power that you can present either audibly or silently as thought messages. You will probably find, however, that silent messages become even more powerful when supplemented by the sound of your own voice.

Positive inner-dialogue is essential to self-empowerment because it provides instant and direct access to the unlimited powers of the subconscious. It includes all the positive messages we send to ourselves through a variety of channels that subsumes not only our verbal expressions but also our beliefs, orientations, aspirations, values, expectations, perceptions, and attitudes. A major advantage of inner dialogue is that it can used almost any time or place.

Among the most effective forms of inner-dialogue are the positive "I am" messages we send to ourselves. Examples are: *I am empowered to succeed, I am destined for greatness,* and *I am a person of worth,* each of which can build powerful feelings of self-confidence and well-being. Even when not directly targeted to the subconscious mind, inner-dialogue will nonetheless be registered there.

A simple positive thought can activate a host of subconscious processes required for your complete success. A college student found that the simple thought, "I am competent," was sufficient to banish stage fright. As president of the university's student government association, she used the simple affirmation, which she silently but emphatically repeated to herself before presentations. In her words, "I was amazed that such a simple message could have such a profound effect. It was not only relaxing, it cleared my mind, built my self-confidence, and connected me to my audience. I soon found myself actually looking for new opportunities to speak publicly!" She discovered that fear, like other disempowering emotions, seeks extinction and welcomes positive intervention. A simple positive message directed inwardly was all it took to replace fear with powerful self-confidence that's so essential to effective communication.

Positive inner-dialogue can be especially effective in coping with feelings of insecurity associated with personal loss as well as career reversal. The owner of a small business used the straightforward message, "I am destined for success," to overcome her feelings of failure that she associated with both a failed marriage and her struggling business. Upon becoming convinced that her business would succeed, she initiated an aggressive promotional program. She overcame her feelings of insecurity and inadequacy and is today the owner of a highly successful retail business firm. She's convinced that empowering dialogue programmed her mentally for complete success and generated an expectancy effect that enriched her life, both personally and professionally.

Positive inner-dialogue can empower you with the coping skills required to meet the demands of even the most distressful situation, including emergencies and other conditions requiring decisive action. When you're faced with disappointment or adversity, the cumulative effects of positive dialogue can be profound. An attorney whose husband was diagnosed with terminal pancreatic cancer found that reassuring each other, "We will get through this together," empowered them to face one of life's most difficult situations. Their mutual reassurances added quality to their relationship during the last stages of their life together. His final words to her were, "We got through this together."

Through the therapist within, you too can experience the highest dimensions of energy and power, even when faced with life's most difficult challenges.

3. Empowering Imagery

Empowering imagery is second only to self-dialogue as an empowerment essential in activating the therapeutic powers of the subconscious. Once you've formulated your goals in positive terms, relevant imagery gives them the substance required for full embracement by the subconscious.

Goal-related imagery can be seen as a present manifestation of a future reality. For instance, if your goal is rejuvenation, imagery of your body at its youthful prime actually activates the subconscious processes related to rejuvenation. By visualizing yourself at your youthful prime while affirming, "I am now empowered with the energies of youth and vitality," you can take charge of the aging process and not only slow aging, you can actually reverse its effects. Living younger, healthier, and happier becomes your destiny.

Along another line, if your goal is to lose weight, visualizing yourself weighing an exact preferred amount while affirming, "This is the true me," can increase your motivation while activating the inner resources required for success. For breaking unwanted habits, such as smoking, visualizing the word "No" while affirming, "I am a non-smoker" can extinguish in an instant the need to smoke.

4. Empowering Symbolism

The use of symbols related to your stated goals can efficiently activate at a moment's notice the subconscious faculties related to even highly complex goals. For instance, if your goal is financial success, simply visualizing a gold coin can increase your motivation and facilitate optimal decision making related to your financial success. Should you decide to do so, you can take that effect a step further by carrying on your person a gold coin and periodically stroking it.

Along a different line, if your goal is to more effectively cope with stress or overcome adversity, visualizing yourself enveloped in a bright glow as a symbol of inner power and protection can energize you with the self-confidence and sense of security required for success. This approach is especially effective when used during any potentially stressful situation, such as a job interview or public presentation. Students have found it highly useful in managing test anxiety and improving their academic performance. A psychology doctoral student reported that his use of this simple approach improved his concentration powers and enabled him to perform at his peak during the defense of his dissertation before a hard-hitting doctoral committee.

5. Self-empowerment Cues

A simple cue, typically a physical gesture, can instantly connect you to the subconscious resources related to your empowerment goal. Among the common examples are the temple touch, finger pad engagement, and toe lift. By incorporating a simple cue into your empowerment program, you can increase the program's effectiveness by using the cue on demand to activate the program's full effects. With practice, the cue usually becomes even more effective. Whether losing weight, quitting smoking, managing stress, increasing self-confidence, overcoming fear, or solving complex problems, a simple cue can unleash a flow of power that ensures your complete success.

Given these five essentials, you have all the elements required to build your own success story. Beginning now, all the resources required, whether conscious, subconscious, or from beyond, are at your command.

CHAPTER SEVEN

SPIRITUAL RELEVANCE OF THE SUBCONSCIOUS:
A Doorway to Spiritual Realities and Interaction with the Spirit Realm

Unfortunately, many people have a peculiar bias that Spiritual matters have little to do with the practical, everyday, <u>material</u> world that includes the physical body, money, Nature, sex, as well as politics, economics, foreign affairs, global weather, health, food sufficiency, or even peace, prosperity, progress, and so on.

It is unfortunate, because everything in the universe does have a common origin, and whatever else it is, that Source is certainly spiritual as well. And, being so, there is no real conflict between material and spiritual—they are just different aspects, and functions, of the same thing, which was Divine in the beginning, is Divine now, and will be Divine at the end—if there is an end.

What there is, and what makes for the apparent conflicts, is human discrimination or lack of it. We have the power of choice, *will*, and need to exercise it. We have the ability to learn, to analyze, to understand, to choose, and to act. We were born to be co-creators—"in His image"—so it is our responsibility to choose and act wisely and with awareness.

WHAT IS SPIRITUALITY?

Our dictionary doesn't tell us much—"the quality or condition of being spiritual"; and then "the property or revenue belonging to a church or church official" (Encarta online Dictionary). We learned that the word "spirituality" comes from the Latin verb *spirare,* which means "to breathe, to live." So, Life and Spirit must be considered together.

We did find, however, one reference of particular interest in the November 8, 2008 *Honolulu Star-Bulletin,* from an article by the Reverend Mike Young:

> *I understand spirituality to refer to living with one's attention on the full experience of being a human being in all its diversity and richness, particularly its interconnectedness, and the discipline of trying to fully live out of that awareness.*

LIVING FULLY OUT OF THE AWARENESS OF INTERCONNECTEDNESS

Quantum theory, as well as world mysticism and our studies of the Subconscious Mind, have taught us that <u>everything is interconnected as it always has been and is from the "Beginning</u>." But, do *we fully live out of that awareness?* There are two propositions here:

1. To be aware of our diversity, richness, and—particularly—our interconnectedness;
2. To fully live out of that awareness.

In other words, our *spirituality calls for us to live in full awareness of this world and our connections to all there is, and then to act fully out of that awareness.* We can't be spiritual while ignoring the world around us. We can't be spiritual by not living—acting—out of that awareness. Spirituality does not wear "blinders," seeing only what we want to call "good" and either ignoring that which doesn't qualify or thinking it has nothing to do with us. Spirituality does not mean that we spend all our time thinking only "pure thoughts," praying to some "higher authority," meditating on "white light," and singing praises to the "being in charge" of it all.

We are perceptive, intelligent people given the responsibility of willful choice. Not only that, we have little-used powers that extend both our awareness and our capacity to act beyond the immediate confines of skin and bones. Through our Subconscious Mind we are in contact with the Universal Consciousness, which likewise includes Awareness and the capacity to Act.

Yes, each of us is "just one," but each of us is connected to many others so that together we are a powerful force that can be united in common cause *merely by doing our part!* Yes, by acting in concert— sharing the planned action and timing it to act together—we may have still more power, but don't let the lack of group planning and leadership stop you from acting alone and at any time. *It works because the power of consciousness is universal and timeless!*

Let us propose two simple exercises:

1. Just sit back, relax, and think of all the scary BIG things going on in the world right now: International Terrorism, Climate Change, Water and Food Shortages, Economic Recession, Rising Cost of Energy, Lack of Education pertinent to the times, Massive Poverty, Severe Weather Phenomena, Pandemics of Disease, Religious Extremism and Cruelty to Women, Abuse of Children—including using them as suicide bombers—Concern for Food Quality, Earth Changes, Drug Cartels, Piracy on the High Seas, Holding People for Ransom, etc. Make your list as long as you can.

2. Now, again sit back and relax, and think of all the times you've had spiritual and psychic experiences: Knowledge of who is calling on the phone, Premonitions, Spirit Communications, Psychic Impressions of a person's character, Feelings about the health of relatives and friends, Out-of-Body Experiences, Miraculous Healing, Levitation, Poltergeist Phenomena, Animal Communication, Knowing about coming weather changes or earthquakes, Mental Telepathy with a Spouse, Forewarnings that saved you from accidents, Remote Viewing, and so on.

Again, make the list as long as you can, and include everything you've heard from friends and others.

What if you could use the powers experienced in (2) above to influence and change those challenges in (1) above? Quantum theory says you can and it is <u>your Subconscious Mind that gives you the means to do so.</u> We are connected to one another, and we are connected to everything that is happening. *By living in <u>full awareness</u> of this, we can and will do something about it. You—as a co-creator, as a god in the making, as one already richly endowed with psychic powers—do have the POWER! Even more, <u>WE have the POWER!</u>*

Everything we've written in this book discloses both the powers everyone is born with, and the greater skills that can come as we consciously develop those powers and focus them on real challenges and problems.

Let's try one more exercise. It's a very simple one, and yet we are still wrestling with a severe problem that could be solved.

Ask yourself: *How is it that all Energy originally came and comes from the Sun, free of charge, and yet our Energy Resources (all derived from the Sun) of Oil, Gas, Coal, Wood, Biofuels, Nuclear, etc. are all expensive, and growing shortages are creating dangerous challenges just about everywhere? How come, with our modern science and technology, and willingness to invest in order to end our dependency on foreign resources, we are more dependent than ever? Why, with the threat of war and the challenge to our prosperity, do we not find new solutions to this old problem?*

Now, what answers did you find? Write them all down.

We are not proposing that you have found the answers to world crisis—you may have, but the challenge is to do something about it.

IT'S ALL TO DO WITH CONNECTIONS!

You've heard that before—that it's who you're connected with—who you know—that can bring about solutions to your needs. It's true about "connections," but it is also true that *you are already well con-*

nected, for you are in touch with the world through your Subconscious Mind.

Yes, you are an individual person, but you are also connected in consciousness to every other person and to their history, experience, and knowledge. And, more deeply yet, you are connected to the foundations of knowledge behind human history, to the ultimate resources by which human history was made, and to the essence of it all from the very beginning.

Every human experience throughout history has created hologram-like energy patterns that can be searched for and read just like information on the Internet. They can be brought to "virtual life" and interacted with just like "spirits" of real people.

You are <u>connected</u>, even though you don't realize it and don't know how to use those connections as needed.

THINKING . . . STARTS THE ACTION

Actually, just thinking about problems and searching for answers initiates a process that stimulates solutions. Questions are balanced with Answers. Problems are balanced with their Resolution. When you think about problems, you are creating psychic and spiritual conditions that lead to their resolution.

Just as observation and measurement at the quantum level causes movement from a sea of possibilities to a state of reality, so does recognizing a problem call its solution into existence. Likewise, ask a question and its answer appears from the universal information field.

Your mind has amazing powers when used properly—and that's what we have to learn.

Alone, or together with others, there is power, but joining with many others likewise concerned to find solutions and meet challenges together creates a positive dynamic in world consciousness that will facilitate resolution of today's greatest challenges.

Going back to the earlier exercises where you recognized the problems we face and you likewise recalled that you do have psychic and spiritual powers that are constantly at work on your behalf, realize now that recognizing problems starts the process for their resolution! We have immense powers that are under-utilized for two reasons:

1. We've been taught to believe we are powerless, and that—in particular—we don't have psychic and spiritual powers.
2. We don't believe we can do anything about world problems so we largely pull the covers over our head and hide from the bad news.

Think! What happens when you ignore or hide from personal problems? They rarely go away, but instead may overwhelm you as they get bigger, and bigger, and **bigger!** We must recognize real problems, whether personal or world-sized. With recognition, we begin the process of mobilizing our resources—both conscious and unconscious—to meet and resolve those challenges.

What are we really doing?

We are bringing problems into consciousness, and making the unconscious part of the process. While we do speak of the Conscious Mind and the Subconscious Mind as if they were distinctly separate, the truth is that separation is like an old fence line that no longer divides property from property. As we act with Wholeness, we bring all the facets of consciousness together to function in unity. Our psychic powers and spiritual skills go to work and we utilize our techniques of dream interpretation, self-hypnosis, dowsing, past-life regression, etc. to consciously unite with the so-called unconscious for successful solutions to our recognized problems or answers to our questions.

We are not powerless, as we have been misled. We can do something about world problems just as we can resolve personal problems by facing them. It is up to us to act with belief in ourselves and not to trust these problems to armies and departments of so-called professionals continuing the problems created by the policies and actions of their predecessors.

It is up to you, and each of us, to resolve these problems directly, acting through our Subconscious Minds to reach the consciousness of

others just like us, who are—in fact—<u>us,</u> to ask Universal Consciousness to resolve a named, specific problem.

PRAYER, MEDITATION, MAGIC, GROUP ACTION

How do we invoke the powers of Universal Consciousness to resolve
problems?

The techniques are familiar, but the realization that you and each
of us can reach out and personally intervene in world affairs is not.
We've been taught to leave it to "others," and when it comes to some
of the most complex problems, the answer those others apply is often
military action. "They" (the other side in the situation) don't do what
"we" want—so the answer is often the command to "bomb them!" If
"they" don't agree with "us"—the answer is to starve them through
"economic sanctions."

Does military action solve problems? Do sanctions bring people to-
gether? Not really. It may seem to, as when the enemy surrenders, but
that is usually followed by still more problems, just as World War II
was followed by the Cold War; just as the Korean Peninsula is still
divided into North and South; just as "the end of military action" in
Iraq was followed by . . . more military action.

Some of what followed military victory was smart, but very costly:
the reconstruction of Japan and Europe after World War II, for example. *What if, however, those sensible efforts could have been applied*
to underlying problems before the resort to war? Or, to put it on a more
personal level, *What if the smell of gas had been followed by repair of*
the gas leak before it exploded and burned down the house? What if that
drinking problem had been recognized before the car accident?

The personal level is often more clearsighted than some big think
tank or layered bureaucracy. But it isn't that <u>we</u> are coming up with
solutions; rather, we must see a scene showing the problem in all its
complexities, and then we must see a similar scene free of the problem.
Then we turn it over to the Subconscious Mind to find and apply the
solution. Seeing the problem with all its complexities is important—
even if we can't see everything and probably cannot comprehend all

the intertwined details. We need to see the "human side" of the problem and the "human side" of its resolution. First, see starving children with bloated bellies, and then, second, see happy children playing together. See the problem at its worst and see its resolution at its best.

THE NECESSITY OF ACTION!

Seeing the problem and its resolution starts a process, but it is your <u>action</u> that triggers movement. Whether you act alone or with a group, action calls forth response. And it isn't necessary to organize a group and time your action in unison when the problem is big enough that you continue your action day after day. The power of thought goes into the universal consciousness and continues reinforcing the movement as people spontaneously add their action to yours.

You are not limited to responding to *human* problems: you can use your same powers to mitigate the weather, and even earthquakes, based on forecasts. But, common sense tells you that the more your action is in advance of the actual conditions leading up to the local effects of the factors involved, the more effective it will be. And, likewise, the more people motivated to act together, the better.

<u>Now, pray</u>! Or whatever you prefer—meditation, creative visualization, ritual magick, group focus. Keep it simple and nonsectarian. For example, a very powerful prayer can be adapted from the traditional "Our Father" without it being either Christian or Jewish.

The Traditional Our Father
> *Our Father, Who art in heaven,*
> *Hallowed be Thy Name.*
> *Thy Kingdom come.*
> *Thy Will be done, on earth as it is in Heaven.*
> *Give us this day our daily bread.*
> *And forgive us our trespasses,*
> *as we forgive those who trespass against us.*
> *And lead us not into temptation,*
> *but deliver us from evil.*
> *Amen.*

A Modified Our Father—focused on peace between Israel and the Palestinians.

> *Our Father/Mother, Who art in heaven,*
> *Hallowed be Thy Name.*
> *Thy Kingdom come.*
> *Thy Will be done, on earth as it is in Heaven.*
> *We pray for Peace and Prosperity*
> *Between Israel and the Palestinians.*
> *Forgive Past Error and Pain*
> *And See a Future of Joy and Gain.*
> *We give our Thanks and celebrate*
> *A lasting Solution!*
> *Amen.*

The same prayer (or a better written one!) could be turned into a group action by making it into song or chant during a circle dance.

The point of our effort is to identify the problem and see as much complexity as possible, visualize how it will be after the problem is resolved but keeping that image simple and nonspecific, and then to turn it over to the Subconscious Mind through simple programming techniques like prayer, meditation, etc.

INTERACTION WITH THE SPIRIT REALM

Throughout this chapter, we have essentially identified Spirituality with the deepest and most comprehensive view of Universal Consciousness. *But, is that the same thing as "the Spirit Realm?"*

Maybe yes, maybe no, but definitely not in the traditional view of some portion of the universe where the "spirits" of the departed abide, and perhaps not in the new sense of a state of consciousness that souls occupy in between lives.

What do we mean by the phrase "Spirit Realm"?

The simple answer would be that it's a place where spirits dwell. But that starts a whole chain of additional questions: *Where is the Spirit Realm? How long do Spirits dwell there? Are we all agreed on what Spirits are? And, do we agree on what the word "Spirit" means?*

We found earlier that our dictionary referred us to the Latin verb *spirare,* which means "to breathe, to live." So, Life and Spirit must be considered together. But, we also understand that Spirit as "the breath of life" may also mean the same thing as the Hindu word *Prana* or the Chinese *Chi*—both words for "life energy." In both traditions, the *life energy* is contained in the air we breathe, but it is not identical with it. Prana and Chi are also in the sunlight.

We think in words, and use words to describe what we mean. We also use signs and symbols to represent bigger ideas, sometimes more concisely than possible with words. Still other times we use analogies to convey—and to develop—ideas, as we did earlier in chapter one with the Great Pyramid for the unit of Personal Consciousness.

But we also encounter the need to stay with the times. Old words, old ideas and symbols, can truly become outdated as we move forward with new knowledge and new technologies, making it desirable to adopt new words and concepts familiar to new generations. In the culture revolving around the Internet and computer we find it easier to express various ideas with words and images adapted from the Cyber World.

We now have various kinds of memories and methods of memory organization and storage, we have "search engines" to tunnel through billions of scanned pages and images at amazing speeds, we have the means to instantly communicate with individuals and communities across the globe, and we can work in virtual offices and command skills we don't personally possess through inexpensive software connections.

The reality is that it doesn't matter whether you perceive "spirit helpers" as the dearly departed or as pure holograms of energy and recorded experience. The universe is set up to bring you these resources. *Ask and ye shall receive!*

"SPIRIT" AND/OR SOUL?

We sometimes use these words interchangeably, but they may not be the same thing, and that could be important to how we become Whole Beings.

Let's face it: *Do you really think the often silly, irrational, incompetent, immoral, ineffective person you know yourself to sometimes be is an immortal SOUL worthy of relationship with the Creator of All?*

Be honest! Place yourself in a situation of pleading your case: *Has your life been so responsible, so worthy, so beneficent, so praiseworthy, so conscientious, and so "spiritual" as to be equated with the SOUL face-to-face with the Creator?*

Or, rather, *can you see yourself as growing to become more of these things in the same way you recognize that the child you once were has become the adult you now are? Can you further see the adult you now are as if just one among a group of students among other classes making up a whole school that together might be equated to a SOUL?*

Is it possible for you to think of the life you are now living as just one of many lives that may be contributing the lessons learned in the School of Life to the essence that is a SOUL that comprehends many lives into a greater unity, just as an elderly person can look back at each of those years of childhood, adolescence, early adult years, middle years, and later years, and see them all merge into the person he is today?

We hope so, for that seems to be both logical and to match with the understanding of most of the great religions of the world—at least those where the spiritual philosophy has not been replaced by political exegesis.

In other words, "you" are not "your Soul" but an *emanation* of it that gathers the lessons of life, like a piece of a puzzle that will eventually be brought together with other pieces to make a whole. But that piece may, at various levels, function as a Spirit, and the "Spirit Realm" may be a place of communication and action between Personal Consciousness and Spirit Beings.

But "you," as an emanation, are just as important now as is your soul. You are the one who is here now, acting and learning. You are real, involved, and "alive," while the Soul is distant and not directly involved. You are the player, and how you play is a measure of a life well lived or not.

It was this emanation of the soul that at conception started the process of attracting elements and memories from the universal consciousness to form the Subconscious Mind that includes all the memories of the soul's previous lives to build the matrix of Personal Consciousness that is the totality of you in the current lifetime, and which is the unit of growth in this incarnation.

Interaction with the Spirit Realm, through carefully crafted questions and statements of problems, can bring the collective wisdom of the cumulative experience to bear on the questions and problems. Your Subconscious Mind is the doorway to this field of interaction.

SPIRIT COMMUNICATION OR SPIRIT INTERACTION?

There are many established ways to communicate or interact with the Spirit Realm. They range from simple to elaborate, from personal to dependent on the involvement of an intermediary person or some kind of device.

One of the most basic is that of the dream. *Ask and ye shall receive!* Think of your question or the problem—whether personal or world-sized—as you slide into sleep. Address "Spirit" if you wish, and state your request. Even better, write it down before you go to bed and expect to record the answer upon awakening.

Even without a formal request, so long as you are earnest and sincere in your concern, you can expect a response. *Why?* Because you are using your Subconscious Mind to connect with Consciousness all about you. Whether there are Spirits of your ancestors or Spiritual Helpers or the spiritual levels of your own consciousness, your request will be answered.

We are all connected, no matter the dimension, and we respond to need.

Suggested Reading List

Newton: *Journey of Souls*
Newton: *Lives Between Lives*
Weschcke and Slate: *Psychic Empowerment for Everyone*

CHAPTER EIGHT

DREAMS—GATEWAY
TO THE SUBCONSCIOUS

For centuries, the mystery and majesty of dreams have intrigued cultures around the world, from the most primitive to the most advanced, but only in recent years have we begun to recognize the relevance of dreaming to self-empowerment. Aside from its essential role in facilitating healthful sleep, the dream experience is a personal gateway to the subconscious with its abundant empowering resources. Better than that, the subconscious by its very nature embraces the dream, not as an unwelcome intruder, but as a welcomed partner and collaborator. Embraced by the subconscious mind, the dream experience becomes a powerful agent for growth and change. In that role, the dream can promote restful sleep while at the same time opening totally new channels for growth and self-discovery.

Dreaming is a basic human need, and although we all dream, we may upon awakening recall only a small fragment of the dream, and that fragment can quickly disappear. But aside from simply recalling the dream experience, a major task we face is unraveling its significance and developing our ability to use the dream experience as a channel for personal growth and empowerment. Fortunately, programs are now available, several of which were developed in our labs, to do just that.

We now know that dreams don't do it for you; they instead work with you. In this chapter, we'll explore the multiple roles of dreams and develop programs that utilize dreams as sources of personal enlightenment and power. By working with your dreams, you can become empowered to solve difficult personal problems, enrich your social relationships, promote career success, activate your psychic potentials, and overcome all blockages to your growth. You can discover new ways of using your dreams to increase creativity, develop highly complex mental and physical skills, build motivation, and actually increase your rate of learning. Through your dreams, you can exercise your psychic skills, including your ability to see into the future and travel out-of-body to distant spatial realities. Beyond these, you can develop your ability to experience firsthand the spiritual realm with its advanced spirit guides and higher planes of spiritual power. All of these you can do for yourself through your interactions with your dreams as interactive channels of power.

THE MULTIPLE ROLES OF DREAMS

The self-empowerment roles of dreams are manifold, to include messenger, motivator, energizer, rejuvenator, protector, therapist, problem solver, and psychic activator, to list but a few. Each role functions often spontaneously and in cooperation with other roles to bring forth new knowledge, power, and change.

Possibly the most common role of dreams is that of messenger. In that role, the dream experience can uncover relevant experiences from your past to include your experiences from past lifetimes and between lifetimes. Your past experiences are forever with you as growth resources. Through increased knowledge of your past, you become empowered with a broader view of your existence and a deeper understanding of the relevance of your past experiences to your present growth and development. You develop a greater understanding of the endlessness of your existence and a deeper appreciation of your life at the moment.

The dream experience can tap into highly specific past experiences, including those of past lifetimes that are critical to your present growth. For instance, a student struggling with persistent feelings of inferiority and depression with suicidal thoughts experienced in a series of recurrent dreams of what appeared to be a past lifetime in which he was betrayed by the woman he loved, an experience so traumatic that it eventually led to suicide in that lifetime. With the retrieval of those painful experiences, the therapeutic function of the dreams clicked into place. He realized at once that his deep inferiority and long history of depression and suicidal thoughts had no relevance to his inherent worth, but were instead the residual baggage of tragedy in a past lifetime. Through the combined roles of his dreams as messenger and therapist, he successfully overcame the feelings of inferiority and developed for the first time (in his present lifetime) powerful feelings of self-worth. By his report, "The message of my dreams literally saved my life."

In another instance of dreams as both messenger and therapist, a social worker's irrational fear of mice seriously constricted her life. Even in situations where mice were unlikely to appear, her fear persisted. For instance, she was uncomfortable sitting in an upholstered chair, fearful that mice might be hidden inside. Finally, she experienced a profound dream in which mice invaded her physical body, but inflicted no harm. Ironically, the intensity of the dream experience proved therapeutic. Upon reflecting on the experience, she knew that, in real life, she was unlikely to experience the extreme conditions depicted by the frightening dream. Her survival of the onslaught of mice in the dream gave therapeutic assurance that she could endure with confidence any invasion of mice in real life. As a result, her fear of mice vanished. Although the extreme contents of the dream suggested a possible past-life origin, the therapeutic role of the dream did not seem to depend upon it.

In yet another example of the therapeutic role of dreams, a college student with a highly specific fear of lighted candles experienced a series of dreams that, step-by-step, extinguished her fear. Although she had no memory of the origin of the fear, she had reportedly been severely burned as a child when her clothing caught fire by an open candle at a birthday celebration. The fear of candles over the years had been generalized to the extent that she was fearful of any open flame. She avoided all social activities that might expose her to burning candles or other open flames. She, in fact, declined an invitation to join a sorority because the initiation ceremony involved lighted candles.

The series of dreams began during her second year of college when she enrolled in a laboratory course that required the use of Bunsen burners. It seemed almost as though the dreams as a therapist literally came to her rescue. In her first dream, she viewed a lighted candle in a window at a distance. Upon awakening, she reflected upon the dream and experienced only moderate anxiety. In the second dream, she entered the room and again viewed the lighted candle situated in the window across the room. As before, upon reflecting on the dream experience, she experienced only moderate anxiety. In the third dream of the series, she walked to the window and picked up the lighted candle. While holding the candle, she felt absolutely no fear. Upon awakening and reflecting on the experience, she knew with certainty that her fear of open flames had been at last extinguished. She completed the laboratory course with no fear of open flames, and later at her church wedding, lighted candles became an important part of the ceremony. Thanks to the series of dreams and her willingness to work with it, she completely mastered her fear of open flames, thus offering convincing evidence that your best therapist, like your best psychic and healer, may very well exist within yourself.

Stage fright, one of the most common phobias known, seems to be particularly receptive to spontaneous intervention by the dream experience. A director of the chamber of commerce whose duties required frequent presentations, typically before small groups, experienced a single dream in which she was the featured guest speaker before an audience of hundreds. Following a highly anxious beginning, she slowly gained command of the situation. By the end of the presentation, she was in complete command with absolutely no anxiety as the audience wildly applauded. Upon awakening from the vivid dream, she knew with certainty that she had at last mastered stage fright and all anxieties related to it. Free of the fright that had limited her life for many years, she is today a frequent lecturer known for her excellent promotional skills. She remarked, "The only mystery of the experience is the fact that it took so long for it to finally occur." We could speculate that the therapeutic effectiveness of dreams includes not only the subconscious mastery of therapeutic skills, but timing in applying them as well.

The motivational role of dreams is often illustrated by dreams related to career strivings. For instance, an elementary education student discovered that her recurring dream of teaching in an elementary school classroom validated her career choice and commitment to her chosen career. But only upon completing her degree and accepting a teaching position was the precognitive significance of the dream manifested. The classroom was identical to the one she had repeatedly experienced in her recurring dream.

In a similar instance, a pre-law student experienced a highly vivid dream in which he visited the law school he would later attend. In that dream, which he described as more like an out-of-body experience than a dream, he observed a collection of rare legal documents on the second floor of the law school's library. Upon later enrolling in the school, he visited the library and, not to his surprise, discovered the exhibit of rare documents on the second floor exactly as seen in his dream. The experience, for him, gave clear confirmation that he was "at the right place at the right time."

The empowering effect of the dream experience was dramatically illustrated by an artist who began to take note of his increasingly colorful dream experiences, which often included highly creative ideas. Upon incorporating his dreams into his paintings, his work took on new and exciting features that critics called a "dramatic transition." With that new-found recognition of his work, he began using a technique he called simply "the creative canvas" in which he visualized a blank canvas during the drowsy state preceding sleep. Even before falling asleep, images of highly creative future works regularly unfolded upon the screen. The simple approach, in his opinion, awakened the creative powers of his subconscious mind and allowed them to materialize upon the canvas of his mind. What began as spontaneous creative dreaming led to the development of a powerful technique that he now regularly uses to activate his creative powers. His dreams worked with him as he worked with them to unleash his creative potentials.

As interaction specialists, dreams can include a variety of communication mechanisms that include symbolism and other forms of disguise such as antithesis and condensation, all designed to increase the dream's effectiveness and promote receptivity to its message. Although a listing of those functions can be exhaustive, awareness of the wide-ranging possibilities can increase your ability to interpret your dreams and apply their messages. Here are a few examples:

Reading a book can signify a search for understanding, quest for new knowledge, or self-discovery.

Taking a trip can signify a new beginning, need for change, or escape from growth constrictions.

A celebration can represent social interaction, need for closure, or future personal gain.

Participating in a competitive sports activity can symbolize personal achievement, determination to overcome barriers, or the need for recognition.

A funeral can suggest the ending of a project, the need to extinguish an unwanted habit, or a new beginning.

Viewing terrain from above can suggest the need for objectivity, disengagement, or feelings of superiority. It can also suggest out-of-body travel.

These few examples are offered as suggested possibilities only. As you will note, a single dream experience can have a variety of possible meanings. By recording your dream experiences in a dream journal immediately upon awakening and reflecting on their significance, you will improve your ability not only to recall your dreams but to better understand them and become empowered by them.

DREAM POWER BY DESIGN

The fact that dreams are often spontaneously empowering suggests interesting possibilities for programs specifically structured to activate the various empowering functions of dreams. Programs have, in fact, been designed to achieve that important goal. Each of the programs presented in the following discussion recognizes the concept that dreams are empowerment driven and are deliberately designed to access the powers of the subconscious mind. Although working with your dreams can be a challenging task, it's rewarding to know that as you work with your dreams, your dreams are at the same time working with you. The result can be an interaction that empowers your life mentally, physically, and spiritually. In the discussion that follows, we'll explore programs designed to facilitate that important interaction.

The Interactive Screen Technique

We mentioned earlier a dream intervention technique in which an artist used an imaginary blank canvas upon which to project creative dream ideas. The Interactive Screen Technique is a similar concept in which a standard white poster board (22"x 28") is used as a tangible blank screen to stimulate goal-related dreaming. The poster-board screen is typically situated on a stand or bedroom wall to facilitate easy viewing prior to sleep. Aside from its usefulness in promoting purpose-related sleep, taking a few moments to simply view the screen before falling asleep is an excellent way to clear the mind of clutter and generate a relaxed state so essential to quality sleep. Here's the program.

Step 1. To begin this procedure, view the screen for a few moments while resting comfortably prior to sleep in a dimly lighted or near-dark room. Almost instantly, you will notice an emerging state of serenity and balance. While viewing the screen, state your goal. Your goal may consist simply of getting a night of restful sleep, or it may involve such wide-ranging objectives as finding solutions to pressing problems, making important decisions, mastering certain skills, exploring relevant past-life experiences, or simply adding happiness and quality to your life.

Step 2. Upon stating your goal, close your eyes and you will note an afterimage of the screen forming clearly in your mind. This may require some practice, but the afterimage usually emerges effortlessly. With the afterimage lingering, use relevant mental imagery to project your goal upon it. For instance, if your goal is to acquire a certain skill, you can project upon the screen a picture of yourself in a situation using that skill while affirming, "I am empowered with success." If your goal is career success, you can visualize yourself in a successful career setting of your choice. If your goal, on the other hand, is simply to improve the quality of your life, you can visualize the word QUALITY projected upon the screen. If your goal is to overcome an unwanted habit, such as smoking, you can visualize the word NON-SMOKER projected upon the screen. Imagery using this technique accompanied with relevant affirmations of success provides a direct route to your subconscious. Accompany each of your images with the affirmation, "I am empowered with success in achieving this goal." You will sense at once the activation of your subconscious resources related to your goal.

Step 3. As drowsiness deepens, you can literally shape your future by generating other relevant images upon the screen in your mind. Goals related to health, fitness, and rejuvenation are especially receptive to this state commonly called "energy infusion." Let the screen become your channel for healthful and rejuvenating energy. You will sense the energy flowing through the screen permeating your total being. To enhance the flow of positive energy, you can introduce relevant color into the interaction. For an abundant flow of healthful and rejuvenating energy, allow the screen to take on the color of iridescent green; for goals related to intellectual functions, introduce glowing yellow; and for stress management allow the screen to take on the serenity of sky blue. At this stage, all the mental, physical, and spiritual resources you need at the moment are at your command.

Step 4. With imagery of your goal lingering in your mind, you are now ready to enter restful, empowering sleep. Sense the powerful merging of both conscious and subconscious resources related to your stated goal. At this stage, let the screen become your gateway to the highest sources of enlightenment and power both within yourself and beyond.

Step 5. Upon awakening, enter your dream experiences in your journal and reflect on their relevance. Conclude by simply affirming, "I am now fully empowered."

The Interactive Screen Technique has been especially effective when used to promote psychic development. For that application, the simple image, PSYCHIC KNOWLEDGE, projected upon the screen and accompanied by the suggestion, "My psychic abilities will be activated as I sleep," is usually effective. You can, however, specify during drowsiness exactly what you need to know, whether about the future or present. Relevant images of both precognitive and clairvoyant significance will often unfold on the mental screen during that drowsy state. A legal assistant enrolled in a continuing education course of dream analysis experienced during the Interactive Screen Technique the exact location of a misplaced document in the office where she worked. Clearly depicted on the screen, even before sleep ensued, was the critical document that had slipped behind a file drawer to become wedged inside the back of the cabinet. Although the cabinet had already been searched, the document had somehow remained hidden.

In an unrelated instance, a fashion designer attributes the wide popularity of her creations to her use of the Interactive Screen Technique. By her own admission, the complete designs are typically depicted spontaneously upon the screen during the very early stages of the procedure. She discovered that even slight modification of the designs reduced their appeal.

In the academic setting, students have found the Interactive Screen Technique useful in promoting both learning and retention. With repeated practice, the technique becomes increasingly effective. Projecting the word LEARNING on the screen before falling asleep has become a common practice among many students to accelerate learning and improve test performance. This approach is often followed by so called "practice dreams" to achieve peak performance, particularly in long-term learning situations. Mastering a new language and acquiring complex technical skills are especially receptive to practice dreaming. Students often note significant improvements in motivation accompanied by the sheer pleasure of learning. Among the most remarkable examples of this effect was a group of high school students participating in a dual-enrollment college science program. The results were so striking that the instructor introduced the Projection Screen Technique into future dual-enrollment programs as an enrichment component.

The Interactive Screen Technique is an excellent approach for exploring past-life experiences related to your present goals and strivings. For that application, simply visualizing the words "PAST-LIFE ENLIGHTENMENT" on the screen, followed by the affirmation that all you need to know about your past will become available to you as you sleep, is usually effective. Resolution of past-life conflicts related to phobias, obsessions, and anxiety is almost always receptive to this program. Though it may seem too good to be true, a single session using this approach can instantly provide the enlightenment and resultant empowerment required to extinguish a long history of disempowering past-life baggage.

Dream Works Program: Interactions with the Spirit Realm

Since the spirit realm is the overarching, energizing force that sustains our existence as evolving souls, it is not surprising to find that dreams often tap into that dimension as an ever-present reality rather than a distant, impersonal dimension. It's a dimension that invites our awareness and interaction, not only during dreaming, but at any moment. The interventions of that dimension into our lives are consistently empowering and probably far more common than most of us realize. They can range from simply the comforting awareness of a caring spirit guide to the powerful intervention of a protective force at a time of great personal danger.

The Dream Works Program recognizes our existence as essentially spiritual and characterized by on-going interactions with the spirit dimension. You are constantly connected to that dimension through the **Center of Spiritual Power** existing in your subconscious mind, as discussed earlier in this book. By actively interacting with that center of power, you have instant and direct access to all the resources of the spirit realm, including spirit guides and growth specialists who are constantly poised to enrich and empower your life. What better way to become intimately connected to the spirit realm and its abundant resources than through the center of spiritual power existing within yourself?

The Dream Works Program is designed to provide direct access to the powers within yourself and, by extension, to the spirit realm at large. Through this program, you can get to know your personal spirit guides and other growth specialists who are constantly poised to enrich your life. You can actively interact with higher spiritual planes to empower your life mentally, physically, and spiritually. Through your interactions with the spirit realm, you can reach your highest pinnacle of growth and fulfillment. Nothing is beyond your reach when you become intimately connected and attuned to the spirit dimension. Here's the program.

1. **Goal Statement.** Although this program requires no goal statement other than to experience the spiritual essence of your existence, you may wish to state in your own words specific outcomes, such as spiritual enlightenment, healing, rejuvenation, happiness, and abundance. Document your goals by recording them in your dream journal. Documentation builds commitment to achieve your goals and positive expectations of success, both of which work together to promote your personal empowerment.

2. **Empowering Imagery.** Upon becoming comfortable and relaxed before falling asleep, visualize the bright Center of Spiritual Power deep within the core of your being. Let yourself experience that center not simply as a part of yourself but as the very essence of your existence as an evolving soul. Note the brilliance of that center radiating throughout your subconscious to energize and illuminate your total being. Visualize distant dimensions of spiritual power, and sense your connection to them. Let yourself become fully enveloped in the glowing energy that typically accompanies spiritual enlightenment. Allow impressions of worth, serenity, and well-being spring forth to accompany that

glow. If your intent is to achieve a more highly specific goal, let relevant images emerge to become a part of your intended destiny for success.

3. **Spiritual Interactions.** At this stage, awareness of a personal spirit guide will often emerge. In the presence of that personal guide, you may experience a profound astral state in which you travel out-of-body to distant astral planes to experience their multiple powers. At this stage, you may also experience interactions with discarnate beings who have crossed over to the spirit realm. It is important, however, to allow these interactions to emerge spontaneously rather than deliberately calling forth a spirit guide or discarnate entity. The key to spiritual empowerment using this program is to maintain a state of spiritual receptivity to the resources available to you from the spiritual realm. Conclude this step by allowing relevant impressions of both present and future relevance to unfold.

4. **Empowering Affirmation.** Upon awakening, affirm in your own words your attunement to the Center of Power within as your connection to the spirit realm beyond. Record the empowering effects of the experience upon awakening in your dream journal.

With practice, you will master your skill in using this approach to increase your awareness of the spirit realm and to build rewarding relationships with your spiritual helpers and guides. Aside from that, you will develop your ability to tap into your subconscious powers, to include those related to healing, rejuvenation, intelligence, learning, memory, and self-development. You will soon discover that all the resources you need are available to you. Through this program, you can now reach out, embrace them, and use them to empower your life.

THE CENTER OF SPIRITUAL POWER: SELF-EMPOWERMENT WITHOUT LIMITS

Could the Dream Works Program with its focus on the Center of Spiritual Power within provide the key to a greater understanding of spirituality and consciousness? In our labs, subjects who participated in our Dream Works studies over the years almost invariably experienced a state they described as *highest* consciousness rather than *higher* consciousness when they interacted with the inner Center of Spiritual Power. Their dream interactions with the center of power were often accompanied with a sense of "complete oneness within and beyond," to use their words. In that context, they often experienced a flow of colorful energies along with musical sounds to create a "celestial symphony" never experienced before. The combination of color energy and music generated unforgettable vibrations that permeated and attuned them to the spirit world, a state they called "authentic oneness." They became convinced that the Center of Spiritual Power offered a breakthrough understanding of "universal consciousness" by connecting them to the limitless resources of the spirit realm. To quote one subject, "I became a co-inhabitant of the spirit world."

Through regular practice of the Dream Works Program, you can connect to your inner Center of Spiritual Power and interact with it as the authentic core of your being. You can get to know your spirit guides and other comforting entities. Through your interactions with that center, you will experience a state of "highest consciousness" and self-empowerment without limits. How could anyone ask for more than that?

CHAPTER NINE

THE EMPOWERMENT REWARDS OF SUBCONSCIOUS KNOWLEDGE

The Subconscious is <u>now</u> your resource of Knowledge and Know-How; it is your Breakthrough to Brainstorming; and it is your vehicle for Exploring the farthest reaches and the greatest depths of the Universe in all its dimensions, inner and outer.

As you have learned to understand the Subconscious Mind as originating out of the Universal Unconscious, out of Consciousness itself, and the individual Conscious Mind as rising up from the Subconscious, you have learned for yourself that there can be no barriers to your attainment other than those you, yourself, impose.

Now, one of your greatest challenges is to know and understand what potentials to Attainment there remain for you and, indeed, for all of Humanity. It's one thing to say there can be no barriers to your Attainment; it is quite another thing to know just how you can become more than you are now. Some things are known—we are aware of "Psychic Powers" that are yet to become fully developed and mastered as dependable "Psychic Skills." And, there is an area of your Personality we have labeled as your "Super-Conscious Mind" in our Great Pyramid model back in chapter one.

Your Subconscious mind is mostly conditioned by the past, and your Conscious Mind by the present. But you were born with a basic purpose, with some specific learning goals for this lifetime. The Super-Conscious Mind is your doorway to and from the future.

The Super-Conscious Mind is the higher self and the source of your inspiration, ideals, ethical behavior, and heroic action, and the very essence that is "the Light of Men" as it was in the beginning and as it is now and as it will always be. . . . Historically it has been suppressed through the denial of knowledge about self and the potentials of the whole person as religious and political authority determined that "common folk" should remain subservient to their self-anointed "nobility."

Even though the Higher Self is also known as the "Holy Guardian Angel," there is value in using a more easily comprehended psychological term. Words are words and there are often many names for the same thing, but each gives a particular shape or color or tone to the thing named to expand our understanding when relating to larger concepts.

YOUR SELF-IMPOSED BARRIERS

Yes, you do this to yourself! And, you are not alone in this. None of us lives up to our potential; none of us are the Super Heroes we can be; not one of us operates anywhere near our real capacity. And the worst thing is that few of us realize that not only is more possible, but that more is better and more is what we owe to ourselves and to humanity and to the Creator. We are intended to evolve into more than we are, but we're told that evolution is finished and that we are the ultimate result. *The truth is far different!*

We are intended for Greatness, but . . . we lack sufficient energy; we don't have drive and persistence; we suffer self-doubt; we lose our vision; we're easily sidetracked; we blame others for our failures and disappointments; we forget our promises to ourselves.

What is the problem?

We do have to place the blame somewhere, but it is really no one's fault. It's everyone's failure to understand the true dimensions of human potential, and then to believe that we can be more than we are, and to set our goals high enough and broad enough. Humanity cuts itself short and our institutions accept those short visions and then profit by them. Too many authority figures want you to settle for less. They institutionalize goals of mediocrity. They fear having one child excel because other children might feel badly. We say: "Don't leave one child behind," but they don't want to push any child ahead. They reward some people for certain popular sports prowess and turn entertainers into billionaires while short-changing science, mathematics, the arts, and subjects that encourage "thinking." They don't want people to think for themselves. They may reward innovation, but they don't want to teach it.

(In 2005, the average Major League baseball player's salary was $2,632,655, while that of a mathematician with twenty years experience was $104,603, $111,769 for a physicist, and $117,570 for an astronomer.)

We have become a society of masses divided into clans and communities rather than of individuals who follow the Great Work, "alone and together." It is as lone individuals that our growth continues. But it is together in true communities (not clans) that we find and contribute support with one another.

EMPOWERMENT AND SUBCONSCIOUS KNOWLEDGE

Both above the level of rationality and below it, there exist for us vital and purposeful areas of psychic activity which are frequently termed "unconscious," not because they are unconscious at their own levels but because the rational mind is unconscious of them. One of the major results to be sought, whether in magical training, in meditation, or for the matter of that in psychotherapy, is to push back the misty boundaries of unconsciousness, both higher and lower. That achieved, the conscious mind is more widely able to recognize the influences which affect it, to understand them and very frequently control them, and so is able to take more intelligent responsibility in the life of the person.

—Osborne Phillips, author of *Aurum Solis: Initiation Ceremonies and Inner Magical Techniques*, pub. by Thoth, UK.

"Intelligent responsibility" as the Conscious Mind becomes aware of Unconscious influences and brings them under control is our means to <u>Self-Empowerment</u>. We may never become simultaneously and fully aware of every single area of the Subconscious any more than we can instantly absorb the contents of the World Wide Web. *But we can manage its contents to meet our needs and desires.*

Knowledge is the source of power but it must be organized, filtered, and handled properly to avoid overload.

What do you know?

You may be able to drone away a few facts, but remembering facts is not knowledge. On January 17, 2009, when Captain Chesley Sullenberger landed his Airbus on the Hudson River, he did not remember and review thousands of facts, but quickly acted and saved hundreds of lives because he had knowledge based on training, experience, and instinct. When your surgeon is replacing your shoulder joint, he does not review a manual that comes with the replacement part, nor does he call up the 283,000 responses from an Internet search.

Specialized knowledge combines a wide education with specialized education, training, practice, review, experience, and "intuition." But **what is *intuition* in a specific situation?** Intuition seems to quickly draw upon the knowledge and experience of others from the Unconscious. It is not a <u>conscious</u> review of facts but it comes because there are facts recorded in the Subconscious Minds of millions of people. It is not a <u>conscious</u> review of experiences recorded in the Subconscious Minds of many individuals. Yet, and this is important, *intuition is not limited to the mind of a single person!* **Intuition somehow "leaps" beyond what is known into that which is as yet unknown!**

When chemist Friedrich von Stradonitz dreamed of a snake eating its own tail, he knew it was the answer to his question about the structure of the benzene ring. It was not information that anyone had ever read or experienced before. At the same time, it was a "leap" that could not have been made without his previous knowledge and experience.

Intuition is a <u>developing</u> psychic power that creates something new that is beyond the cumulative base of memory and experience carried in the Subconscious Mind. Intuition is an example of *evolution actually happening.* The Conscious Mind asserted a need—in this case a quest for new knowledge—and the Subconscious responded through the vehicle of a dream to provide an answer totally new in human knowledge and experience.

OVERCOMING GROWTH BLOCKAGE

Because of our continuing evolution and the role that properly evoked intuition can play, there is no known limit to our growth. We encounter "blocks" of various origin—from physical and emotional to financial and professional—but overcoming resistance builds muscles, overcoming blockage develops persistence, and sometimes blocks are signs from our Subconscious that we are on the wrong track.

LET YOUR SUBCONSCIOUS DO THE TALKING

When you encounter blockage, it is time to "regroup" and look at the situation from alternative positions. *Let your Subconscious do the talking.* Stubbornness is not the same thing as persistence. Don't let stubbornness deter you from looking for and taking a new direction. Don't let weakness, or lack of know-how, or shortage of capital stop you if the idea is good, but a shift in thinking may uncover other problems, or other solutions.

Don't merely buck against a fixed obstacle or merely give up. (Two buck deer can lock antlers fighting each other, and starve to death; two bucking rams can knock themselves silly.) Ask your Subconscious Mind for guidance in meditation, in prayer, or through dreams. Or use self-hypnosis to search for an answer. (See *Self-Empowerment through Self-Hypnosis* by Slate and Weschcke, Llewellyn, 2010.)

RESOLVING CONFLICT

People often complain that there is too much conflict in their lives. What they seem to mean is that they don't always get their way! But, too often, they don't really know what it is they want, or why.

Our first job is to determine what the supposed conflict is about, to understand the issues and positions of the parties involved, decide on what is really important to us, and then to negotiate from that position.

In truth, we may decide that we don't really have a position. All conflict is self-imposed acceptance of limitation: remove the perception of limitation, and conflict goes away.

How we accomplish this is through acceptance of our subconscious knowledge of the situation. Sometimes we will find that we no longer care, that we've moved on, or that other parties have moved on. The Conscious Mind sometimes locks us into positions, and the Subconscious Mind can really say it doesn't matter.

Once again, let your Subconscious Mind do the talking. Relax, settle back, ask yourself the basic question, and calmly wait for the answer. Use the Wisdom of the Ages to resolve yesterday's conflict, and just move on to tomorrow.

SELF-ENLIGHTENMENT

There is a long history of enlightenment attained by initiatory rituals involving a guru/teacher who hands on that which he himself received from his guru/teacher within the same esoteric tradition. There is a presumption that neither spontaneous nor self-initiation is possible, nor—from the perspective of the particular tradition—desirable.

What, then, is Enlightenment, and what is Self-Enlightenment?

A common definition of enlightenment is "Self Realization." We become "self-centered," meaning that we have found our "self" and live by our own real values rather than those imposed or "preached" by others. But that "self" is what we have elsewhere referred to as the Big Self as opposed to the smaller self. It is the Whole Person we are yet becoming. It is the "core" of our being beyond "name, number, and rank." It is truly the "man without a country" because self is not defined by nationality, race, age, relationship, religion, or anything other than self.

Being self-centered is not to believe the world revolves around our self-interests, but to find our self that is deeper and larger than the world, a self centered in love of all things without demand or interest, a self that is timeless.

Essentially, this Self is found through the next step in our evolution as we become more than we are now, more whole, and as we move into our Super-Conscious Mind. <u>Self-Enlightenment</u> is <u>Self-Empowerment</u>. No one can give it to you. No one can take it away from you. But it is a process that is never finished. As we take the next step, as we evolve to become more than we are now, we think we're there only to find that we haven't arrived.

We take another next step, and grow in consciousness, and then another, and another. Each step, each initiation, is progressive and a stage of never-completed fulfillment. Growth, self-development, and enlightenment are all part of our purposeful life journey, our adventure, the fundamental reason of our existence. The process is endless until Time itself ends for us.

HAPPINESS AND SUCCESS

Of course, you say, we all desire happiness and success in what we do. But, when you look around at those people you know well, and finally when you can look at your own life without bias, do you really find many happy and successful people? And, don't you often wonder about those—especially the celebrities—that supposedly do live charmed lives? Why, if they are so happy, do they have drug problems and marital problems? Why do many have problems with the law? And why do those who have achieved success in their respective fields of business, science, the arts, politics, and so on likewise seem to be unhappy and often judge themselves as failures?

Is it because they don't really judge themselves but from their perspective of what they believe others think, of how they may compare to others and are insecure, fearing that what they have can be taken away?

What do we mean by "Happiness"? What do we mean by "Success"?

These are judgments that only you can make for yourself based on the criteria of your choice—not that of others—but it does seem clear that setting your goals as Happiness and Success is likely to doom you to disappointment and failure because there is nothing definitive about them. What marks success today is unsatisfactory tomorrow. It's like Wealth—people will say that you can never have enough.

But you can be happy and successful in your life and work if you define these as simple enjoyment of what you do best. Success, then, is accomplishment—and Happiness is your enjoyment of Success. We enjoy the fruit of our labor. We bask in our own security. We build from our heart and not the yearnings of others. We can ignore the advertisements for more of this and that, for the latest and best, and for what others feel they need, and live by our own needs.

But, we say your purpose in life is to grow, to become more than you are, to turn your innate powers into reliable skills, to fulfill the potentials the Creator built into the structure that is your being.

Exactly! These are inner accomplishments and not outer ones—although they will bring outer rewards as well. Outer accomplishments may be seen as marks of success by others, but the only real judge is the inner you. Happiness comes when you can consciously unite with your Subconscious Mind and say "I AM happy!" and know it is true.

Think for yourself.

One of the richest men in the world still lives in a small house in a small Midwestern city. He's a man who is always smiling. He doesn't see his wealth as a means to power. In fact he's already given most of it away.

We don't work to become happy. We don't accumulate wealth or things to become happy. We don't accumulate academic degrees, hang certificates on our walls, pin medals to our chests, and otherwise demonstrate success and accomplishment to become happy.

But we do become happy by living a good and fulfilling life marked by growth and development.

Happiness is not a goal; happiness just is.

WE'RE READY TO TAKE THE NEXT STEP

We, the people, are ready to move forward, not because we've finished anything or passed a grade allowing us to move on, but because we're being called to do so. Our Consciousness is calling to us and a Great Shift of energies is preparing the way to a new evolution in our state of being.

It's now time for the appearance of the Super-Conscious Mind.

CHAPTER TEN

THE SUPER-CONSCIOUS MIND

We've learned a lot about the nature and "powers" of the Subconscious Mind in this book. And we've learned that it is through "managing" these powers that we can become Self-Empowered and "captains of our own ship."

The Subconscious Mind is always awake and always aware, and as a result is a storehouse of personal experience from preexistence to the present. It is also attuned to many processes and functions for making conscious its unconscious elements composed around personal and collective memories from the beginning to now. These include most particularly techniques of meditation, self-hypnosis, dream interpretation, interactions with Nature, and spirit communication.

In addition, over tens if not hundreds of thousands of years, people have developed special systems of employing subconscious powers in understanding personal experiences and surrounding current and future events. These systems include Tarot, Runes, the Yi King, the interpretation of astrological charts, and more.

In a sense, there is no end to the powers of the subconscious because all levels of consciousness are really one. As we become better able to consciously manage these powers of the Subconscious, we can achieve out-of-body experiences, we are able to integrate mind and body in healing and rejuvenation, deploy amazing applications of energy in levitation and movement of objects and people, and engage in all types of problem solving and creativity.

It is through the increasing integration of these levels of consciousness that we grow, evolve, become more enlightened, and discover our own personal success and happiness.

We've explored the amazing potential of not just the personal Subconscious Mind but its access of Universal Consciousness through the Collective Unconscious. To access all this potential we have to *communicate* through certain "emergent thresholds" seemingly dividing Conscious and Unconscious levels of the inner world of the psyche that find replication in the outer worlds of our universe as described in the ancient formula: *As Above, so Below.*

We are not going to cover all forms of this communication in detail in this book, but will explore three in particular: Self-Hypnosis, Meditation, and Dreams. For more information on Psychic Development and what we describe as psychic tools, we refer you to our previous books: *Psychic Empowerment for Everyone, Self-Empowerment through Self-Hypnosis, Rejuvenation, Aura Energy,* and the forthcoming *Llewellyn Complete Book of Psychic Empowerment.*

THE ORIGIN OF CONSCIOUSNESS AND EMERGENT THRESHOLDS

Consciousness, Energy, and Matter compose the fundamental trinity with us since the "Beginning." Just as Energy and Matter have taken many forms and levels, so has Consciousness. From their *raw* initial beginning there emerged more complex states, expanding awareness, and affording evolving life with challenges and opportunities for accelerating development.

While human life did not emerge whole, all at once in the complete form we know today, we only concern ourselves with the evolution of human consciousness in this book to better understand the continuing process occurring now.

As human consciousness evolved from Universal Consciousness there emerged family, clan, and tribal awareness, alongside evolving individual self-awareness. As human evolution continued, we developed Personal Consciousness consisting, at first, of just what we now refer to as the Subconscious Mind characterized by the qualities of:

a. Perception—sensing.

b. Memory—recording.

c. Feeling—evaluating.

d. Desiring—wanting.

Subconsciousness, however, was still an island in the sea of universal consciousness but with self-awareness the Conscious Mind appeared. With focus on the individual, the Conscious Mind emerged by developing the qualities of:

a. Logical thinking—organizing data meaningfully.

b. Abstract thinking—relating to concepts unlimited in time and space.

c. Analytic thinking—formulating strategies based on past experience.

d. Innovative thinking—new ways to do old things.

In our Personal Consciousness, combining expanding world awareness with self-awareness, the Subconscious Mind and Conscious Mind interact through the evolving functions of Imagination and Fantasy, producing mythical understanding of the Universe around us, the functions of memory recall and analytic thinking produce Creative Thinking, while the functions of abstraction and desire lead towards Innovation and Intuition.

We find a slowly emerging Super-Conscious Mind characterized by these qualities:

a. Symbolic thinking—replacing objects, people, and concepts with symbols that can be placed in formulae representing existing or alternative relationships.

Symbols engage a different part of the brain than does ordinary writing or language. It addresses the intuitive, nonverbal, visually based right hemisphere of the brain, which deals with spatial and abstract relationships, intuition, and the subconscious. It is the part of the brain that is not bound by rational and linear thought and perhaps the area of the mind that is host to our higher self, that instinctively seeks out divinity. The language of symbolism serves as a bridge between the two types of intelligence humans are endowed with, rational and intuitive. As such, the symbol goes beyond language, promoting cooperation between and the unification of the brain's two hemispheres (from Edward F. Malkowski: *Before the Pharaohs—Egypt's Mysterious Prehistory,* Bear & Co., 2006).

b. Creative thinking—using intuition to act from a higher perspective. Connecting to the Soul.

It is at this level that we see the Conscious Mind bringing the Subconscious Mind into conscious awareness with the ability to focus its powers as necessary, while the Super-Conscious Mind emerges as "manager" of the entire field of personal consciousness, integrating Conscious and Unconscious, seeing the entire human entity and perceiving the Great Plan of evolution and its goals that was "outlined" with the Beginning "Word."

EXTENDED AWARENESS AND FOCUSED ATTENTION

We're arriving at new levels of expanded consciousness as part of the transition into new phases of the "New Age." Yes, the New Age may have gained a bad rap in recent years as numerous people justified all kinds of *fluffy thinking* as "wisdom transmitted from far, far away in other galaxies."

The truth is far more exciting. As you review the years of the last half century, you can see a steady extension of common awareness to comprehend more of Humanity, more of the life and consciousness of our planetary home, and the assumption of more personal involvement with personal and world health and well-being.

It is this movement of extending personal awareness with focusing attention on areas of personal action that builds the <u>Super-Conscious</u> Mind as we take a dramatic new step in evolution. Some of the signs of this New Age include:

- Increasing interest in and openness to the study of paranormal phenomena, in the development and training of psychic powers and skills, and the broader aspect of spiritual growth itself.

- Cross-Cultural Awareness and more openness to experiencing other cultures' religion, art, music, and folk magick. There is a conscious effort to make our own culture inclusive rather than exclusive, and to make art an instrument of globalism. An example of this: In 1985, Michael Jackson and Lionel Richie wrote the song "We are the World" that was recorded by a group of forty-five musicians performing as USA for Africa, and produced and conducted by Quincy Jones, to raise money for famine relief in African countries decimated by drought.

- Green Thinking. In combination with growing understanding of Global Warming and the 2008-2010 World Recession, governments and individuals have reduced hazardous waste and dangerous pollution, switching from dependencies on chemicals used in growing and preserving food to local and organically grown foods, investing in cleaner fuels and cars, and houses that incorporate "green" awareness. Recognizing the intimate connection between Man and Nature, people undertake personal involvement in local politics regarding air and water quality, land use, and architectural design.

- Innovative and Intuitive Thinking seen most dramatically in alternative applications of technology, healing practices (both traditional and modern), in the "new" sciences of Quantum Theory and Transpersonal Psychology, and the recognition of underlying consecutiveness of the parts in the unity of the Whole.

- Business legislation and practices that encourage small and independent businesses as well as larger producers, regulations for ethical as well as economic justification, and creative financing for new entrepreneurs in Africa, China, India, and other emerging economies.

- New spiritual traditions that are personal rather than institutional, that value Divinity within rather than the intermediacy of priest and prophet, that develop inner growth over outer aggrandizement, and that factor both solitary and group practices.

• Laws and Ethics vs. Edicts and Corruption, secular vs. parochial education, democracy vs. theocracy, and administration vs. bureaucracy.

CHALLENGE AND RESPONSE

Evolution occurs in response to outer Challenge and Opportunity and inner Response and Effort. The common presumption is of evolution as a purely historical process uninvolved with present-day personal action, but the reality is that every deliberate act we take impacts the future and shapes mind and body.

As we respond to challenge—whether climatic, medical, political or economic, and as we seize opportunities to expand our "dialogue" with Nature through genetic and other fundamental research—we become part of that evolutionary process as it happens right now. And when we make an <u>inner</u> effort fueled by personal intention, the effect is immediate even if invisible to the short-term view. Each personal effort is like a single stone of the many used in building a great structure.

One of those personal efforts is a spiritual technique based on a Kabbalist exercise known as "the Middle Pillar." In the traditional form, which can be found in an excellent book, *The Middle Pillar: Balance Between Mind and Magic* by Israel Regardie, edited and annotated with new material by Chic and Tabatha Cicero (Llewellyn, 2002), the images and words used are in Hebrew, while the form given here used Latin words and American images for those not trained in the Kabbalah.

The method of the exercise is to stimulate the six Psychic centers (chakras) of the physical/etheric body energizing the aura, to circulate energy and awareness throughout the aura, to expand the aura and awareness to encompass all the Earth, and then while withdrawing back to your own center to rain love and blessings down on the Earth and all living within Her.

The intention of the exercise is to actually extend your <u>awareness</u> to encompass the whole Earth itself. Of course, your <u>attention</u> cannot be everywhere, but you can learn to focus it in response to awareness. It's like peripheral vision—you note something out of the corner of your eye, so you turn your full attention to that one thing. By extending your awareness, you become part of the planetary consciousness, able to intentionally influence happenings. The individual effect may be minimal, but it can also be cumulative as others practice similar extensions.

It's a big order of business! But you have the power to do it. Everyone has the power to bless because it follows the intent to do so. You were formed in the image of God and so it is that you have God's capacity to love and the power to bless.

THE AMERICAN MIDDLE PILLAR AND AURIC ENERGIZER

These psychic centers are truly psychic, but their position is associated with areas of the physical body. We need to "open" them in several stages. And it is to be noted that this is an exercise that can be undertaken individually or in group practice as a fundamental ritual of unification.

Location	Name*	Sepheroth
Above the Crown of the Head	*Magnus Spiritus*	Cosmic Center, Kether
Brow, between the Eyes	*Mater Stellarum*	Control Center, Binah/Chokmah
Throat	*Puer Maris*	Bridge Center, Daath
Heart	*Aquilla Bellatrix*	Sun Center, Tiphareth
Genital area	*Alba Domina*	Moon Center, Yesod
Feet together, at the insteps	*Mater Libertas*	Earth Center, Malkuth

---

* A note on pronunciation of these names, for they each invoke a particular vibration that is to be felt in the associated body area. In each case you want to break

The language used for the Psychic Centers is not important in itself. Hebrew and Greek are often preferred because of long usage and the ease of numerical associations in Kabbalistic practice. Latin is used here because of its basic familiarity to English language speakers and yet it is not "common" to them: hence it has more magical, or sacred, potency than would plain, ordinary English. And, of course, Latin was long the sacred language used by the Catholic Church, adding that potency as well.

There is also the value of familiarity with the language as we associate the words with actual American images, as follows:

Name*	Images
Magnus Spiritus	Great Spirit, the "Manitou," Sky Father
Mater Stellarum	Mother of the Stars, the Star Goddess
Puer Maris	Child of the Waters
Aquilla Bellatrix	Warrior Eagle, the American Bald Eagle
Alba Domina	White Lady, the Moon Goddess
Mater Libertas	Mother Liberty, the Earth Mother

These images are not the same as the particular symbols to be associated with the body locations of the psychic centers themselves, which will be given next. However, these images should be sensed appearing in front of you as if "invoked" by the names as *sacred words of power*. The images should appear facing the same direction as you are for they are part of you.

---

the words down into syllables, and giving each syllable the same weight, *chant* each syllable the same length of time. Always take a full and deep breath before pronouncing the name, and try to be at the end of that breath as you complete the word/phrase. As you speak the name, you want to *vibrate** (**Vibration is accomplished by a "quiver" at the back of the throat to energize the word.)* each syllable in a tone that is slightly lower than your normal speaking voice. Additional information on the origin of these names appears at the end of this chapter.

The psychic centers themselves are not to be visualized as images or symbols, but rather as colored spheres of intense light, each about one and one-half inches in diameter, located—as indicated—either as a full sphere external to the body, or as a half sphere partially within the body and partially projecting out in front of the body. Nevertheless, you know and feel the half sphere as a whole one—the other half being internal. The actual center should be perceived as glowing as colored lights.

Name*	Location	Color
Magnus Spiritus	Sphere—six inches above head	Intense White light
Mater Stellarum	Half sphere—center of brow	Pearl Gray
Puer Maris	Sphere—just in front of throat	Purple
Aquilla Bellatrix	Half sphere—center of chest	Yellow/Gold
Alba Domina	Half sphere—genital area	Lavender/Violet
Mater Libertas	Sphere—half below ground, half above—at feet	Rainbow of Colors

The centers are activated sequentially from just above the crown of the head down to just below the feet. As they are activated, a beam—or pillar—of white light is seen and felt to descend from above the head down through the center of the body and just into the earth at the feet. This "Middle Pillar" descends to the point corresponding to the area of the center being activated, and remains there while you are vibrating the name, and then descends further as you proceed to the next center in the sequence.

Once completed, the Middle Pillar is to be seen and felt to have circulation both upward and downward as it connects the Heaven and Earth poles of the human electrical circuit.

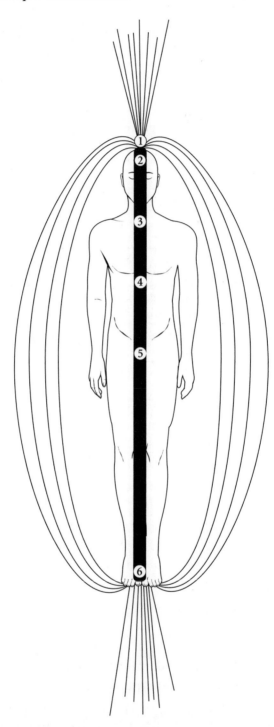

Figure 10A: The Six Centers

Now that you have the picture and all the instructions, let's do the exercise step-by-step.

1. Form the mental image of a sphere above the crown of the head in intense white light. Take a deep breath and vibrate *Magnus Spir-it-us* as you exhale. Inhale and reform or reinforce the sphere and vibrate the name again. Repeat a third time. As you vibrate the names, feel the center itself vibrating. In your mind's eye, see it vibrating. Feel the power in the center.

2. Upon an exhalation, see the Middle Pillar of white light descend from the Crown center to the level of the Brow center. See it, feel it, and continue to hold it there.

3. Form the image of the sphere of pearl gray light in the Brow center—half in and half out. Take a deep breath and vibrate the name *Ma-ter Stell-ar-um* as you exhale. As you inhale, reform and reinforce the sphere of light at the brow center, and then again vibrate the name for a total of three times.

4. On an exhalation, bring the Middle Pillar down to the throat level.

5. Form the Throat center sphere in purple—totally outside, just in front of the throat as indicated—and vibrate the name, *Pu-er Mar-is*. Repeat as previously for a total of three times.

6. Bring the Middle Pillar down to the Heart center as previously instructed.

7. Form the Heart center sphere in yellow/gold in the center of the chest, and vibrate its name, *A-quil-lah Bel-la-trix,* three times as previously instructed.

8. Bring the Middle Pillar down to the Genital center as previously instructed.

9. Form the Genital center sphere in lavender/violet in the genital area and vibrate its name, *Al-ba Dom-in-a,* three times as previously instructed.

10. Bring the Middle Pillar down to the Feet center as previously instructed.

11. Form the Feet center sphere in a spinning rainbow of colors in the insteps and vibrate its name, *Ma-ter Li-ber-tas,* three times as previously instructed.

12. Finish at the Earth center between the feet, and see the Middle Pillar extending as a column of white light and vibrating energy from just below the feet up through the center of the body and out the top of the head.

13. Now, as you inhale your breath, see and feel energy rise up the Middle Pillar from just below the feet to "fountain out" just above the head as you exhale. See light descending from above your head to join that from your Middle Pillar, flowing down on all sides of the body to sweep back in at the feet so that you have an egg-shaped oblong sphere around you.

14. Again inhale, feeling more energy from the Earth rising up the Middle Pillar adding more and more strength to the power you are circulating. Likewise feel more energy and light being added at the crown as you start each exhalation.

15. Circulate the light and energy up the Middle Pillar and out and down the egg-shaped aura for as long as you can feel energy still being added to the circuit you have developed. Make this such a positive image that you can form the aura about you at any time without going through the whole exercise.

16. If working alone, you can end the exercise at this point, but it will be ideally repeated once daily.

17. If you are working with a group of individuals, each doing the same thing together in concert following the pattern as set by a leader, you can now bring the individuals together in a circle, arms joined shoulder to shoulder or hand to hand as you prefer, and form a single Middle Pillar at the circle's center for the entire group and a common aura about the group, and raise energy from the common Earth center of the group Middle Pillar to fountain above and joining with more descending

light from above to flow down the group's aura and back in at the Earth center.

18. Upon common agreement, you can change the direction of the circulating energy from vertical to horizontal, moving clockwise around the group, and expand the circulating group aura outward to the far horizons of your locale, region, nation, and the world as desired.

19. See the far horizons in the mind's eye, and pour blessings upon the Earth like rain falling upon parched soil. Continue for as long as you feel comfortable, and then bring the aura back to the group, identify with the Middle Pillar of the group, and then separate and reidentify with your personal Middle Pillar and aura, and then close down.

20. It is possible for the group leader to visualize the entire exercise without the members being together if the group is firmly established and the members have given their individual permission. It's better if those members know of the leader's plan so they can participate in absentia. This will be more completely treated in a separate book on the Group Mind.

21. The exercise can also be modified for use by an intimate couple in a procedure basically like that for the group. Standing face to face, arms on each other's shoulders, with the Middle Pillar visualized between you and a single aura around you, circulate the energies as before, first vertically and then horizontally. You can expand your joint aura to encompass family, home, the entire home property, a family business, and your financial estate. This will be more completely treated in a separate book for the Intimate Couple.

22. You can also modify the Middle Pillar for the Intimate Couple prior to sexual union. After building the Middle Pillar and Aura separately, standing face to face, come together as above with the Middle Pillar visualized between you, your arms on each other's shoulders, circulate the energies vertically. Then the male should focus on the Brow center and project energy to the female's Brow center. She receives it and brings it down

through her spinal column to her Sex center where she projects it to his Sex center. He brings it up through his spinal column to his Brow center, and projects it to hers as before. Repeat as long as desired, and then complete with sexual union.

23. It is possible to perform the Middle Pillar exercise for the Intimate Couple even when they are separated by distance, visualizing each other and circulating the energies as if the visualized person was present. It does not require the other person to do the visualized exercise simultaneously.

24. It is desirable to end the exercise, whether group, couple, or solitary, with some positive act of body consciousness such as stamping your feet on the ground, shaking your hands, calling out "It is finished!" or having a long drink of water.

The real value in the exercise is the expansion of consciousness that comes with expansion of the aura. In that sense, it's similar to other exercises that train the physical senses, strengthen and stretch muscles, and train your ability to observe and remember scenes in your imagination along with the ability to accurately visualize images "with your mind's eye."

There are many exercises to develop the creative powers of the Subconscious Mind, just as there are those that develop and train the physical body as an instrument of self-expression. Many of these will be found in *The Magician's Companion* by Bill Whitcomb (Llewellyn, 2002).

It is also interesting to reach out with your aura to any specific location to observe activities as in remote viewing.

There are many other variations that can be practiced as you gain experience, remembering that you are—particularly as practiced regularly by yourself—developing your Super-Conscious Mind. You can, for example, center your awareness on any particular Psychic center and *feel* it for its own power and character. This is particularly of value in connection with the Brow center. Learn to feel the "space" that is back of the eyes, see that space fill with "light," learn to project light out from the center, etc. Each center has its own Power, and as each becomes activated this power becomes yours. Because you are working within a balanced exercise, you need not be concerned with any danger of "ego inflation" or coming into contact with forces you can't handle.

As a group exercise, it's an ideal exercise for the development of the Group Mind.

There is one more set of correlations we would like to provide for these six centers that will illustrate the further possibilities inherent in the system. These are familiar American symbols with very powerful energies attached to them.

Name	Symbol	Elucidation
Magnus Spiritus	A Spirit Power in the Sky	Possibly "Uncle Sam" might be associated here, but it would seem more appropriate to have a stern "presidential" head in clouds.
Mater Stellarum	"The Star Spangled Banner," or a woman soldier with flag leading troops into battle	Could also be thought of as the Egyptian sky goddess, Nuit.
Puer Maris	The embryo shown at the end of the *2001* sci-fi movie	New beginnings.
Aquilla Bellatrix	The American Bald Eagle	Great strength and far vision.
Alba Domina	Woman in white robes reclining on a crescent moon	A Huntress. Woman of allure. Woman as Lover.
Mater Libertas	Earth Goddess in the form of the Statute of Liberty.	Earth Mother is always pictured showing benevolence and concern.

There are no structures in the physical brain that correspond to these three levels of Mind or Personal Consciousness, but it is sometimes useful to feel that the lower or Subconscious Mind is generally below the chin, while the middle or Conscious Mind occupies the general "headspace," and the space above the head is the general location for the higher or Super-Conscious Mind.

Physical evolution follows that of consciousness, but how the body may be shaped by this development is anyone's guess.

At the more esoteric level, we've discussed the basic construct of the Personal Consciousness Unit as having arisen out of the field of Universal Consciousness to individually empower each human entity (leaving aside nonhuman entities for the moment). Based on a presumption of a triune model, we've arrived at something like this:

a. The Subconscious Mind, arising out of Universal Consciousness but still connected to it mainly through what is called the Collective Unconscious.

b. The Conscious Mind, arising out of the Subconscious Mind and functioning as the manager of the person.

c. The Super-Conscious Mind, arising out of the Universal Consciousness to contain both the Subconscious and Conscious Minds.

Just as (a) the Subconscious Mind remains in direct connection with the Universal Consciousness mainly through the Collective Unconscious, we will find that (c) the Super-Conscious Mind has a connection with the Soul. Thus, each human being functions through a:

• Physical/Etheric Body that relates to the physical and energetic universe.

• Astral Body that relates to the Subconscious Mind and corresponds to the Lower Self.

• Mental Body that relates to the Conscious Mind and corresponds to the Middle Self.

• Spiritual Body that relates to the Super-Conscious Mind and corresponds to the Higher Self.

• Soul that relates to Source.

It remains important, vitally important, for each person to remember that he or she is a whole person functioning as a unit and not a collection of bodies, each living a separate life. Most of us are not fully conscious all the time on these different levels, but the more broadly we learn to think of the physical world about us and the more we are aware at these different levels of consciousness through the subtle bodies, the more opportunity we provide for our personal growth and development.

The Subconscious Mind is with us all the time, and does provide us with a rich heritage of personal history and vast psychic powers. Integration is not a process of psychotherapy as practiced in the last century, but of conscious psychic empowerment practice and experience in the twenty-first century.

While there is a kind of psychic "pressure" pushing from the "lower level," it is really through conscious effort and practice of spiritual technologies that we undertake the next step of evolutionary development in this New Age.

It's all happening now! And you are part of it.

NOTES

The names of Middle Pillar centers and their associated images were developed by Carl Llewellyn Weschcke and Osborne Phillips, co-author, with Melita Denning, of "The Magical Philosophy" series, working together nearly forty years ago. The concept, however, is age-old, and draws upon both Western and Eastern traditions combined with modern psychotherapeutic experience.

APPENDIX ONE
Self-Empowerment and Self-Hypnosis

Self-Empowerment is a way of life, a belief in Self (big "S") and a belief in Humanity's continued evolution and personal growth. We want you thepowers into conscious skills. We want you to believe that you can become more than you are now. We want you to believe in your own power and your own authority to take command of your life. We want you to expand beyond your present artificial limitations and become the whole person you are in potential.

Self-Empowerment means that you take charge of your own Destiny and that you work to fulfill your existing potential so that we all benefit from what each of us becomes—a greater Whole Person.

To meet the challenges to humanity and to our planet in the immediate future, we have to quickly grow to become more than we are now.

That may well mean making drastic changes in your familiar ways and in the ways in which you have seen the world about you. Our world is changing and that makes changes in our ways necessary whether we are discussing world politics, world economics, new approaches to health and education, conflict among the organized religions of the world, the challenges of climate and extreme weather patterns, the changes in national economies, *or* if we are looking at our personal nutritional and social ways.

In the final analysis, it all comes down to adopting better habits and making our innate but underused powers into conscious skills opening to the Whole Person we are destined to become.

I will only write this as a personal belief—but I think there are those who prefer that we do not grow and develop powers, that prefer to reserve such advancement for themselves as an elite minority at the top of the hierarchies of organized religion and certain political and economic entities. I believe the immediate future presents immense challenges to those who do want to grow and develop for themselves and to share in the technology of growth and development with as many people as possible. I believe our very survival depends upon more people "growing up" and become the Whole Person we are intended to be.

GUIDED SELF-HYPNOSIS
AND MEDITATION PROGRAMS

Self-Empowerment is the fulfillment of our inherent potential. Evolution, however you define it and whichever mechanisms you consider, has brought humanity to its present overall level, but particular people have learned techniques to accelerate their personal growth. Evolution is a slow and uneven process—sometimes providing a general spurt over a short period but at other times, without the stimulus of sometimes catastrophic events, growth remains static.

The meaning of Self-Empowerment is the taking of conscious control of various presently subconscious processes. It happens slowly, naturally, but it can happen faster.

Self-Empowerment can be more skillfully achieved through self-hypnosis. Simply stated, guided programs of self-hypnosis and meditation accelerate what otherwise may require years of study and practice. Everything you need to benefit from self-hypnosis is included in the text of this book. Special self-hypnosis Scripts are included in our previous book, *Self-Empowerment through Self-Hypnosis*, and other books widely available.

However, we have to face the fact that some of us are lazy and lacking in self-reliance and self-discipline. You've read the book, but have you started doing anything with the knowledge we've given you? Possibly you've tried a little bit, but then fell asleep or skipped to the next day. You read the book, but you may be failing in its application.

But, as the commercials on television repeat, "Wait, there's more!"

We've produced a special audio CD just for readers who do want to benefit from the Self-Empowerment program. It's an hour-long CD with guidance and appropriate pauses for your response whether spoken aloud or silently. Timing is extremely important. The voice and script is that of Dr. Joe Slate. The CD is richly supported by specially produced background music that deepens your self-induced trance. The music and audio production is by Larry Smith at AUOH Productions in Moulton, AL 35650.

This CD is designed for use with this book and others in the Self-Empowerment series. You will find information on where and how to obtain this CD in the back pages.

Why do we use self-hypnosis for Self-Empowerment? We need to reach the nearly unlimited power in the Subconscious Mind that normally isn't available to us. Through self-hypnosis we bring about a productive partnership between the Conscious Mind and the Subconscious Mind directed by your focused will and intention. Focus, or Concentration, is the key here, and self-hypnosis is our method for its accomplishment.

THE SELF-HYPNOSIS SCRIPT

Now, here's the full script itself. You can apply it yourself, or even record it yourself. However, you would then not benefit from Dr. Slate's experience and expertise in the careful pacing of suggestion and response, and the specially developed background Music enriching the trance experience.

Hello. I'm Dr. Joe Slate.

I want to take a moment to refresh you on what we are accomplishing in this *Self-Empowerment through Self-Hypnosis* program.

This program introduces you to the best of personal hypnotists, the one existing within yourself. Through that inner hypnotist, you can achieve a highly attentive, focused state of self-hypnosis that empowers you to uncover your subconscious potentials and use them to achieve your highest goals. Through self-hypnosis, you can accelerate learning, improve memory, promote creativity, and increase motivation. You can break unwanted habits, banish negative stress, extinguish phobia, and overcome all blockages to your growth. You can facilitate your career success and enrich your social interactions. You can generate an attuned, empowered state of mind, body, and spirit that promotes health and fitness and even slows the aging process. You can develop your psychic powers and use them to bring new knowledge, happiness, and success into your life. You can retrieve experiences lost to conscious awareness, including those related to your past lives. All of these, you can do for yourself through self-hypnosis.

The script that follows provides a step-by-step guide designed to introduce the trance state and *connect* you to the subconscious powers related to your stated goal. The script is followed by an aura energy exercise that reinforces the effects of self-hypnosis and establishes a mental, physical, and spiritual state of personal empowerment that simply cannot fail.

For the typical session, set aside at least an hour in a quiet, comfortable setting, free of distractions. Your willingness to respond to your own suggestions is the key to success using this program. You may find that your receptiveness to hypnosis will vary depending on the time of day, with late afternoon and evening hours typically more conducive to self-hypnosis. It's important never to use self-hypnosis while driving, operating machinery, or engaging in any activity requiring concentration or attentiveness.

For best results, limit each self-hypnosis session to only one major goal. Before beginning the session, clearly formulate your goal in positive terms and write it down, preferably in a self-hypnosis journal using the first person. Begin with, "My goal is…" and describe it if possible in behavioral terms. After clearly formulating your goal, take a few moments to develop images and affirmations of success related to it. For instance, if your goal is to lose weight, specify your desired weight and visualize yourself standing before a mirror weighing that exact amount while affirming, "This is the true me." If your goal is career success, visualize yourself succeeding in your chosen career, while affirming, "I am empowered to achieve my career goal." If your goal is rejuvenation, visualize yourself at your youthful prime while affirming, "Time is now slowing down. Living younger, longer, and happier is my destiny." If your goal is to overcome stage fright, visualize yourself before an audience receiving an enthusiastic ovation for your presentation, while affirming, "I am in command." The use of creative visualization and relevant affirmations during self-hypnosis gives added substance to your stated goal and builds the commitment and confidence required to achieve it.

This program embraces the *I Am Principle* of self-empowerment that recognizes your power, not only to induce the trance state, but to take command of your life and your destiny. Each suggestion in the script is presented in the first person and followed by sufficient time for you to repeat it either silently or aloud. Although the sound of your own voice can be a powerful induction force, you may prefer the silent approach. Center your full attention on each suggestion and let yourself respond to it. The post-hypnotic cue presented near the end of the trance can be used on demand to trigger in an instant the full empowering effects of the session. With repeated practice, you will develop your ability to enter the trance state at will.

To begin the trance, settle back into a comfortably seated or reclining position with your legs uncrossed so as not to cut off circulation and your hands resting at your sides or on your thighs. With your eyes closed, listen carefully to each of the suggestions, and then repeat it either audibly or silently. You can repeat it exactly as presented, or if you prefer, you can revise it and state it in your own words. The pause following each suggestion allows plenty of time for you to repeat it at least once, and then to center your full attention upon it.

You can increase the effectiveness of self-hypnosis by using your imagination and focusing on images related to your suggestions. For instance, you can accompany your suggestions of relaxation with visualization of yourself in a relaxing natural setting, such as strolling along a serene nature trail or viewing a fluffy cloud drifting slowly against a clear blue sky. You can accompany your reverse counting with suggestions of "going deeper and deeper" combined with imagery of slowly descending a staircase step-by-step. You may find that simply visualizing each number in a favorite color against a blank background as you count downward can effectively deepen the trance state. Here's the script:

As I now settle back with my eyes closed, I give myself permission to enter the trance state.

By taking in a few very deep breaths and exhaling slowly, I am becoming more and more comfortable and relaxed.

Now breathing slowly and rhythmically, I am clearing my mind of all anxiety, clutter, and fear.

Soothing relaxation is now soaking deeper and deeper into every muscle, from my forehead right into the tips of my toes.

By now focusing my full attention on a peaceful, relaxing scene of my choice, I am becoming even more relaxed and receptive to each of my suggestions.

As I now count slowly downward from ten, I will become even more relaxed and receptive to my suggestions. Upon the count of one, I will be in a successful trance state.

Now in the trance state, all my cares have melted away—I am at total peace with myself and the world around me.

Here in my own words is my personal goal.

By now clearly visualizing my goal, I am unleashing all the power I need to successfully achieve it.

I am now fully empowered to achieve my goal. Complete success is my destiny.

I can at any moment activate the full effects of this trance experience by simply touching my forehead and affirming, "I am empowered."

I am now ready to end the trance state and return to the normal state of empowered awareness by counting slowly from one to ten.

Now fully conscious, I am empowered with self-confidence, security, and complete success.

With the trance state now successfully ended, take a few moments to reflect on the experience. Remind yourself that you can activate in an instant its full empowering effects by simply touching your forehead while affirming either mentally or audibly, "I am empowered."

You can stabilize the empowering results of self-hypnosis by attuning and balancing your personal aura, that field of energy enveloping your physical body. Begin by simply turning your palms upward, and with your eyes closed, visualizing bright beams of energy from a distance entering your hands and then spreading throughout your body. Think of your hands as your body's antennae to the universe with power to both send and receive energy. Allow the energy entering your hands to infuse your total being—mentally, physically, and spiritually. Visualize a bright glow of radiant energy enveloping your full body and reaching outward to infinity. Take a moment to sense your connection to the highest dimensions of energy and power.

With the infusion of new energy now at its peak, take a few minutes to attune and balance your aura system through the Aura Energy Massage. Begin the massage by first placing either hand, palm side down, at a few inches from your solar plexus, the central core of your aura energy system. While carefully not touching your physical body, use small circular hand motions and gradually expand them. Almost instantly, you will sense the balancing and attuning effects of the massage throughout your aura system. Conclude the massage by bringing your hands together and affirming, "I am now balanced and attuned, mentally, physically, and spiritually." You will experience during the massage a powerful sense of security and well-being. This simple massage is especially effective in activating the aura's rejuvenating powers. Through its regular use, you can take command of the aging process and, in some instances, literally reverse the effects of aging.

Finally, you can protect your aura energy system from the onslaught of stress or any other disempowering influence through the so-called finger-interlock gesture. Begin the gesture by simply joining the tips of your thumb and middle finger of each hand to form two circles, and then bringing them together to form interlocking circles. While holding the finger-interlock gesture, affirm: "I am now fully empowered. Nothing is beyond my reach. Greatness is my destiny." Use this subtle gesture as needed to generate an instant state of mental, physical, and spiritual empowerment. You can use the gesture almost anywhere and anytime.

Conclude this program by further reflecting on the experience. Write a summary of the session in your self-hypnosis journal and periodically document your progress in achieving your personal goal. Keep in mind that *the power is within you*. You are now in full command of it.

You can repeat this script as needed for other personal goals. You will find that, with repeated use, the script becomes increasingly effective. You will also find that there are no limits to the powers within yourself.

Thank you for listening. Best wishes for your new life of Self-Empowerment.

You can do it yourself!

Yes, of course you can record this script yourself for yourself. While it is copyright protected against copying and selling for profit, we extend permission for personal recording and self-usage. You can read it to yourself, or have someone else read it to you. You can adapt it as you wish—and, of course, it has those personal elements you must write for yourself.

Nevertheless, there are considerable advantages to working with a professionally produced product. And we will be producing other Self-Empowerment audio products in the future available from Llewellyn Worldwide.

GLOSSARY & SUGGESTED READINGS

Many of these terms do not actually describe "things" so much as they do "functions." Just as a hand can be described as a *fist,* or an *open palm,* or a *light hand* or a *heavy hand,* and so forth—these describe functions of the hand. You don't have a fist, but you have a hand that can function as a fist as well expressing emotion, communicating, functioning as a sign, and so on.

Most words describe things, or actions, but in this book we are dealing mostly with consciousness, or—if you prefer—with the inner dimensions of the paranormal and psychology.

Functions are not easily definable and mean different things to different people, yet we have to make the effort to use our terms consistently within the limited context of discussion in particular subject areas.

So it is that one function of your Personality is described as the *Ego*—that which <u>confronts</u> the outer world. Another function is described as the *Psyche*—that which <u>expresses</u> the feeling of selfhood.

But we have various challenges because we have also to deal with the ways in which the reader may be accustomed to use particular words and allow for other words that may be more descriptive. For example, the Subconscious Mind is also called the *Unconscious,* and sometimes the *Personal Unconscious.* And, unfortunately, some writers have confusingly identified it as the *Soul.*

As an overall view, the Subconscious Mind is the *lower* part of the Personality containing forgotten and repressed feelings and memories;

those feelings that make up the fundamental Belief or Operating System that filters Reality to our perceptions of the world; that collection of guilt feelings called the "Shadow"; the "Anima" or "Animus" collection of feelings representing our idealization or fear and sometimes even hatred of the opposite gender; and the various Archetypes and Mythic images formed through the long history of human experience, all of which can operate as gateways to the Collective Unconscious, to the astral world, and connect us to the higher or super-consciousness. The Subconscious Mind is also home to our instincts and the autonomic system that cares for the body and its operation.

But it is also much more. It is the nascent Super-Conscious Mind.

In truth, all our divisions of Consciousness are arbitrary, and the reality is that we are each a unit of Consciousness in the process of integrating the parts and becoming more developed without losing our unique identity. Although there may come a time in our far-off future when we willingly sacrifice what may be left of our separate identity in order to return to our Source, it is not now.

Affirmations. (Self-Hypnosis) As used in Self-Hypnosis, these are positive assertions of that which is desired *as if it is already realized.* This is vital to the involvement of the subconscious mind.

Suggested Reading—Hewitt: *Self-Hypnosis for a Better Life*
Slate & Weschcke: *Self-Empowerment through Self-Hypnosis*

Akasha. The element of Spirit, one of the five tattwas or elemental forces—the others being Air, Fire, Water, and Earth, which are derived from Spirit. It is symbolized by an indigo-colored egg shape.

Suggested Reading—Mumford: *A Chakra & Kundalini Workbook*

Akashic Records. The collective unconscious is a kind of group mind that is inherited from all our ancestors and includes all the memories and knowledge acquired by humans and sometimes is called the "Akashic Records." It is believed to exist on the higher astral and upper mental planes and to be accessible by the super-consciousness through the subconscious mind in deep trance states induced through hypnosis, self-hypnosis, meditation, and guided meditation.

It is a function of the Astral Light to retain all that has ever happened in thought and deed; hence the Akashic Records are the enduring records of everything that has ever happened and the repository of all knowledge and wisdom, and the files of every personal memory.

Being able to call up infinite information and integrate it into your present life needs is of enormous benefit—similar to but beyond the capacity of any present-day Internet search engine.

Suggested Reading—Dale: *The Subtle Body—An Encyclopedia of Your Energetic Anatomy*

Alpha Level. The brain generates weak electrical impulses representative of its particular activities. As recorded by the electroencephalograph (EEG), they fall into particular levels assigned Greek letters. Beta, at 14–26 cycles per second, is our normal waking state including focused attention, concentration, thinking, etc. Alpha, 8–13 cycles, is the next level down, characteristic of relaxation, alert receptivity, meditation, and access to the subconscious mind. It is at 8 cycles per second, the border between alpha and theta, that Trance occurs. Theta, 4–7, is lower yet and occurs just before (hypnopompic) or after (hypnagogic) sleep and is characteristic of light sleep, deep meditation, vivid imagery, and high levels of inner awareness. Delta, 0.5 to 3, is characteristic of deep sleep.

Altered State of Consciousness (ASC). Wakefulness and sleep are the two most familiar states of consciousness. Others include dreaming, meditation, trance, hypnosis and self-hypnosis, hallucination, astral projection, etc. ASCs can be induced by sleep deprivation, chanting, fasting, ecstatic dancing, drumming, sex, psychedelic drugs, and conscious self-programming. Once you've been "there," it is easier to get there again.

Anahata. The chakra located at the heart, color green, associated planet Sun or Venus, associated Sephirah: Tiphareth.

Suggested Reading—Dale: *The Subtle Body—An Encyclopedia of Your Energetic Anatomy*

Anatomy of the Body of God. If we accept the possibility of "truths" expressed in sacred literature we have to be open to non-literal interpretations. It is hardly sensible to think we are "created in God's image" and then look for such identity just in our physical bodies. Rather, knowing that Consciousness, along with Energy and Matter, have to come "in the Beginning with the Word," we can think of the unit of consciousness that is ours as modeled after God as Consciousness, hence "the Anatomy of the Body of God" is our consciousness as programmed for our development.

In *Self-Empowerment and Your Subconscious Mind* (co-authored with Joe H. Slate), Carl Llewellyn Weschcke draws upon a personal visionary experience in which the Great Pyramid of Giza becomes a model for Personal Consciousness expressed as the Subconscious Mind, the Conscious Mind, and the Super-Conscious Mind, and connections to Soul and to the Collective and Universal Unconscious.

The major point is the realization that in our Personal Consciousness we are modeled after the Universal Consciousness set at the Beginning. As a model, we are constantly growing to fulfill that potential and in doing so we are fulfilling the Great Plan set forth in the "Word."

Anima. The Woman in every man. In Jung's psychology, it is the mythic ideal of the feminine that a man projects on to women. It manifests in fantasy, romance, sexual behavior, the estrogen hormone, and in feminine energy.

Animus. The Man in every woman. In Jung's psychology, it is the mythic ideal of the masculine that a woman projects on to men. It manifests in fantasy, romance, sexual response, the testosterone hormone, and in masculine energy.

Anima/Animus. The formula of relationship between men and women is that of "Giving and Receiving"—or Projection and Reception. And yet it must be remembered that in each is the opposite for we are both complete in union and in our selves.

Apas. The tattwa of elemental Water. It is symbolized by a silver crescent with the horns pointing upward, as if a container.

Application Programs. The aptitudes and capabilities you demonstrate. Many self-improvement classes give you new aptitudes that augment your "Application Programs."

Archetype. A universal image and center of psychological function and energy, mostly similar across nationalities, races, cultures, and historical times. Generally speaking, "Mom" is the same mom everywhere. Nevertheless, there may be some minor variation across long-established cultures as expressed in dominant religions, and personal variants may be the source of traumatic disturbances as when a real-life mom fails to fulfill her archetypal stature.

The archetypes are the foundation of major mythologies, and correspond with gods, goddesses, and mythic heroes. They are found in the major arcana of the Tarot, may be seen and experienced through Kabbalistic pathworking and shamanic trances, and are often met in dreams and projected on to real-life figures in times of crisis. One of the goals is every program of self-knowledge is to gain understanding of our particular interaction with them, and possibly to change those interactions from a childish to a more mature level.

The archetypes may be the "gods," each charged with particular responsibilities in the natural world. See also "Noosphere."

As Above, so Below! The key phrase found in the Emerald Tablet that recognizes the dynamic formula established when "God created Man in his own image." Simply stated, the human person is the Microcosm and the Universe is the Macrocosm. Not only is their identity between Man and Cosmos but there is a continuity correspondence of action between the two.

Ask, and you will receive. Remember that your Personal Human Consciousness is modeled on the Body of God. The Powers of the Universe are yours to learn and earn. You do have the Power, but you have to learn it, understand it, believe it, use it, and—above all—have *faith* in its reality.

Assiah. In the Kabbalah—Tree of Life—the World of Action. The fourth and lowest of the Kabbalistic worlds corresponding to the material level, the world of sensation, the dominion of Primordial Earth and its four elements. Assiah is pictured either on the Tree of Life as Malkuth only, or as a fourth Tree of Life below the other three.

Suggested Reading—Regardie & the Ciceros: *A Garden of Pomegranates*

Association. Connection and relationship between similar items such that thought about one calls up others. It is not the same as "correspondence," which occurs at the universal macro level, whereas association is generally related to personal and human experience. It is often used in dream interpretation.

Astral Body. The third body or level of consciousness, also called the Desire or Emotional Body. In the process of incarnation, the astral body is composed of the planetary energies in their aspects to one another to form a matrix for the physical body. This matrix is, in a sense, the true horoscope guiding the structure of the body and defining karmic factors.

The Astral Body is the Lower Self of Emotion, Imagination, Thinking, Memory, and Will—all the functions of the mind in response to sensory perception. It is the field of dreams and the subconscious mind. It is the vehicle for most psychic activities.

Yet, a distinction must be made: The Physical Body is the field of ordinary conscious mind and the Astral Body is that of the subconscious mind, and a doorway to the super-conscious mind and the collective unconscious.

Astral Doorways. Meditation on certain objects may function 1) to induce an alternative state of consciousness or 2) to bring access to certain areas of the subconscious and the astral plane. Among the first are fascination devices that focus awareness and induce trance—crystal balls, magick mirrors, swinging pendulums, pools of ink, etc.—allowing the user to receive impressions. Among the second are Tarot Cards, Rune Symbols, I Ching Hexagrams, Egyptian Hieroglyphs, Hebrew Letters, Tattwas, and Yantras etc. used in meditation that open certain astral circuits and gain access to specific parts of the Astral Plane and to subjective states of consciousness.

Suggested Reading—Tyson: *Soul Flight, Astral Projection & the Magical Universe*

Astral Light. The "substance" of the Astral Plane through which "intentional thought" has its effect, as in magical operations. It is approximately equivalent to Ether, Mana, Vital Fluid, etc. holding the impressions of thought and emotion and feeling, forming memory.

Suggested Reading—Regardie & the Ciceros: *The Tree of Life—An Illustrated Study of Magic*

Astral Plane. The second plane, sometimes called the Inner Plane or subjective world, is an alternate dimension both coincident to our physical world and extending beyond it. Some believe it extends to other planets and allows for astral travel between them.

It is that level of concrete consciousness between the Physical/Etheric, the sphere of ordinary consciousness, and the Mental and Spiritual levels. It is where dreams, visions, and imagination are experienced and magical action shapes physical manifestation.

Astral Projection and Astral Travel. It's desirable to treat these two subjects together because of the confusion in terminology over the years. Astral projection is a particular state of consciousness in which the astral body separates from the physical and is able to travel on the astral plane, obtain information, communicate with other beings, and return to the physical with full memory. It is commonly understood that the astral body separates from the physical during sleep, but does not travel. Nonphysical movement in the familiar physical world is more likely to involve the <u>etheric</u> body than the astral. The etheric is the energy double of the physical body, able to function separately from the physical body while connected to it with the "silver cord" that transfers energy and consciousness between the two.

The etheric body can travel anywhere in the physical world, moving with the speed of thought, and can interact with the physical in a limited manner.

The astral body does not leave the physical body because it is not really an independent body but is the subconscious mind and "moves" within the field of consciousness without moving at all. Consciousness is everywhere, and in consciousness you can be anywhere. To the extent you want a body, you need to create a "Body of Light" in your imagination and then just imagine it doing what you want, going where you want.

But, the astral plane is not the physical world, and it lacks the "solidity" of the physical plane even though there is replication. However, things may appear on the astral that are not in the physical plane.

Suggested Reading—Bruce & Mercer: *Mastering Astral Projection,* book and CD companion

Denning & Phillips: *Practical Guide to Astral Projection, the Out-of-Body Experience*

Goldberg: *Astral Voyages, Mastering the Art of Interdimensional Travel*

McCoy: *Astral Projection for Beginners—Six Techniques for Traveling to Other Realms*

Phillips: *Astral Projection Plain & Simple—the Out-of-Body Experience*

Webster: *Astral Travel for Beginners, Transcend Time & Space with Out-of-Body Experiences*

Astral World. Just as we can speak of the physical plane and the physical world, so can we speak of the astral plane and the astral world. A "plane" (like a "level") is descriptive of the characteristics of the things that make up a world—the substance, energies, laws, etc. A "world," in contrast, is descriptive of how the things are put together, hence the landscape, the life-forms, the climates, and so forth.

The astral world has its own landscape, generally replicating the physical world, but is far more extensive, reaching wherever consciousness reaches. It has its own inhabitants, which include the astral bodies of the inhabitants of the physical world. Those astral inhabitants also include forms that have never incarnated into physical bodies as well as temporary inhabitants created by humans through the power of imagination, emotion, and fantasy.

It is also possible that some creatures, like certain paranormal entities, such as UFOs, aliens, the Loch Ness and other "monsters" that slip in and out of the physical world, have their origin in the astral, and that mythical beings like dragons also exist in the lower astral close enough to the physical that they sometimes appear to the physical world inhabitants.

Astrology. Astronomy brought down to earth. It is the science that relates planetary patterns measured by positions in the sky and mapped in relation to the physical location and time of birth of a person or an event in a very long tradition of observation and interpretation to describe the character of the person or event.

While considered as an ancient form of divination, it is today used as a scientific approach to self-understanding and the forecasting of mundane events: weather and climate changes, earth movements, economic and political events, and cultural trends. The horoscope provides a map of planetary energies at any specific time and as projected at a particular location. That map is correlated with the meanings of those planetary energies as established through thousands of years of observation and the now established principles of horoscopic analysis and interpretation.

A horoscope calculated for the exact moment and place of birth is like a photograph taken of the complex relationship of planetary forces as reflected in the astral body. Since the astral is formative to the physical, this photograph tells the tale of the physical incarnation and of the Personality. Solar Return (birthday) horoscopes show the annual progression from the birth chart.

This scientific astrology has little to do with the simplistic "birth sign" horoscopes found in popular media, which lump together approximately one-twelfth of the population as alike, based purely on the position of the Sun in a particular zodiacal sign on their birthday. Thus, while there are some general similarities commonly shared by those of the same Sun Sign, there are nearly as often powerful planetary factors involved providing a substantial deviation from some of the generalities.

Suggested Reading—George: *Llewellyn's New A to Z Horoscope Maker & Interpreter, A Comprehensive Self-study Course*

Riske: *Llewellyn's Complete Book of Astrology, the Easy Way to Learn Astrology*

Attention. Focused awareness. Concentration. To pay attention is a conscious choice to limit perception and the work of consciousness to something specific.

Attraction. The principle involves believing yourself worthy and already in possession of those things you want. It functions best when used as a goal in our Self-Empowerment through Self-Hypnosis technique, which fully mobilizes your inner resources and leaves no doubt of your success.

Atziluth. The first and highest Kabbalistic world, the divine world of the Archetypes. The domain of Primordial Fire. It corresponds to Kether, Chokmah, and Binah.

Aura. An egg-shaped sphere of energy extending as much two to three feet beyond the physical body and viewed by clairvoyants in colorful layers that may be "read" and interpreted.

It includes layers outward from the physical: the Etheric, Astral, Mental, and Spiritual bodies. The aura is also known as the "magical mirror of the universe," in which our inner activities of thought and feeling are perceived in colors. It is also the matrix of planetary forces that shapes and sustains the physical body and the lower personality.

Clairvoyants may analyze the aura in relation to health, ethics, and spiritual development, and the aura can be shaped and its surface made to reflect psychic attacks back to their origin.

Suggested Reading—Andrews: *How to See and Read the Aura*

Slate: *Aura Energy for Health, Healing & Balance*

Webster: *Aura Reading for Beginners, Develop Your Psychic Awareness for Health & Success*

Aura Reading. Clairvoyant "reading" of the aura to determine the health, character, and spiritual development of the person (or animal) by the colors seen.

Suggested Reading—Andrews: *How to See and Read the Aura*

Smith: *Auras—See Them in Only 60 Seconds*

Webster: *Aura Reading for Beginners, Develop Your Psychic Awareness for Health & Success*

Automatic Writing. A form of channeling in which a person, sometimes in trance, writes or even keyboards messages generally believed to originate with spiritual beings, or with aspects of the subconscious mind.

Autonomic Nervous System. The "lower intelligence" that safely runs the body functions without conscious awareness.

Awake. In contrast to being asleep, being awake supposedly says we are alert and perceptive to sensory input and the ongoing functions of ordinary consciousness. Nevertheless, self-observation will clearly show that there's more to being awake than having your eyes open! It's somewhat like having a dimmer on your light switch. Learn to turn up the intensity to become fully awake.

Awareness. Awareness is the focus of consciousness onto things, images, ideas, and sensations. Awareness is more than what we physically sense. We do have psychic impressions independent of the physical apparatus. And we can focus our awareness on memories dredged up from the subconscious; we can focus on symbols and images and all the ideas, and memories, associated with them. We can turn our awareness to impressions from the astral and mental planes, and open ourselves to receiving information from other sources from other planets, other dimensions, and other minds.

Awareness is how we use our consciousness. It is just as infinite as is consciousness, just as infinite as is the universe in all its dimensions and planes. When we speak of expanding or broadening our awareness, we are talking about paying attention to new impressions from new sources, and other ways we can use our consciousness. Awareness is like the "Operating System" that filters incoming information, sometimes blocking "what we don't believe in."

Become more than you are. You—we all—are a "work-in-progress" towards fulfilling the potential of the Whole Person already existent as a "matrix" of consciousness into which we are evolving.

To "Become more than you are" is the goal of everyone who accepts the *opportunity* and *responsibility* of accelerated development and Self-Empowerment.

Belief System. The complex of "feelings" that defines the way we perceive reality. Also see "Feelings" and "Operating System." Belief is also described as "Faith" that filters our perception of reality as defined by religious institutions.

Suggested Reading—Braden: *The Spontaneous Healing of Belief, Shattering the Paradigm of False Limits*

Body of Light. Sometimes used as an alternative term for the Astral Body, but more correctly as an image created ritually out of the astral light through the power of imagination and used by a magician as a vehicle for conscious perception and action.

Suggested Reading—Ashcroft-Nowicki & Brennan: *Magical Use of Thought-Forms—A Proven System of Mental & Spiritual Empowerment*

Brainstorming. Commonly a group search for new ideas, or for new applications for old ideas. It's best done as a rapid-fire, free-for-all, idea jam session opening the psychic faculties to inspiration. See "Inspiration."

Briah. The second of the Kabbalistic four Worlds, the archangelic and creative world of pure intellect. The world of Creation and the dominion of Primordial Water. It corresponds to Chesed, Geburah, and Tiphareth on the Tree of Life.

Captain of Your Own Ship. The personal "commandment" that each person should take full authority and responsibility for his or her being. Without question, it involves more than the modern perceptions of democratic government and capitalism, for it also makes demands upon both to provide each individual with certain basics of education, the rule of law, security of person, health, public services, etc.

To be "captain of your own ship" calls for a partnership between individual and government, with government guaranteeing both independence and opportunity for the individual in exchange for loyalty and tax payments.

The concept is developed as fundamental to "self-empowerment" in several books by Carl Llewellyn Weschcke and Joe H. Slate.

Censorship in Religion. All organized religions experience a program of codification in which certain practices and literature are approved by a controlling body while other practices, books, myths, and lore are disapproved and sometimes officially banned. Initially, much of this had political motivation—to bring the faithful under a single roof and to eliminate deviancy and competition to Roman rule in the case of early Christianity.

Until the middle of the twentieth century, certain books were listed as "sinful" for Catholics to read, and such banning was not limited to books with sexual themes although that was the common interpretation.

Only in recent years has there been widespread opportunity to explore alternatives in Christianity, and—to a lesser extent—in Islam and Judaism. In some cases, it has been archaeological finds that brought old ideas into new perspectives. For Christians, the primary findings have related to Gnosticism and Neoplatonism.

Change. There is always change. In Self-Empowerment, instead of letting life happen to you, you can make life happen your way. But you have "to take charge" and "state your intentions." There is recent scientific evidence showing that change in your own thoughts make changes in your brain's circuitry.

Channels. (1) An alternate name for a medium, and (2) a specific connection similar to a television channel for astral and mental plane communications. It is this connection that is the function of a carefully constructed Thought Form.

Suggested Reading—Denning & Phillips: *Foundations of High Magick*

Channeling. Receiving information from a discarnate entity or a higher spiritual being. It may also refer to communication with an aspect of one's own subconscious mind. It is similar to, but not necessarily the same as, the spirit communication of mediumship. In both, however, one person serves as bridge between a spirit or spiritual intelligence and people of ordinary consciousness. In spirit communication, the medium is more often unaware of the communication; in channeling of spiritual intelligence, the channeler is more often aware and sometimes a participant.

Automatic Writing is a form of Channeling in which a person, sometimes in trance, writes or even keyboards messages generally believed to originate with spiritual beings, or with aspects of the subconscious mind.

Suggested Reading—Wiseman: *Writing the Divine—How to Use Channeling for Soul Growth & Healing*

Channeling the Subconscious. While possibly related to "channeling" and "mediumship" in technique, the intention is to open the Conscious Mind to the Subconscious and experience the unity of consciousness as indeed there truly is.

Within that unity—just as there is in the ocean everywhere on Planet Earth with its layers, currents, variations in temperature, etc.—there will often be practical barriers preventing the free flow of information from the one to the other. Through our disciplines we must do the same kind of thing done with wireless communications technology: establish a channel of our own that is "interference free." We calm the mind through ritual, breath control, meditation, and routine. We isolate our channel from the noise of others and direct it towards known sources.

In studying both channeling and mediumship, we can benefit from the cumulative experience of many thousands of practitioners recorded in studies, journals, folklore, and expositions of theory, practice, and application.

No matter which approach we adopt, it is what the practitioner does that "powers up" the actual process and this is done with defined intention to establish the *channel* and then to clear it of all interference. The "channel'" may be the various tools, or the tools may only use the mentally created channel. Again, it is the practitioner's intention that matters.

The conscious mind can create the channel as an act of creative imagination in which a gate, door, natural stream, road of light, tunnel, etc., can serve as an "information highway," or it can just feel the intention itself, or your own journal will itself serve as a channel (as in dream processing and in automatic writing). Find what has the strongest appeal to you, something that satisfies your sense of drama or propriety.

Clearing the channel of interference is commonly accomplished by keeping the whole operation secret, or revealed only to a group of supporters so that no expression of amusement, criticism, contrary images, or doubts interferes with your own sense of correctness.

The choice of either direct experience or a divinatory or communication tool will, to some degree, shape the remaining elements of composition, transmittal, receiving, and interpretation.

Clairaudience. The psychic ability to hear things inaudible to most people, such as the voices of spirits, and sometimes sounds of inanimate objects such as crystals, minerals, artifacts, etc.

Clairvoyance. Sometimes called "ESP," the psychic ability to perceive things invisible to most people, such as auras, various health indicators, spirits, as well as things at a distance in space or time. It includes skrying (which see).

Both clairaudience and clairvoyance, and other psychic skills, have been induced through hypnosis and self-hypnosis.

Suggested Reading—Katz: *You Are Psychic, The Art of Clairvoyant Reading & Healing*

Owens: *Spiritualism & Clairvoyance for Beginners, Simple Techniques to Develop Your Psychic Abilities*

Slate & Weschcke: *Psychic Empowerment for Everyone*

Clan Consciousness. In humanity's early stages of development, individuals functioned primarily as part of the clan and not as individual persons. As such, there was little personal consciousness, very little "conscious mind."

Co-Creators. Here's the realization: we have all along been unconscious co-creators, and now we have the growing realization that we must be <u>conscious</u> co-creators, broadly aware of our own transgressions of natural law, or else the human experiment will end in failure.

Cognitive Relaxation. Inducing physical relaxation through intervention into the mental functions related to relaxation. Common examples are the use of visualization and suggestion to induce a peaceful, relaxed state.

Collective Unconscious. That function of the Personal Consciousness that bridges to the collective racial, cultural, mythic, and even planetary memories and the world of archetypes of the Universal Consciousness, making them available to the Psyche mainly through the Subconscious Mind.

   The memories of all of humanity, perhaps of more than humans, and inclusive of the archetypes. The contents of the collective unconscious seem to progress from individual memories to universal memories as the person grows in his or her spiritual development and integration of the whole being. There is some suggestion that this progression also moves from individual memories through various groups or small collectives—family, tribe, race, and nation—so the character of each level is reflected in consciousness until the individual progresses to join in group consciousness with all humanity. This would seem to account for some of the variations of the universal archetypes each person encounters in life.

Conscious Mind. The "middle" consciousness—the "ordinary" consciousness, the "objective" consciousness, the "aware" consciousness—with which we exercise control and direction over our "awake" lives.

   With your Conscious Mind you can take charge of the great resource of the Subconscious Mind. Information is constantly coming in, more than you can take full cognizance of, and so much of it is automatically diverted to the Subconscious Mind. The Subconscious Mind is more than a passive collection of memories, it is also your personal connection to the Universal Consciousness containing all that is from the very Beginning. Within this are all the potentials for all that you may become. This includes what we call "powers"—generally thought of as *psychic* powers. But before these powers are fully meaningful, they must be developed to become consciously directed <u>skills</u>.

But wait, as they say in television commercials, *there's more!* All that is the Conscious Mind—with its magnificent potentials for rational thinking, for creative development, for abstract analysis, for organization, for the use of imagination, for planning, and all those skills that make it possible for the human being to manage the resources of the natural world—rose out of the Subconscious Mind. Outwardly, that's what we do; inwardly, we manage Consciousness, because that is what we are. In particular, the job of the Conscious Mind is to manage the Subconsciousness and develop its innate powers into skills that we can then deploy consciously with awareness and intention to work with the Great Plan of evolving life. In another sense, it is to make Conscious the Unconscious through careful management of its resources.

When you take deliberate charge of the subconscious, your life takes on a new dimension of both meaning and power. Rather than a risky existential leap into a dark cavern of the unknown, your probe of the subconscious is an "inward leap of power" that clarifies the nature of your existence and reaffirms your destiny for greatness and meaning. It's a leap of progress that not only accelerates your growth, but guides you toward greater happiness and fulfillment as well.

As we became more aware of ourselves as individuals and operated more in the Conscious Mind, developing personal memory, rationality and new ways of thinking, we perceived ourselves in relationship to the natural world rather than as part of it. We learned to store knowledge in our memory rather than having immediate "feeling" access to it. Rather than relating internally to the rhythms of the Sun, Moon, and Planets, we saw them externally and developed sciences of astronomy, astrology, and agriculture. And we became aware of linear time.

Nature can show the ways to knowledge and understanding of her secret powers when you learn to listen. The Sun, the Moon, and the Planets, too, have powers to share with Man in his wholeness.

As Manager, it is the job of the Conscious Mind to know, understand, and direct all these resources. It's the most exciting, most gratifying, most rewarding and grandest job you will ever have, and it's one that is yours forever! You can't be fired, nor can you abdicate.

Consciousness. Everything that is, out of which Energy and Matter manifest and Life evolves. Consciousness is the beginning of all things and part of the trinity of Consciousness, Energy, and Matter. "Consciousness just IS!" We can't really define consciousness because we are nothing but consciousness and consciousness cannot really define itself. "I AM THAT I AM."

Our personal consciousness includes all states of awareness and our experiences of fear, love, hope, desire, happiness, sadness, depression, ecstasy, mystical union, etc. We experience connectedness through consciousness

Consciousness is not a "thing" nor is it a function of a "thing" called the brain. Killing the brain doesn't kill consciousness but it limits its expression in the familiar physical world. Consciousness is expressed through the brain, but it exists outside the brain. Consciousness acts upon the physical world, like a "force," as in telekinesis.

There are three levels of consciousness:

I for Instinct, a function of the lower subconscious.

I for Intelligence, a function of the ordinary consciousness.

I for Intuition, a function of the super-consciousness.

Control. The spirit that acts as a kind of manager through which other spirits communicate to the medium during a séance.

Creativity. A desirable characteristic in your resumé. *But what is it?* Our standard response largely relates creativity to the capacity to have new ideas and to create unique expressions. It's innovation and inventiveness—to look at a problem and come up with a new way to solve it; to take an old concept and come up with a new model; to take an old look and come up with a new one. But, creativity must also be applicable to a situation. Generally, at some point, it needs to be practical and attainable.

Destiny. While related in meaning to "fate" and "karma," destiny has a less rigid feeling. Each person is born with a life "pattern" that can be seen in a birth horoscope. We each have a genetic heritage, the love of our parents, the immediate environment, etc., but as we grow older those surrounding factors are replaced with new ones that may change what seemed to be an expected pattern. Education and social environment may become powerful influences for change.

The empowered person takes charge of his or her destiny, making conscious decisions rather than letting change passively affect life.

Suggested Reading—Finley: *Design Your Own Destiny—Shape Your Future in 12 Easy Steps*

Developmental Process. From even before birth, we grow into our *Psyche* just as we also grow into our *Psychic Potentials.*

Our childhood experiences are the foundation of the Personality, but we live most our lives as adults and not as children. As the Bible says, we have to put aside childish things (and even many perceptions of our young adulthood) and learn to see and think as an adult. But, to put our "childish ways behind" sometimes requires our conscious remembering and recognition of those childhood perceptions in order to see them freshly as an adult.

After all, you don't want to spend your adult life as a *Big Baby!* Yet, when you see news of barroom fights, child molestation, rape, road rage, mass shootings and suicides, sports violence and violent demonstrations, and more—not to even get into the matter of mass terrorism, piracy on the high seas, dictators who are responsible for mass murder and genocide, and demand for nuclear weapons—you realize the terrible consequences that can be associated with the adult child. Don't blame the Subconscious Mind for any of these bad things. It just does its job of remembering everything. It's up to the adult Conscious Mind to do its job and change childish conditioning into adult strength and wisdom. And, as a knowledgeable adult, it is your responsibility to do so.

Divination. Prophesy and information by "occult" methodologies.

By reading naturally produced signs ranging from the shape of clouds to the positions of planets (astrology).

By reading artificially produced signs ranging from the patterns of tea leaves to the throwing of dice or dominoes.

By reading symbols such as the Tarot cards or the I Ching hexagrams.

By reading visions as seen in Dreams or in Trance.

In each situation, something experienced is interpreted, usually by means of long-established rules justified by many years of observation across many cultures. In most cases, these interpretations are supplemented by psychic factors of impressions or intuition naturally arising in either conscious or subconscious (trance) states.

Suggested Reading—Cunningham: *Divination for Beginners—Reading the Past, Present & Future*

Dream Book or Dream Journal. Record the elements of a dream immediately upon awakening (see Dream Recall below), but do not stop to interpret them. Later, you will also record your interpretation, and start a "dictionary" of the symbols and other elements that seem meaningful to you, and what they seem to mean.

The dream experience is a personal gateway to the subconscious with its abundant empowering resources. Embraced by the subconscious mind, the dream experience becomes a powerful agent for growth and change. In that role, the dream can promote restful sleep while at the same time opening totally new channels for growth and self-discovery.

But aside from simply recalling the dream experience, a major task we face is unraveling its significance and developing our ability to use the dream experience as a channel for personal growth and empowerment. We now know that dreams don't do it for you; they instead work with you. Through your dreams, you can exercise your psychic skills, including your ability to see into the future and travel out-of-body to distant spatial realities. Beyond these, you can develop your ability to experience firsthand the spiritual realm with its advanced spirit guides and higher planes of spiritual power.

Dream Interpretation. An important factor in Self-Empowerment is the more complete utilization of lines of communication between levels of consciousness. While commercial "dream dictionaries" may have limited application, one that you compile yourself may be immensely helpful. Through the regular use of a Dream Journal, you become familiar with your own symbol meanings and can explore each further for more insight. When you actually pay attention to your dreams, they start to pay attention to you and can deliver information and even guidance of immediate application.

Suggested Reading—Gongloff: *Dream Exploration—A New Approach*
Gonzalez-Wippler: *Dreams and What They Mean to You*

Dream Recall. The most important parts of the process are to tell yourself to remember your dreams just before falling asleep, and that you will wake up from those dreams and immediately record the details you can remember. At this time, no effort is made to interpret the dream. Dream interpretation can wait for a day or more. If there is no immediate recall, then assume you did dream and just don't remember it. Lie there and ask yourself questions about the unremembered dream—*what was it about, were there people, what was the time period of the dream, were there messages in the dreams and so on.* If no dreams are recalled, ask one more question: *why can't I remember?* Record that answer.

Your recall, recording, and interpretation of dreams is part of an overall process of building lines of communication between the conscious mind and the subconscious, and ultimately with the super consciousness. Part of the process of dream recall is developing your own personal dream dictionary (don't presume that your dream dictionary is universal and offer it for publication! It is your dream dictionary, and no one else's) is bring order to the chaos of forgotten memories and childish experiences. As you do so, you are also engaging in the 'house cleaning' necessary before total integration is attempted.

Dreaming True. Programmed dreaming where a question or an intention is formulated before sleep, and left to the subconscious mind to respond with an answer or an action. It can also be effectively programmed with self-hypnosis.

Dreams. Stories experienced during sleep. Some dreams seem merely to be translations of physical experiences, others seem to be ways we assimilate new information. Dreams are also a function of the subconscious mind and deliberate dreaming is a doorway into the subconscious and its connection to the Collective Unconscious.
Suggested Reading—Gongloff—*Dream Exploration, A New Approach*
Gonzalez-Wippler: *Dreams & What They Mean to You*

Earth. Planet Earth is alive—and that includes the entire electromagnetic system that reaches out from the planet's core to the Moon and beyond. The Solar System is alive, and with it vast fields of energy connect from all planets and other solar bodies to Moon and Earth, and the inhabitants of Earth. We are part of the Whole, and the Whole is within us.

Ego. That function of the Personal Consciousness that confronts the outer world.

Emotion. "Energy in motion." Emotion is a dynamic and powerful response to something perceived that connects to universal human experience and archetypes. Emotion is the energy "powering" most intentional psychical and magical operations, the energy responsible for many types of psychic phenomena, possibly including hauntings, poltergeists, rapping, etc., where there is potential for the emotion to have been "recorded" in the woodwork of the building. Emotion is found in Netzach as part of Ruach, the Conscious Self.

Empowering Imagery. Empowering imagery is second only to self-dialogue as an empowerment essential in activating the therapeutic powers of the subconscious. Once you've formulated your goals in positive terms, relevant imagery gives them the substance required for full embracement by the subconscious.

Goal-related imagery can be seen as a present manifestation of a future reality. For instance, if your goal is rejuvenation, imagery of your body at its youthful prime actually activates the subconscious processes related to rejuvenation. By visualizing yourself at your youthful prime while affirming, "I am now empowered with the energies of youth and vitality," you can take charge of the aging process and not only slow aging, you can actually reverse its effects. Living younger, healthier, and happier becomes your destiny.

Empowering Symbolism. The use of symbols related to your stated goals can efficiently activate at a moment's notice the subconscious faculties related to even highly complex goals. For instance, if your goal is financial success, simply visualizing a gold coin can increase your motivation and facilitate optimal decision making related to your financial success. Should you decide to do so, you can take that effect a step further by carrying on your person a gold coin and periodically stroking it.

Etheric Body. The second, or energy body that is closest to the physical body. As with all the subtle bodies, it has two layers:

The first, sometimes called the "Etheric Double," is fully coincident with the physical body in health and extends about an inch beyond physical skin. It is the psycho-physical circuitry of the human body (the chakras, nadis, and meridians) through which the lifeforce flows under direction of the astral matrix. To clairvoyant vision, it is the health aura and appears as very fine needles of radiation—standing straight up in health and lying down in illness.

The second layer, along with the astral and mental bodies, forms the egg-shaped aura surrounding the human body. It is an interface between the individual and dynamic planetary energies and cosmic forces that sustain life.

The Etheric Body can be projected (see "Etheric Projection") and can be molded by intense thought and thus shape the physical body.

Etheric Plane. The Energy Plane between the Physical and Astral planes, although from another perspective it is part of the Physical. Its energies are in constant movement, like tides and currents, ruled by the Moon, Sun and Planets and moving in cycles.

Etheric Projection. A portion of the etheric body, sometimes along with other etheric material for added substance, can be formed as a vehicle for the operator's consciousness and projected to other physical locations. Being of near -physical substance and energy, it is sensitive to certain physical materials, like iron and silver. It can be injured, and such injuries will repercuss back to the physical body.

The etheric body can also be shaped to resemble other entities, and is a factor both in the lore of werewolves and were-leopards.

Evolution. Unlike the Darwinian concept that focuses primarily on the physical form, esotericism extends that concept of evolutionary change to every aspect of life and consciousness including the Soul, and sees a constant movement of growth and development throughout the Cosmos, both visible and invisible. Evolution is not a thing of the past but continues, both in physical response to the environment and also in fulfillment of a primal program set forth a the "Beginning."

For the human being, the evolutionary process is primarily in the fulfillment of the potentials of the Personal Consciousness, in particular in the fulfillment of the Whole Person and the growth and development of the Super-Conscious Mind.

Many in the esoteric community believe that the beginning of the New Age in the 1960s—whether or not coincident with the influx of Aquarian Age energies—brought an expansion of awareness and an actual change in consciousness that is having an increasing effect on personal and social development.

In the personal area, this is having an immediate effect in the development of innate unconscious psychic powers into conscious psychic skills. In the social area, it is expected to translate into world government and global economy, law, and human rights.

As a factor in human consciousness, the evolutionary impulse is not limited by the physical structure, but rather can mold it as needed by the emergent psychic faculties.

Expectancy Effect. The effect of expectation on the future, to include personal performance and outcomes, with expectations of success typically facilitating success.

Extrasensory Perception (ESP). The awareness of, or response to, events, conditions, and situations independently of known sensory mechanisms or processes.

Fate. *Don't be a victim!* A common perception is that our fate—our destiny—is fixed and unchangeable. The new concept of self-empowerment is that each person can "take charge" of personal life and influence it with conscious intention.

Even the horoscope is not seen as a fixed pattern but rather as a personal field of opportunities. The more you understand these opportunities, the greater your control over your personal life and the greater its fulfillment.

Feelings. An instinctive response conveying some "truth" about a person or situation. It is a kind of filter through which we experience reality. Also see "Operating System."

Forgotten Memories. Are retained in the subconscious and may be recalled using various techniques including word association, asking questions, dialogue, and "sleeping on it." Nothing is truly forgotten, but things may have been insignificant at the time, painful and so repressed, overshadowed by larger events, etc. Memories can be recovered if you know what you are looking for and if you know they are pertinent. Sometimes, events will remind you and otherwise tell you that something significant is missing.

God's Image. We are told that we are made in God's image: "So God created man in his own image, in the image of God he created him; male and female he created them." (Genesis 1:26-27) Therefore we are to understand that the pattern of our Personal Consciousness was structured by Mother/Father/Creator/Source at the beginning of Existence itself.

Great Plan, the. Some esoteric groups believe that there is a Plan guiding the evolution of human consciousness to its eventual re-union with the ultimate Source. They further believe that Humanity has a role to play as co-creators able to accelerate the Plan in its application to human consciousness.

Great Work, the. The path of self-directed spiritual growth and development. This is the object of your incarnation and the meaning of your life. The Great Work is the program of growth to become all that you can be—which is the realization that you are a "god in the making." Within your being there is the seed of Divinity, and your job is to grow that into the Whole Person that is a "Son of God." It is a process that has continued from "the Beginning" and may have no ending, but it is your purpose in life. It is that which gives meaning to your being.

In this new age, you are both teacher and student, and you must accept responsibility for your own destiny. *Time is of the essence!* Older methods give way to new ones because the entire process of growth and self-development has to be accelerated. Humanity has created a *time bomb* that's ticking away, and only our own higher consciousness can save us from self-destruction. But—have faith and do the Great Work for it is all part of a Great Plan.

Suggested Reading—Denning & Phillips: *Foundations of High Magick*

Group Mind. The collective consciousness of a group or team of people working together on projects or studies. It may be a spontaneous function of a group of like-minded people or deliberately created by a magical group or a functional organization such as a business corporation or working partnership. It was part of the teachings of Napoleon Hill, author of *Think and Grow Rich*.

Guided Imagery. The use of suggestion and visualization to guide thought processes, typically to promote a positive state of physical relaxation and personal well-being. Guided imagery can, however, be used to induce a trance state or as a goal-oriented technique for managing stress or pain, overcoming fear, breaking unwanted habits, slowing aging, and promoting wellness, to mention but a few of the possibilities.

Guided Meditation. A meditation led by an experienced guide following established inner pathways to access particular iconic collections of knowledge and experience. A typical example would be found in Kabbalistic pathworkings progressing on the Path from one Sphere to another on the Tree of Life.

Suggested Reading—Clayton: *Transformative Meditation, Personal & Group Practice to Access Realms of Consciousness*

Lorenzo-Fuentes: *Meditation*

Mumford: *Yoga Nidra Meditation—Chakra Theory & Visualization—Audio CD*

Healing through Self-Hypnosis. (Self-Hypnosis) Based on the premise that a supreme healing force exists in everyone, healing through Self-hypnosis accesses that force and focuses in on specific goals related to healing, both mental and physical. This concept also recognizes the existence of healing dimensions beyond the self and our capacity through self-hypnosis to tap into them.

Suggested Reading—Slate & Weschcke: *Self-Empowerment through Self-Hypnosis*

Health Diagnosis through Self-Hypnosis. (Self-Hypnosis) This concept is based on the premise that you alone know yourself best. Through self-hypnosis, you can not only identify the conditions relevant to your health, you can intervene directly in ways that promote healing. Various techniques are employed, but the most common includes a visual (inner) survey of the body itself with the expectation that the subconscious mind will seize the opportunity to call attention to areas of the body needing medical intervention.

Suggested Reading—Slate & Weschcke: *Self-Empowerment through Self-Hypnosis*

Higher Self. The third aspect of personal consciousness, also known as the Super-Conscious Mind. As the Middle Self, or Conscious Mind, takes conscious control of the Lower Self, or Subconscious Mind, the Higher Self becomes more directly involved in functioning of the Personal Consciousness.

Even though the Higher Self is also known here as the Holy Guardian Angel, there is value in using a more easily comprehended psychological term. Words are words and there are often many names for the same thing. But each gives a particular shape or color or tone to the thing named to expand our understanding comprehension when we are relating to larger concepts.

Kabbalistically, it is the Super-Conscious Mind in Tiphareth that mediates between the Divine Self and the Lower Personality.

Hypnoproduction. New abilities that may occur through self-hypnosis include instantaneous command of a new language and sudden mastery of an artistic or scientific skill, each of which could be explained as the retrieval of skills acquired in a past life.

Hypnosis (see also "Self-Hypnosis"). An Altered State of Consciousness that provides a bridge to the subconscious mind by which conscious suggestions mobilize subconscious resources including current and past life memories, and exercise certain control over physical body responses to external stimuli and internal functions, access areas of the Collective Unconscious, and channel communication between astral and mental levels and the physical level. The hypnotic trance has been associated with various psychic abilities.

As the historical and scientific advancements in hypnosis continue, interest in hypnosis has slowly expanded to include self-hypnosis and its applications, particularly toward *self-development and personal empowerment.* That trend is due in large part to the recognition that hypnosis, to be effective, depends not only on the skill of the hypnotist, but even more importantly, on the receptivity of the participant. That recognition places the participant, rather than the hypnotist, at the center of the induction process. The result is a moving away from an authoritative, often dramatic induction approach that *commanded* the participant to respond toward a more permissive, person-centered approach that *permitted* the participant to respond. That change is based on the premise that <u>hypnotic suggestions become effective only when accepted and integrated by the cooperative participant</u>.

Suggested Reading—Hewitt: *Hypnosis for Beginners, Reach New Levels of Awareness & Achievement*

Hypnotic induction. (Self-Hypnosis) The procedures preliminary to the actual hypnosis session, starting with relaxation of the body and calmness of mind, focus on the established intention of the session, and development of a concise statement of that intention as accomplished.

I AM. This phrase invokes the higher self in a powerful self-affirmation used in self-hypnosis.

Icons. It is through symbols and images, and icons, that we open the doors of our inner perception. The great secrets of magicians, shamans, and modern scientists are in the associations they attach to such icons, and in the power of certain signs and formulae to function as circuits and pathways—not in the brain but in consciousness.

"Identity." We have many identities—some of them are psychological masks or "personae" we adopt for our dealings with the world, in our relationships, and sometimes—unfortunately—to hide behind within our own Personality. In other words, those masks can be either practical or self-deceitful.

As a business person, for example, we should *dress* according to our role and that includes the mask that represents that role. It identifies our expertise and function, and is practical and is not deceitful. As a parent, we adopt another mask of the good mother or father—a mask that fulfills a function for the child as well as a constant reminder of the changing nature of the important role we play for the growing child.

As a lover, we adopt another mask, but there we have to be more careful that it is not deceitful about the depth and reality of our obligations in a loving relationship, which does include honesty about our self but also a "living up to" the promise and nobility, the caring and devotion to the beloved, etc.

But, for ourselves, we adopt a "self-image" that must be true and honest as well as ideal. We need to work to fulfill that ideal as part of the Great Work of building an inner relationship between the middle self of Personality and the Higher Self that is also our Holy Guardian Angel.

Images. It is through symbols and images, and icons, that we open the doors of our inner perception. The great secrets of magicians, shamans, and modern scientists are in the associations they attach to such icons, and in the power of certain signs and formulae to function as circuits and pathways—not in the brain but in consciousness.

Imagination. The ability to form and visualize images and ideas in the mind, especially of things never seen or experienced directly. The imagination is an amazing and powerful part of our consciousness because it empowers our creativity—the actual ability to create. Imagination is found in Tiphareth as part of Ruach, the Conscious Self.

Imagination is the making of images, and magick is accomplished by making images and their movement real. Some of that reality comes in the process of charging those images with energy, but more comes by the acceptance of their reality on the astral plane. As images are charged in the astral world, they can be drawn into the physical world, or have an effect on the physical plane.

Induction. See "Hypnotic Induction."

Information. Programs of instruction and memories that control the transfers of energy and matter.

Information Packets. Combinations of programs controlling a numbers of processes. In the body, they instruct how each tiny cell functions, how every organ does its work, how every nerve and every vein carries energies and hormones to designated places, and how everything relates together to make a functioning and healthy body.

Inner Dialogue. Positive inner-dialogue is self-empowerment at its peak. It can be defined simply as *the empowering messages you send to yourself.* Once you've formulated your personal goals, inner-dialogue can activate the resources required to achieve them. Think of your dialogue as personal affirmations of power that you can present either audibly or silently as thought messages. You will probably find, however, that silent messages become even more powerful when supplemented by the sound of your own voice.

Positive inner-dialogue is essential to self-empowerment because it provides instant and direct access to the unlimited powers of the subconscious. It includes all the positive messages we send to ourselves through a variety of channels that include not only our verbal expressions but also our beliefs, orientations, aspirations, values, expectations, perceptions, and attitudes. A major advantage of inner dialogue is that it can used almost any time or place.

Among the most effective forms of inner-dialogue are the positive "I am" messages we send to ourselves. Examples are: *I am empowered to succeed, I am destined for greatness,* and *I am a person of worth,* each of which can build powerful feelings of self-confidence and well-being. Even when not directly targeted to the subconscious mind, inner-dialogue will nonetheless be registered there.

Inner Divinity. The belief that each person has a "Divine Spark" or part of the Divine Creator at his core. As the person evolves and grows in wholeness, he becomes more and more closely identified with his Divinity until an ultimate unity is accomplished.

Inner Therapist. Your best therapist, like your best hypnotist and healer, exists within yourself as a functional, advanced part of your subconscious. It is your direct link to the resources required to advance your growth and enrich the quality of your life. As a fundamental part of your being, it recognizes your basic nature as a person of dignity and incomparable worth.

Inspiration. Usually a sequence of ideas suggesting particular actions, originating at the psychic level. It is often associated with brainstorming, and is especially productive in a group setting. See "Brainstorming."

Suggested Reading—McElroy: *The Bright Idea Deck*
McElroy: *Putting the Tarot to Work*

Integration. Integration is more than a bringing together: it the uniting of parts into a new whole. It is used to describe the goal of psychological development in Jungian Psychology culminating in the person actually becoming the Higher Self rather than the personality.

It is a difficult concept because it is a change of identity from the "I" of the personality into a new "I" that incorporates the transformed elements of the old personality into a new Whole Person centered on the Higher Self.

"Who am I?" requires a new answer.

International Parapsychology Research Foundation (IPRF). Established at Athens State University in 1970 by Joe H. Slate, Ph.D., this foundation is committed to the study of parapsychology and related topics. It has conducted extensive research and established student scholarships in perpetuity at Athens State University and the University of Alabama. The president of the foundation is District Judge Sam Masdon of Montgomery, AL. For more information, contact Joe H. Slate, Ph.D. at joeslate@aol.com

Intuition. A blinding flash of insight answering a question or solving a problem originating at the Soul level of consciousness. A developing psychic power drawing upon the knowledge and experience of others, living and dead.

Jungian Psychology. Also called Analytic Psychology—the system developed by C. G. Jung. After studying with Freud, he advanced a more spiritual approach to psychotherapy evolving out of his studies of occult traditions and practices including, in particular, alchemy, astrology, dream interpretation, the I Ching, the Tarot, and spiritualism.

For Jung, the whole range of occult and religious phenomena have evolved out of the relationship between the individual consciousness and the collective unconscious. While the personal unconscious or subconscious mind is the lower part of the individual consciousness, it is through it that we also experience the elements of the collective unconscious—most importantly the role of the archetypes.

The archetypes are "collectives" of images and energies relating to (1) role-specific functional, formative, and universal experiences such as Mother, Father, Lover, Judge, Hero, etc., (2) those that are more personal with karmic content including the Shadow (repressions), the Anima (expressions of the Feminine in men), the Animus (expressions of the Masculine in women), and (3) the Self (the evolving Whole Person that overshadows the Personality).

Kabbalah. A complete system of knowledge about all the dimensions of the universe and of the human psyche organized into "the Tree of Life" diagram showing the inner construction and the connections between levels and forms of consciousness, energy, and matter. It provides a resource for understanding and applying the principles of Magick, for understanding the dynamics of the psyche, and for interpreting human history and action. The present-day Tarot specifically relates to the Tree of Life. See also "Qabala."

Suggested Reading—Christopher: *Kabbalah, Magic, and the Great Work of Self-Transformation—A Complete Course*

Dennis: *Encyclopedia of Jewish Myth, Magic and Mysticism*

Godwin: *Godwin's Cabalistic Encyclopedia—A Complete Guide to Cabalistic Magick*

Gonzalez-Wippler: *Kabbalah for the Modern World*

Gonzalez-Wippler: *Keys to the Kingdom—Jesus and the Mystic Kabbalah*

Malachi: *Gnosis of the Cosmic Christ—A Gnostic Christian Kabbalah*

Regardie & the Ciceros: *A Garden of Pomegranates—Skrying on the Tree of Life*

Regardie & the Ciceros: *The Middle Pillar—the Balance Between Mind & Magic*

Stavish: *Kabbalah for Health and Wellness*

Trobe: *Magic of Qabalah—Visions of the Tree of Life*

"Know Thyself." This motto was inscribed on the sixth century BCE temple of Apollo at Delphi and quoted by several ancient writers, some of whom attributed it to Solon. It has been since quoted by thousands if not millions of self-help, motivational and spiritual writers and teachers.

Know Yourself. The process of self-discovery, of self-knowledge, of self-understanding is endless until such time as we become one with the Highest Self. The process of self-knowledge is the process of becoming more than you are.

Levitation. Non-supported elevation of physical objects and persons. (1) Partial elevation is common to "Table-tipping" in which the attendees place fingers lightly on a table and ask questions of supposed spirit presences. The table responds by lifting two or three of the four legs and taps answers. (2) In some cases, the entire table has elevated. (3) During spiritual séances, various objects are elevated and move about the séance room. (4) During séances, the medium has actually been elevated and even moved outside the room through one window and returned through another. (5) During meditation and prayer, some people "bounce" and in other cases fully levitate.

Life Between Lives. Following the belief in reincarnation, there is a period between the previous life and the next life during which the past life is reviewed and the next life planned.

Suggested Reading—Newton: *Destiny of Souls, New Case Studies of Life Between Lives*

Newton: *Journey of Souls, Case Studies of Life Between Lives*

Newton: *Life Between Lives, Hypnotherapy for Spiritual Regression*

Newton: *Memories of the Afterlife—Life Between Lives Stories of Personal Transformation*

Life-journey. The "journey'" through life that each person makes. It is the story of one single lifetime.

Life Purpose. We are here to grow, to become more than we are. Each of us has the ability to apply our inherent powers and our emerging skills to the challenge of accelerating personal growth.

Lucid Dream. A particularly vivid dream in which the dreamer himself appears. It is believed to be a form of astral projection, and if the dreamer can take conscious control of the dream, it then becomes a full out-of-body experience.

Suggested Reading—McElroy: *Lucid Dreaming for Beginners*

Magical Personality. It is a constructed personality, given a magical name, that can be compared to the created avatar in cyber games. It is an idealized self-image for the Whole Person you are coming to be.

Matrix. The background framework for all and any manifestation. It is a union of Consciousness in the Universal Field of primary energy/matter potentials. The universal matrix is the pattern for the evolving universe and all within it. The individual matrix is the pattern of energy/matter guiding the development and function of each lifeform. It is mostly a function of Mental, Astral and Etheric levels of consciousness guided by an intention expressed at the Soul level. It functions as the Etheric Body.

Suggested Reading—Bradden: *The Divine Matrix, Bridging Time, Space, Miracles, and Belief*

Meaning to Life. One of the most challenging questions any of us will ever confront. We can say that our Life's Purpose is "to grow, to become more than we are," but purpose and meaning may not be exactly the same thing. "Meaning" may be either personal or for all of us—either way, it is probably best discovered for oneself. Meditate on it often.

"Meaning" at the level of the Subconscious is always personal, never abstract.

Meditation. (1) An emptying of the mind of all thoughts and "chatter," often by concentration only on the slow inhalation and exhalation of breath, and is characterized by slow alpha and theta waves. It induces relaxation and a "clean slate" preparatory for receiving psychic impressions. (2) A careful thinking about a particular sub-ject in a manner that brings access to physical memories as well as astral and mental level associations of knowledge about that sub-ject. (3) A state of consciousness characterized by relaxed alertness reducing sensory impressions with increased receptivity to inner plane communications.

Suggested Reading—Chadwick: *Inner Journeys—Meditations and Visu-alizations*

Clement: *Meditation for Beginners, Techniques for Awareness, Mindfulness & Relaxation*

Paulson: *Meditation as Spiritual Practice*

Medium. See also "Channel." Most mediums enter a trance state and then—often through the agency of a "control" or "guide"—to en-able communication with a discarnate person. Often the Control speaks for the Spirit seeking communication.

Suggested Reading—Mathews: *Never Say Goodbye, A Medium's Stories of Connecting with Your Loved Ones*

Mediumship. The study and development of the skill necessary to function as a spiritual medium facilitating communication be-tween the worlds of spirit and the living. See also "Spiritualism."

Suggested Reading—Eynden: *So You Want to be a Medium? A Down-to-Earth Guide.*

Mental Body. The fourth body. The mental body "thinks" in abstract rather than emotional form. The lower mental body unites with the astral and etheric bodies as the personality for the current in-carnation. The higher mental body is home to the Soul between incarnations.

Mental Plane. The third plane up from the physical/etheric, between the Astral and the Spiritual Planes. It is the plane of abstract con-sciousness, where we find meaning, patterns, the laws of nature and mathematics, number, and form. It is the plane where all thought is shared. It is the upper home for the Akashic Records, shared with the astral.

Mental Telepathy. Mind to mind communication by nonphysical means. Usually, an image of the intended receiver is held in mind while a simple message, such as "Call me," is projected. Once the message is sent, it is important to let go of it rather than doing constant repetition.

Mind-Body Connection. It is only recently that science has recognized that there is somewhat of a two-way street between Mind and Body. Both are far more complex than earlier perceived and more intimately connected through energy and hormonal exchanges. With this recognition, we have the beginning of mental healing, where visual images are found to influence the body. And, with meditation or hypnosis (and self-hypnosis, of course), imagined exercises and movements were found to result in muscular developments.

Equally interesting, with Reichian Therapy, deep massage and certain exercises involving specific muscle groups were found to release emotional traumas and bring memories of their origins to the conscious awareness.

Suggested Reading—Reich: *Character Analysis*

New Consciousness. In just the last few decades, there has been a whole new perception of the subconscious mind as a resource of considerable power, and a realization that "consciousness" itself is bigger, older, and more fundamental than previously perceived.

Consciousness is even more elemental than Energy and Matter and extends throughout Time and Space. Modern science, and in particular quantum physics and what we now dare to call "new age psychology," along with paranormal studies, have restored balance to our cosmology. We see Life and Consciousness as universal and limitless.

We are evolving into a new relationship between different levels of personal and extended consciousness, with the conscious mind as manager able to call upon the resources of the extended range of consciousness to tap into memories, knowledge and perceptions. The new relationship is a two-way communication with the conscious mind calling up specified content from the subconscious, the collective unconscious, and the greater universal consciousness, and using nearly forgotten psychic powers to expand awareness beyond the limitations of the physical senses.

The divisions between the conscious mind and the subconscious mind are becoming less substantial and are merging towards Wholeness, with the conscious mind functioning more like a Managing Director and the subconscious as a Director of Resources. While the conscious mind is still the functional director, the relationship to the subconscious is becoming more one of interactive teamwork than previously.

Evolution for humanity is continuing and accelerating. It is driven by purpose and meaning, and not only by chance and Darwinian natural selection. Evolution is not founded in biology but in consciousness, and continues to build upon a long-ago programming for which no end is in sight.

Noosphere. The network of human thought surrounding the Earth. See also "Collective Unconscious."

Operating System. Inside every computer there is a software package providing the instructions for the hardware to carry out the work requested by application software packages like Microsoft Word and Excel. The operating system is the interface between the computer hardware and the world, while the application packages are like the skills and training we learn by study and experience. Like every other computer, the human brain requires an operating system that interfaces with the world and filters our perceptions to correspond to what we are conditioned to expect through parental guidance, our life experiences, education, training, interaction with authority figures, social expectations, and to far lesser extent by our genetic heritage and past-life memories. This operating system also conditions and directs the way we respond to external stimuli. Much of this operating system functions in the subconscious mind. Like computers, the operating system can be modified, updated, changed, and even replaced. Self-understanding is learning about our operating system; self-improvement is about modifying and changing our operating system; self-transformation is about up-dating and largely replacing our old operating system.

Pain Management. Pain Management is one of the greatest personal challenges. Too often we meet that challenge by the use of medications that sometimes become addictive, other times have adverse side effects, and still other times are withdrawn from use because of demonstrated harm.

Pain can also be managed by diverting awareness away from the painful area of the body or away from thought of the emotional source of pain. While this can be a simple focus of attention elsewhere—absorption in a good novel or other entertainment, mental exercises of visualization, repetition of prayer or mantra, inner dialogues, etc.—at other times it may require a greater depth of subconscious management accomplished through meditation or self-hypnosis.

Suggested Reading—Slate & Weschcke: *Self-Empowerment through Self-Hypnosis.*

Past-Life Regression. A technique involving hypnosis, self-hypnosis, or meditation to reexperience past-life events in order to resolve traumatic reactions, recover lost memories and skills, and resolve certain recurring problems.

Suggested Reading—Andrews: *How to Uncover Your Past Lives*

Grimassi: *The Cauldron of Memory—Retrieving Ancestral Knowledge & Wisdom*

Webster: *Practical Guide to Past Life Memories, Twelve Proven Methods*

Slate & Weschcke: *Doors to Past Lives*

Personal Consciousness. Your Personal Consciousness, which was once part of the Universal Consciousness, remains forever connected to it. It is created in the image of God—its matrix is "the anatomy of the Body of God," *Lower, Middle* and *Higher* Consciousness. Subconscious Mind, Conscious Mind, and Super-Conscious Mind. We are born with a "matrix" to be filled in by experience. Look at the Pyramid (see diagram, page 11) as the entirety of Personal Consciousness and consider that it represents the anatomy of the Body of God, *which is our own body of consciousness shaping our world of physical, emotional, mental, and spiritual experience.*

Personality. The immediate vehicle of personal consciousness we believe to be ourselves. It is a temporary complex drawn from the etheric, astral, and mental bodies containing current life memories, the current operating system, *"the totality of somebody's attitudes, interests, behavioral patterns, emotional responses, social roles, and other individual traits that endure over long periods of time.* (*En-*carta on-line dictionary, copyright © 2008 Microsoft Corporation)

Physical/Etheric Body. When awake, the physical and etheric bodies are inseparable, although an adept is able to project parts of the etheric body in magical operations. Asleep, it is possible to partially separate the etheric body from the physical for travel on the physical plane.

Precognition. The psychic awareness of the future, to include knowledge of events, trends, and conditions.

Psychic Body. Generally conceived as the Etheric and Astral bodies together.

Psychic Empowerment. Generally the following of a specific plan or program—sometimes involving self-hypnosis and meditation—for the development of innate psychic powers into dependable skills. With empowerment, the psychic or spiritual bodies can be integrated into the Whole Person.

Suggested Reading—Slate & Weschcke: *Psychic Empowerment for Everyone*

Psychic Powers. All the abilities, especially as trained skills, associated with the paranormal, including Astral Projection, Aura Reading, Channeling, Clairaudience, Clairvoyance, Extrasensory Perception, Mediumship, Mental Telepathy, Psychokinesis, Remote Viewing, Spirit Communication, Spiritual Healing, Telekinesis, Teleportation, etc.

Suggested Reading—Denning & Phillips: *Practical Guide to Psychic Powers, Awaken Your Sixth Sense*

Slate & Weschcke: *Psychic Empowerment for Everyone*

Webster: *Psychic Development for Beginners, An Easy Guide to Releasing and Developing Your Psychic Abilities*

Psychokinesis (PK). The movement of objects without physical contact.

Psychometry. The reading of emotional and psychic energies impressed on an object such as a watch, jewelry, etc. to reveal its history and ownership.

Suggested Reading—Andrews: *How to Do Psychic Readings Through Touch*

Qabala. There are various alternative spellings of the words, *Qabala* and *Qabalistic.* The most common are "Kabbalah" and "Kabbalistic;" another is "Kabala," and then "Cabala" and "Cabalistic." All are transliterations of the Hebrew word QBLH meaning "an unwritten tradition transmitted orally from teacher to student." "Kabbalah" and "Kabala" generally refer to the original Jewish version, "Cabala" refers to the Christian version, and "Qabala" and Qabalah" to the magical or Hermetic version.

The Kabbalah—no matter how spelled—is probably the most complete "preview" of the world as perceived and experienced through spiritual vision that we have. It is a systematic organization of spiritual reality into a manageable formula for human study along with a methodology of "correspondences" to organize all of human knowledge.

It is a treasure trove for practicing magicians and the most expert self-study program of progressive meditation the world has ever seen.

Qabalistic Pathworking. Generally, a progressive system of guided meditations following the connecting "paths" on the Sephiroth of the Tree of Life. Through systematic "travel," the student builds pathways in the Subconscious Mind providing structure for the developing Super-Conscious Mind.

The Tree of Life is described as a "filing cabinet" organizing all of life's experiences, memories, and knowledge into sets of "correspondences" such that new experiences automatically reveal their "inner secrets" and integrate their powers.

Suggested Reading—Regardie & the Ciceros: *A Garden of Pomegranates—Skrying on the Tree of Life*

Reality. The personal world as seen through our belief system. While it mostly coincides with that of other people, self-analysis will show deviations and distortions reflecting the "feelings" of the person.

Regression. (Self-Hypnosis) The recovery of past memories through hypnosis or meditation. To generate the regressed state, we use suggestions of traveling back in time to a stage of youthful prime. The program found that lingering in that regressed state of peak youthfulness tends to be rejuvenating.

Reincarnation. The belief that the Soul experiences multiple lives through newly born physical bodies and personalities. Upon death of the physical body, the personality withdraws to the astral and then mental plane while the essential lessons of that incarnation are abstracted to the Soul.

Suggested Reading—Slate: *Beyond Reincarnation, Experience your Past Lives & Lives Between Lives*

Slate & Weschcke: *Doors to Past Lives*

Rejuvenation. The condition of becoming youthful again, or the process of making a person young or youthful again.

Suggested Reading—Slate: *Rejuvenation: Strategies for Living Younger, Longer & Better.* Book with audio CD

"Self." We distinguish between a little self (small "s") and a big Self (large "S"). The small self is that of the personality, the person we think we are, and in fact are until we identify with the big Self that is also the "Higher Self," the permanent Self existing between incarnations.

Self-Development. The work, also called "the Great Work,'" of developing the little self into the big Self.

Self-direction calls for acting with awareness of the consequences of our decisions.

Self-Empowerment. A synthesis of Occultism, Psychology, and Self-improvement in a functional lifestyle that is both practical and spiritual. Its goal is the fulfillment of the innate potentials leading to the Whole Person. Through the use of self-hypnosis, it condenses traditional esoteric programs by activating the subconscious mind and drawing upon the collective unconscious.

The self-empowerment perspective recognizes the subconscious as an interactive phenomenon in which various subconscious processes work in concert with each other to promote our personal empowerment. The self-empowerment perspective focuses on your capacity alone to experience the subconscious, activate its powers, and focus them on self-designed goals. That's what self-empowerment is all about!

It follows that our personal empowerment depends largely on our capacity to interact with the subconscious. Therapeutic techniques based on this view include hypnosis, dream analysis, free association, and various forms of meditation that focus on specific subconscious processes.

The self-empowerment view recognizes the subconscious as a storehouse of knowledge not yet manifest to conscious awareness. As we dive deeper into the subconscious, the more we learn about ourselves and the more empowered and balanced we become. Amazing though it may seem, complex bodies of new knowledge have been accessed and transferred to conscious awareness through appropriate empowerment programs, including hypnosis.

Self-Hypnosis. *"Self-hypnosis can be best defined as a self-induced state of altered consciousness that gives direct access to the vast reserve of resources and underdeveloped potential existing in everyone. It's a strategy based on the premise that you alone are your best personal hypnotist and growth specialist."* (from Slate & Weschcke: *Psychic Self-Empowerment for Everyone*)

The self-induction of hypnotic trance and the **catalytic power of direct self-programming** through simple but carefully developed affirmations mostly expressed as already accomplished "I AM" conditions, such as "I AM slim."

Suggested Reading—Park: *Get Out of Your Way, Unlocking the Power of Your Mind to Get What You Want.* Includes audio CD of self-hypnosis programs

Slate & Weschcke: *Self-Empowerment through Self-Hypnosis—Harnessing the Enormous Potential of the Mind*

Self-Improvement. We can always change for the better; we can improve ourselves physically, mentally, and spiritually; and no matter what the challenges may be, we can try to meet them on our own terms. Self-improvement starts with knowing where we are now and understanding how our current situation limits us. Then comes examination of where we can go from the current position and what steps we can make to move forward, and, finally, the decisions to be made and the costs to be assumed.

Self-Knowledge. Self-knowledge means knowing just who you are—free of the gloss of what other people say and think, free of the bounds of family and place, and aware of the role of education and environment in your current conditioning.

Self-Programming. We make many programming choices, and the more understanding we have of the external programming placed upon us and knowing the opportunities we have to choose new programming, the greater our freedom to become more than we are.

Self-Talk, Self-Dialogue. Discussion with your self as if you are several people—which you are. Through such dialogue you isolate those different personae—masks—from one another until you know who you are and how you can make use of the different persona in your relationships with the outer world. You are the director and producer of the drama that is your life, and you are also all the main characters in the drama. They are the different persona that you can become at will as you gain knowledge and understanding.

Self-Understanding. Self-understanding is different from self-knowledge. Knowing who you are is different than understanding who you are. Understanding involves "why" you are who you are—the karma leading up to now, the planetary factors in your horoscope, and the impact of your environment on who you are. Self-understanding also brings understanding of what the choices your have before you actually involve.

Shadow. In Jung's psychology, the Shadow is a somewhat independent splinter personality representing those elements that have been deliberately or unconsciously repressed and denied expression in your life, or that are dormant and unrecognized. It is the Nephesh located in Yesod, the Lower Self or lower subconscious with primal instincts and drives, most of which have been unconsciously banished in the drive for conformity and approval by the authorities in one's life.

With repressed elements, there is a lot of emotional energy locked up. It's like prisoners in jail—human energy denied freedom. Sooner or later, we need to confront these repressions and release those of childhood trauma, understand those repressed in the name of conformity, rationalize those that represent sensible behavior and customs. and get rid of the rest, while coming to terms with any that remain.

Yes, perhaps there is some inner "demon" left that calls for professional help. Your subconscious will tell you if need be. Just listen for advice from your Inner Voice or Spirit Guide.

Skills. Trained powers.

Skrying. Sometimes spelled "Scrying." The psychic techniques of reaching into the subconscious mind by means of fascination devices such as crystal balls, magick mirrors, pendulums, etc., and focusing devices such as dowsing rods, shells, oracular dreaming, Ouija™ boards, aura reading, or psychometry, **as an aid to concentration to allow visions** and automatic writing and speaking, etc.

Suggested Reading—Tyson: *Scrying for Beginners, Tapping into the Supersensory Powers of Your Subconscious*

Skrying in the Spirit Vision. Skrying using a symbol. See "Astral Doorways."

Suggested Reading—Regardie & the Ciceros: *The Tree of Life—An Illustrated Study of Magic*

Soul. The essential self behind all personal manifestation. It is not the personality but it absorbs the core lessons learned in the life of each personality created in a series of incarnations.

Spark of Divinity. In our core of our consciousness, we have a spark of Divinity that gives us, in our Consciousness, the power to shape the future and even to change the present. We will earn that power through the techniques of Self-Empowerment and the Self-Improvement programs presented in books on Self-Empowerment by Dr. Joe H. Slate and Carl Llewellyn Weschcke.

Spirit. Used variously to (1) identify the Spiritual Body, or Soul; (2) the essence of the deceased person in communication with the living or appearing as a "ghost"; (3) the "collective" of etheric, astral, mental, and spirit bodies other than the physical; (4) entities from other dimensions or planets channeling to humans; (5) nonhuman inhabitants of the astral plane; (6) a collective term for nonindividual spiritual power and intelligence, probably an aspect of the Collective Unconscious or Universal Consciousness; (7) the fifth element from which the lower four—Fire, Air, Water, and Earth—are derived. In addition, there is the "Holy Spirit," which may be the Primal Consciousness or Matrix that can be activated by prayer or other affirmative thoughts.

Spirit Body. In the hierarchy of subtle bodies, Spirit is higher than Mental, Astral, Etheric, and Physical. There is lack of specific definition, but it could be that the Spirit Body is first in the process of the descent of the Soul into physical incarnation. In this scheme, the Soul creates the Spirit Body, which then serves as a kind of matrix for the Mental Body formed of mental "substance," then the Astral Body of astral substance, etc.

Spirit Communication. Generally, the communication between living people and the spirits of the deceased. Also may include communication with other spiritual entities—Guides, Angels, Masters, etc.
Suggested Reading—Buckland: *Buckland's Book of Spirit Communications*
Konstantinos: *Speak with the Dead, Seven Methods for Spirit Communication*
Livon: *The Happy Medium—Awakening to Your Natural Intuition*
Parkinson: *Bridge to the Afterlife—A Medium's Message of Hope & Healing*
Slate and Weschcke: *Psychic Empowerment for Everyone*

Spirit Guide. An entity manifesting on the astral or mental plane exhibiting high intelligence and wisdom with a personal interest in the welfare of the individual experiencing the more or less constant presence of the Guide.
Suggested Reading—Andrews: *How to Meet and Work with Spirit Guides*
Webster: *Spirit Guides & Angel Guardians, Contact Your Invisible Helpers*

Spirit World. The nonphysical world. The subconscious is, in fact, in continuous interaction with the higher realms of power to meet your empowerment needs, including protection in time of danger, comfort in times of grief, and hope in times of despair. Through your connection to the spirit realm, you will experience the full beauty and power of your existence— past, present, and future—as an evolving soul.

Spiritual Body. The highest aspect and consciousness of the human being. See "Spirit Body."

Spiritual Genotype. The individual's unique spiritual or cosmic makeup that remains unchanged from lifetime to lifetime.
Suggested Reading—Slate: *Beyond Reincarnation*

Spiritual Plane. The highest level of creative being from which the lower planes are derived.

Spiritualism. Generally the practice and the religion associated with spirit mediumship and communication, and the belief in the survival of the individual after physical death as spirit.
Suggested Reading—Owens: *Spiritualism & Clairvoyance for Beginners—Simple Techniques to Develop Your Psychic Abilities*

Spiritualist. We are using this term not to identify persons interested in the practice or the religion of Spiritualism, but rather persons interested in exploring spirituality and the spiritual nature of the person, of humanity, and of the Cosmos itself.

Spirituality. The study and exploration of the spiritual nature of the person, of humanity, and of the Cosmos itself. The study includes the foundations and nature of religion, the nature of man in relation to Creator, and the connections of Spirituality with metaphysical subjects.

Spirituality calls for us to live in full awareness of this world and our connections to all there is, and then to act fully out of that awareness. We can't be spiritual while ignoring the world around us. We can't be spiritual by not living—acting—out of that awareness.

Spirituality does not wear "blinders"—seeing only what we want to call "good" and either ignoring that which doesn't qualify or thinking it has nothing to do with us. Spirituality does not mean that we spend all our time thinking only "pure thoughts," praying to some "higher authority," meditating on "white light," or singing praises to the "being in charge" of it all.

We are perceptive, intelligent people given the responsibility of willful choice. Not only that, we have little-used powers that extend both our awareness and our capacity to act beyond the immediate confines of skin and bones. Through our Subconscious Mind we are in contact with the Universal Consciousness which likewise includes Awareness and the capacity to Act.

Subconsciousness. Also called "the Unconscious." It is the *lower* part of the Personality containing forgotten and repressed feelings and memories, feelings and the fundamental Belief or Operating System that filters Reality, that collection of guilt feelings called the "Shadow," the "Anima" or "Animus" collection of feelings representing our idealization or fear and hatred of the opposite gender, the various Archetypes and Mythic images formed through the history of human experience, all of which can operate as doorways or gates to the astral world and connect to the higher or super-consciousness. The subconscious is also home to our instincts and the autonomic system that cares for the body and its operation. The subconscious mind is accessed by various techniques including hypnosis, prayer, and ritual, and during sleep.

Subconscious Memories. While the subconscious retains memories of everything, its feeling associated with that memory. In general, however, we are mostly concerned with childhood memories, fears, and misunderstandings that have been—often—repressed. As childish memories, they live on and may still influence our adult understanding and feelings erroneously and painfully. By recalling those memories, an adult perspective can replace the childish one and at the same time release energies tied up in those childish fears and misunderstandings.

Subconscious Mind. The subconsciousness—never asleep, always aware. The Nephesh. That part of the mind below the threshold of consciousness. Normally unavailable to the conscious mind, it can be accessed through hypnosis and self-hypnosis, meditation, automatic writing, etc.

"The subconscious is not only a content domain but a dynamic constellation of processes and powers. It recognizes that the wealth of our subconscious resources is complementary to consciousness rather than counteractive. It's a powerful component of who we are and how we function" (from Slate & Weschcke: *Psychic Self-Empowerment for Everyone*).

The Subconscious Mind has no ethics or morals; it is your Conscious Mind that must make choices and impose order on chaos, develop distinct channels to reliable resources, and otherwise understand and learn that your Subconscious Mind is your key to the infinite resources of the Universe. Helping you to build the relationship between the Subconscious Mind and the Conscious Mind is the purpose of *Self-Empowerment And Your Subconscious Mind*, by Weschcke & Slate.

But the major message we want to give you is that the Subconscious Mind is an unlimited resource, not only of memories and information but also of powers and skills. It the foundation and matrix to all we are and all that we will become. Our personal unit of consciousness is part of the Universal Consciousness so we have unlimited potential and have yet to discover any limits to our capacity or ability to use that potential. Our goal is to become adept at calling upon these powers and resources to match our needs and interests, and to keep "pushing the envelope" toward yet greater capacity and ability.

Aside from the integrative process, there's evidence suggesting that the subconscious can literally generate new potentials and growth energies independent of our conscious interactions through processes not yet fully understood, possibly through the synergistic or holistic results of the integrative process alone. What we need to understand is that the Subconscious Mind is not a passive bystander, but always aware and always active. As you grow in consciousness and integrate more of your psychic and other powers into your Whole Person, the Subconscious Mind grows and contributes more to the Whole Person you are becoming.

Understanding these creative processes of the subconscious mind is among our greatest challenges with potential for enormous benefits. The point here, as elsewhere, is always that the greater our understanding, the greater the benefit, but even as we face the continual challenges, the very attempt at understanding stimulates positive developments.

Contrary to some views, the subconscious is "the essential you," the essence of your being as an evolving soul. Without the subconscious, you would not exist at all. It's the vast totality of your existence: the "old you" of the past, the "dynamic you" of the present, and the "infinite you" of the future.

According to the self-empowerment perspective, the subconscious never sleeps—it's in continuous interaction with consciousness. It embraces the physical, spiritual, and psychical nature of our existence. Awareness of future events, telepathic communications, and clairvoyant insight are all among its powers. The subconscious welcomes our probes and challenges us to use its powers.

Subconscious Resources. The subconscious, with communication to the Collective Unconscious and the Super-Consciousness, has very nearly unlimited resources available to you through your Guide.

Super-Conscious Mind. Your subconscious mind is mostly conditioned by the past, and your conscious mind by the present. But you were born with a basic purpose, with some specific learning goals for this lifetime. The Super-Conscious Mind is your doorway to and from the future. The super-conscious mind is the higher self and the source of your inspiration, ideals, ethical behavior and heroic action, and the very essence that is "the Light of Men" as it was in the beginning and as it is now and as it will always be . . . .

The Super-Conscious Mind is the *higher* level of personal consciousness with access to the universal Collective Unconscious. It is where the "gods" or powerful archetypes and spirit guides can be found, and where the Akashic Records are accessed.

Our goal is to intentionally make use of psychic skills for our practical benefit—*and in developing these psychic powers into skills, we are fulfilling the potential of the Whole Person and developing the Super-Conscious Mind.*

Superman. A fictional character and comic book super hero created by Jerry Siegel and Joe Shuster in 1932. Superman first appeared in Action Comics #1 (June 30, 1938) and helped to create the modern superhero genre.

There have always been superheroes in myth and sometimes in real life. As such, they have an archetypal quality going beyond gender. Today Wonder Woman is as strong an archetypal power as is Superman.

Symbols. It is through symbols and images, and icons, that we open the doors of our inner perception. The great secrets of magicians, shamans, and modern scientists are in the associations they attach to such icons, and in the power of certain signs and formulae to function as circuits and pathways—not in the brain but in consciousness.

Table-Tilting, Table-Lifting, Table-Turning. The partial or complete lifting of a table in a séance setting, used in communication (most in response to yes/no questions with one tilt or two) with spirits.

Tarot. A vast system of Archetypal Knowledge condensed into a system of seventy-eight images on cards that can be finger-manipulated and then laid out in systematic patterns to answer specific questions or provide guidance to the solution of problems. While it is a form of divination, it is one of the most sophisticated and carefully developed systems of images and relationships following the structure of the Kabbalah's Tree of Life. Going beyond divination, it is also a system to access the Unconscious, and to structure magical ritual.

It's a powerful Western esoteric system comparable to the Eastern I Ching.

Suggested Reading—Amber K & Azrael Arynn K: *Heart of Tarot, an Intuitive Approach*

Ciceros: *The New Golden Dawn Ritual Tarot—Keys to the Rituals, Symbolism, Magic & Divination*

Ferguson: *The Llewellyn Tarot*, 78-card deck and 288-page book

Hollander: *Tarot for Beginners—An Easy Guide to Understanding & Interpreting the Tarot*

Telekinesis. The psychic skill to move the location or change the shape of a physical object. See "Psychokinesis."

Telepathy. See "Mental Telepathy." Mind-to-mind communication or thought reading, more commonly experienced during trance.

Teleportation. The dematerialization of a person and rematerialization at a different location.

Thought. Astral and mental collections expressed mostly in words to represent a particular opinion, intention, or plan of action. We *think* thoughts. We *feel* emotions.

Thought Form. (1) An astral image created by concentrated thought intended to accomplish a specified objective. When reinforced with emotion and charged with etheric energy, it will become physically manifest. (2) A spontaneous image created in the imagination that is charged with emotional energy. Either can be perceived by a clairvoyant and felt by ordinary people with some degree of psychic sensitivity. A carefully constructed mental image that is charged with emotional energy can become a manipulative tool used in product marketing, political action, and religious domination.

Suggested Reading—Ashcroft-Nowicki & Brennan: *Magical Use of Thought Forms, a Proven System of Mental & Spiritual Empowerment*

Three Levels of Consciousness.

I for Instinct, a function of the lower subconscious.

I for Intelligence, a function of the ordinary consciousness.

I for Intuition, a function of the super-consciousness.

Training Programs. Examples of simple programs to train the memory and the ability to visualize include:

Recreating your room. Simply look about the room you are in right now, and any time you have the opportunity in different rooms, then close your eyes and visually recreate it. With your eyes closed and looking at your imagined image of the room, pick out something significant in all six parts of the room: ceiling, floor, and all four walls. Look for colors and shapes, note textures and the play of light and shadow. Estimate the room's measurements and the sizes of objects. Play a game with yourself and pretend you are going to be paid money for everything accurately remembered.

Then open your eyes and look for those significant areas and see how well you did, and even more importantly, how well you did with the areas adjacent to those significant areas. Repeat often. Later, when you are away from the room, close your eyes and recreate it again, and when you return, verify as many of the details as possible.

Self-Imaging. Take a simple statement, like "I AM slim," or "I AM strong," and picture yourself accordingly. Do not think of the process of becoming slimmer or stronger, but just a simple image that is you as stated. Now, write a description of what you saw, in detail. Repeat often.

Recreate an event. Think of a recent event at which you were present, and picture it in detail. See where you were and see what you were doing. See where other people were and what they were doing. Note what people are wearing, and especially jewelry and watches. Now, listen, and hear the sounds and voices of that event.

Recreate a story. Take a scene from a novel you recently read, and recreate the story in your imagination. Fill in the detail for what wasn't described in the printed version. Add sound effects, listen to the voices, and hear the sounds of the environment. Pretend that you are watching a movie made from the story and see the actors, see their hair, their clothes, how they move, feel their emotions.

Remember the day backwards. See yourself as you prepared to go to sleep, undressing from the day, having dinner, coming home from work, finishing up work, your work that day, etc. all the way back to having breakfast, dressing for the day, using the toilet, washing and showering, getting out of bed, and waking up. Note anything you wished you could change, and intentionally do so in your imagination. This especially concerns feelings where you have regret or even guilt for something said or done to others, and hurt and pain from things others said or did to you.

You don't need to carry pain or guilt around with you. Undo these matters in your imagination with strong feelings of intention to remove the pain, whether yours or others. Such emotion is a barrier to your empowerment.

Create a Memory Palace. I mentioned this earlier. Don't use your own living quarters but create an apartment inside a building, and pretend you are both architect and interior designer. Construct and decorate a room for each major category of your life where you will store objects representing actual memories. Have a room representing marriage, for example, and start it with a wedding picture. Add memories using objects even if you have to imagine one, such as a photo you didn't take, and place it appropriately in the room.

Create another room representing your job, another for your hobby, another for each subject you've studied, and so on.

Now, keep adding memories to your palace. As you review your day, select things to be permanently filed for future reference and create an "icon" to contain everything important about each such thing.

Journal it. These are all exercises that can be continued, but it's these last two that I really recommend becoming a permanent activity. And how will you enable that? Journal it! Nearly every self-improvement system, whether it is esoteric or mundane, recommends that you keep a journal or diary. Why? Because the act of recording solidifies everything about the recorded event, and what you intend to do about it. If you regret something you said or did, record that you are undoing it. If you are happy about something and want to affirm it, record that too.

Trance. A state of consciousness in which awareness is concentrated, focused, and turned inward to the subconscious mind, either unconsciously through repetitive stimuli or consciously induced in a similar technique in hypnosis, meditation, or religious or shamanic practice. During a trance state, carefully designed programs of suggestion and affirmation can lead to dramatic changes in conscious behavior and perceptions.

Transmuted. To be "transmuted," is to be changed in an evolutionary manner. Just as the alchemist sought to transmute base metal into gold, the goal of the Great Work is to transmute the lower self into the higher.

Tree of Life. (Qabalah) A glyph with ten spheres and twenty-two connecting paths that functions as a "filing cabinet" for you to file corresponding facts and experiences with others of the same nature, along with the information similarly filed by millions of other students over hundreds of years.

Ultimate meaning to your life. That in fulfillment of the Great Plan pronounced in that Beginning Word, you become not only fully empowered but a conscious co-creator with the Divine Source of life and purpose of this great planet that is our home.

Unconscious. (1) A lack of consciousness. (2) An alternate word for the subconscious mind. (3) A particular reference to the personal Unconscious region of the mind where suppressed desires, memories, and feelings reside. In common usage, the personal unconscious is somewhat lesser than the subconscious mind. Some theoreticians believe that at least some psychic phenomena rise from these areas of the personality as quanta of energy/matter packets manifesting in poltergeist-like phenomena.

Universal Consciousness. "In the Beginning is the Word." But before the manifestation of the physical cosmos, there was the emanation of Consciousness and the Great Plan that first guided the formation of Spirit and then of Space/Time and Energy/Matter, leading into the Big Bang of physical creation. With physical creation we have Universal Consciousness (or the Unconscious, or the Great Unconscious) functioning in the background of all there is, and permeating every life visible and invisible and every thing visible and invisible.

Vibration. When pronouncing a word or phrase for psychic effect, it must be done (1) at a lower octave than normal; (2) louder than normal but without stress; (3) with a vibratory feeling—sort of a trembling or buzzing sensation throughout the body. With practice the effect should be noticeable wherever the words are projected inside or outside the body.

Suggested Reading—Regardie & the Ciceros: *The Tree of Life—An Illustrated Study of Magic*

Visualization. Create a vivid image in your mind, before your closed eyes, of whatever is called for—a pictured object, person, word, symbol, alphabetical letter, deity, etc., make it glow, and then retain that image as you open your eyes. Using the imagination to create vivid images of desired conditions or objects to attract those goals. Creative Visualization is a practical system for personal success.

Visualizing Scenes. The same process as above, but creating images of actual scenes rather than single objects. The scenes may be static or in motion depending upon the need.

Vital Body. Same as the Etheric Body, which see.

Waking Trance. Whenever you pay close attention to an idea, to conversation, to an object, or to your imagination, you are in an awake trance. The greater your depth of attention, the focus of your awareness, the deeper is your trance. The deeper your trance, the more you are directing your consciousness to the object of your attention.

Whole Person. An expression to represent the entirety of our potential and inclusive of all the subtle bodies. In "becoming more than you are," you are fulfilling the innate potentials that you have. You are born a potentially whole and complete person, with undeveloped powers. The meaning of life is found in developing those powers, turning them into skills, and fulfilling all your potentials. That will make you a Whole Person.

Wholeness. The conscious mind and the subconscious mind, together, are the Lower Self while the super-conscious mind is the Higher Self. Our goal is to link the two together in Wholeness.

Will. (Kabbalah) Will is found in Geburah as part of Ruach, the Conscious Self. It is that part that decides on action and what that action will be, channeling all our energies towards a specific goal.

Suggested Reading—Regardie & the Ciceros: *The Tree of Life—An Illustrated Study of Magic*

Word. *In the Beginning there <u>was</u> the Word,* but that Word—as "programming"—continues to guide the Great Plan in action and evolution.

INDEX

A

Abstract Thinking, 53, 137, 177, 195

Action, 24, 53–55, 84, 86, 95, 101, 103, 105–107, 109, 126, 138, 140, 165, 167, 172, 182, 193, 211–213, 217

Adult Child, 4–5, 179–180

Affirmation, 51, 94, 118, 120, 122, 215

Aging, 82–83, 96, 156, 159, 183, 187

Akasha, 162

Akashic Records, 2, 22, 44, 162–163, 196, 211

Alba *Domina*, 141–143, 149

"Alone and Together," 103, 106, 126–127, 146

Alpha Level, 163, 195

Altered State of Consciousness (ASC), 163

Anahata, 163

Analytical Thinking, 36

Anatomy of the Body of God, 9, 16, 163–164, 199–200

Ancestral Heritage, 25–26

Ancient Wisdom, 8

Anima, 4, 162, 164, 193, 208

Animus, 4, 162, 164, 193, 208

Anima/Animus, 4, 162, 164, 193, 208

Apas, 164

Application Programs, 165

Aquilla Bellatrix, 141–143, 149

Archbishop of Canterbury, 30

Archetypes, 2–4, 22, 40, 70, 162, 165, 170, 176, 182, 193, 208, 211

"As Above, so Below!" 17, 21, 135–136, 164–165

"Ask, and ye shall receive," 108, 110

Assiah, 165–166

Association, 22, 34–35, 55, 81, 84, 89, 94, 166, 185, 203

Astral Body, 4, 18, 30–31, 150, 162–163, 166–167, 169–172, 183–184, 188, 190, 195–196, 200, 206–208

Astral Doorways, 166, 206

Astral Light, 162–163, 166–167, 171–172, 212

Astral Plane, 166–168, 173, 183, 190, 195–196, 200, 202, 206–207

Astral Projection & Astral Travel, 166–168

Astral World, 4, 31, 150, 162, 166–169, 172, 190, 200, 206–208

Astral World, 4, 31, 150, 162, 166–169, 172, 190, 200, 206–208

Astrology, 28, 65, 74–75, 169–170, 178, 180, 192

Athens State University, 54, 58, 192

Attention, 27, 50–51, 74, 80, 89, 100, 138, 141, 157–158, 163, 170–171, 181, 187, 199, 217

Attraction, 26, 170

Attunement, 48, 50–51, 62, 89, 122

Atziluth, 170

Aura, 52–53, 136, 140, 146–148, 156, 159, 170–171, 183, 200, 205

Aura Reading, 170–171, 200, 205

Auric Energizer, 141

Automatic Writing, 4, 69, 73–74, 171, 174–175, 205, 209

Autonomic nervous system, 171

Awake, 16, 23, 33, 135, 171, 176, 200, 217

Awareness, xv–xvi, 20, 23–24, 42, 48–49, 51, 67, 72, 83–86, 88, 90–91, 99–102, 116, 120, 122, 136–141, 148, 156, 158, 163, 166, 170–171, 177–178, 184–185, 189, 196–200, 203, 208, 210, 215, 217

Azurite, 59

B

Back Office, 43

Beginning, xiv, xvi, 2, 9, 13, 19, 29–31, 40–41, 97, 99–100, 103, 114, 116, 126, 135–136, 138, 156, 164, 177–178, 184, 186, 197, 211, 216–217

Belief System, 4, 162, 172, 202, 208

Bias of Physical Perception, 29

Bible, 4, 30, 179

Big Bang, 26, 29, 216

Blockages, 45, 48–49, 87, 112, 156

Blue, 53, 118, 157

Body of Light, 9, 99, 142–143, 146, 148, 162–163, 166–168, 170–172, 207

Brain, 66, 68, 84, 137–138, 149, 163, 173, 178, 189–190, 198, 211

Brainstorming, 76–78, 125, 172, 192

Briah, 172

Bridge, 2, 62, 138, 141, 173, 188, 207

C

Calendar, 32–33

"Captain of Your Own Ship,"
xiii–xiv, xvi, 172

Catholic, 30, 142

Censorship in Religion, 173

Center for Higher Good, 53–56,
189

Center of Healing Power, 52–53,
55, 120–122

Center of Intellectual Power,
52–53

Center of Multiple Powers,
53–55, 121

Center of Power, 19, 21, 47,
52–57, 120–123, 140–141,
145–148, 157, 165, 189

Center of Rejuvenating Power,
52–53

Center of Spiritual Power, 47,
52–56, 120–123

Centers-of-Power Program,
52–56*

Chakra, 21, 68, 162–163, 187

"Challenge and Response," 72,
140

Change, xiii–xiv, 5, 8, 20, 47,
58, 65, 85–86, 91, 101–102,
111–112, 116, 147, 165, 173,
179–180, 184–185, 189, 192,
204, 206, 212, 214

Channel the Answer, 73–74, 181

Channels, 7, 25, 27, 45, 48, 94,
111–112, 173, 180, 191, 209

Channeling, 70, 72, 74, 171,
173–174, 200, 206, 217

Channeling the Subconscious,
70, 72, 174–175

Chi, 108

Childhood Memories, 2, 4–5, 24,
34, 39, 91, 109, 209

Childish Ways, 4, 179, 182

Christianity, 30, 173

Clairaudience, 84, 175, 200

Clairvoyance, 59, 69, 84, 175, 200,
207

Clan Consciousness, 65–66, 85,
136, 175

"Clean Slate," 23, 37, 195

Clearing, 50, 56, 73, 158, 175

Co-Creators, 40, 85, 99, 176, 186

Codes, xiii–xiv, 23, 25

Cognitive Relaxation, 176

Color Visualization, 56, 61

Collective Unconscious, xvi, 2–3,
6, 14, 19–20, 22–24, 26, 28, 40,
65–67, 135–136, 150, 162, 164,
166, 176, 182, 188, 193, 198,
203, 206, 211

Compose the Question, 73, 75

Conclusion, 51, 56

Conflict, 45, 71, 99, 129–130, 153

Connections, 22, 24, 100, 102–
103, 108, 164, 193, 208

Conscious Awareness, xv–xvi, 19,
22–24, 41–42, 48, 50, 66–67,
72, 83–85, 88–89, 91, 136–139,
155–156, 166, 170–171,

176–178, 185, 188, 197, 199, 203, 210

Conscious Memory, xvi, 23–24, 32–33, 39, 48, 59, 65, 67, 128, 136–137, 155, 166, 177

Conscious Mind, xiii–xvi, 1–2, 4–5, 7, 9, 14–19, 22–24, 26–29, 32–33, 37, 39–44, 48, 50, 55, 61, 65–70, 72–75, 77, 79, 83–85, 104, 125, 127–130, 135–138, 149–151, 155, 163–164, 166, 174–181, 188, 195, 197–199, 203, 209–211, 215–217

Consciousness, xiv–xv, 1–7, 9, 14–19, 21–24, 26, 28–29, 31, 37–38, 40–45, 47, 52, 57, 60, 65–72, 75, 84–85, 89–91, 101, 103–110, 123, 125, 131, 133, 135–138, 141, 148–151, 161–168, 170–171, 174–178, 181–182, 184–190, 192–193, 195–200, 203, 206–211, 213, 215–217

Constantine, 30

Control, xiv, 70, 73, 80, 85, 127–128, 141, 154, 174, 176, 178, 185, 188, 190, 195–196

Cosmos, 7–8, 165, 184, 208, 216

Create a Memory Palace, 214

Creative Thinking, 137–138, 177, 207

Creativity, 45, 65, 76, 78, 86, 112, 135, 156, 178–179

Cultural Heritage, xiii, 25

Cyber World, 108

D

Dark Matter, 27, 177

Destiny, xiii–xiv, xvi, 37, 47, 96, 122, 153, 157–159, 177, 179, 183, 185–186, 194

Developmental Process, 4, 43, 89, 179

Diversity, 25, 90, 93, 100

Divination, 4, 80, 169, 180, 212

Divine, xvi, 31, 99, 170, 174, 188, 191, 195, 216

Divine Will, xvi, 31, 99, 174, 195

Dream Book, 81, 115–116, 120, 135, 180

Dream Interpretation, 73–74, 81, 104, 135, 166, 175, 180–181, 192

Dream Journal, 74, 116, 119–122, 180–181

Dream Power, 89, 91, 111, 116, 120–123, 180–181, 203

Dream Recall, 111, 116, 180–182

Dream Works Program, 81, 120–123

Dreaming True, 119, 182

Dreams, xvi, 4, 22–23, 28, 39, 44–45, 48, 57, 66, 70, 80, 89, 91, 111–117, 119–120, 129, 136, 165–167, 180–182

E

Earth, xv, 9–10, 14–19, 21–22, 35, 60–62, 69, 73, 101, 106–107, 140–143, 146–147, 149, 162, 166, 169, 174, 182, 198, 206

Edict of Milan, 30

Ego, 3, 18, 149, 161, 182

Electromagnetic, 21, 182

Emergent Thresholds, 136

Emotion, 17, 22, 29, 66, 161, 166–168, 182–183, 212, 214

Empowering Affirmation, 94, 121–122

Empowering Imagery, 95, 121, 157, 183

Empowering Symbolism, 95–96, 115, 183

Energy, xiv–xv, 8, 11, 22, 26, 29, 31, 34, 52–54, 56–57, 59, 61, 67–71, 82, 84, 93, 95, 101–103, 108, 118, 121, 123, 126, 135–136, 140, 146–147, 156, 159, 164–165, 167, 170, 178, 182–184, 190, 193, 195, 197, 205, 212–213, 216

Enlightenment, 6, 21, 45, 48–49, 52–53, 56–57, 88, 111, 118, 120–121, 130–131

Etheric Body, 18, 30–31, 140, 150, 167, 170, 183–184, 195–196, 200, 206, 217

Etheric Plane, 167, 183–184, 195–196, 200, 206

Etheric/Physical Body, 18, 30–31, 140, 150, 167, 170, 183–184, 195–196, 200, 206

Etheric Projection, 167, 183–184, 200

Ethics, 7, 140, 170, 209

"Everything is Alive!" xiv–xv

Evolution, xiv, 30, 41, 67, 126, 129, 131, 133, 136, 138, 140, 150, 153–154, 184, 186, 198, 217

Existence, 8–9, 47, 54, 57, 82, 88, 90, 103, 112, 120–121, 131, 177, 186–187, 207, 210

Expectancy Effect, 93, 95, 185

Extrasensory Perception (ESP), 185

F

Fantasies, 2, 17

Fate, xiv, 79, 179, 185

Feelings, 4, 17, 33–34, 51–52, 62, 66, 88, 90, 94–95, 101, 112–113, 116, 161–162, 172, 185, 191, 202, 208–209, 214, 216

Feminine Magnetic Energies, 17

Firewall, 24

Focusing, 50, 56, 89, 138, 157–158, 205

"For dust thou art," 21

Forgotten Memories, 4, 28, 34, 39, 66, 161, 182, 185, 198, 208

Fourth Dimension, 31

G

Gaia, 22

Galaxy, 22, 36

"Garbage Dump", 5, 66

Genesis, 9, 21, 186

Genetic Heritage, xiii, 179, 198

Gnostic, 30, 193

God's Image, xiv–xv, 9, 30–31, 164, 186

God's Word, xv, 30–31, 164

Gods in the making, 40

Goal Statement, 56, 93, 121

Grand Gallery, 9, 11–13, 16, 18–19

Great Mysteries, 6–7, 11–12

Great Plan, the, xiv, xvi, 10, 41–42, 138, 164, 176–177, 186, 215–216

Great Pyramid, 9–16, 19–20, 23, 42, 69, 108, 125, 164

Great Work, 1, 6, 24, 108, 127, 176, 186, 189–190, 193, 202, 215

Green, 53, 55–56, 118, 139, 163

Green Thinking, 53, 139

Group Action, 105–107, 109, 140

Group Mind, 3, 73, 77, 101, 106–107, 140, 146–149, 162, 175–176, 186–187

Growth, xiv, 8, 23, 43–45, 47–49, 53, 82, 87, 89–90, 92, 110–112, 116, 120–121, 127, 129, 131–132, 139–140, 151, 153–154, 156, 174, 177, 180–181, 184, 186, 191, 195, 203, 210

Growth Blockage, 129

Guided Imagery, 162, 187

Guided Meditation, 45, 154, 162, 187, 195, 201

H

Happiness, 2, 45, 47–48, 54, 87, 93, 117, 121, 131–132, 136, 156, 177–178

Healing through Self-hypnosis, 57, 92, 135, 187

Health, 37, 45, 49, 53, 55, 62, 65, 71–72, 79–81, 99, 101, 118, 138, 153, 156, 170–172, 175, 183, 187, 194

Health Diagnosis through Self-hypnosis, 187

Hidden programming, 37

Higher Consciousness, 1, 4, 18, 21, 90, 100, 123, 138, 150, 162, 173, 181, 186, 188–190, 192, 196, 199, 207–208, 211, 215

Higher Self, 90, 126, 138, 150, 188–190, 192, 202, 211, 217

Holy Guardian Angel, 126, 188, 190

Horoscope, 23, 70, 74, 166, 169, 179, 185, 205

Hydraulic ram, 20

Hypnoproduction, 49, 91, 188

Hypnosis, 4, 9, 22, 34, 45, 49, 51, 89, 91, 156, 162–163, 175, 188–189, 197, 199, 202–203, 209, 215

Hypnotic induction, 188–190

I

I AM, 31, 57–58, 75, 93–96, 118–119, 132, 156–159, 178, 183, 189, 191–192, 204, 213

Icons, 189–190, 211

Identity, 90, 162, 164–165, 189, 192

Images, 4, 22, 31, 50, 61, 72–73, 75, 80, 108, 115, 118–119, 122, 140, 142–143, 148, 151, 156–157, 162, 171, 175, 189–190, 193, 197, 208, 211–212, 217

Imagination, 42, 73–74, 80, 86, 137, 148, 157, 166–168, 172, 175, 177, 190, 213–214, 216–217

Indigo, 52–56

Individual Memories, xv, 3, 65, 175–176, 195

Induction (See Hypnotic Induction), 190

Information, xiv, xvi, 18, 23, 28, 37, 41, 44, 70, 73, 76, 79, 103, 128, 136, 142, 155, 163, 167, 171, 173–176, 180–182, 190, 192, 210, 215

Information Packets, 190, 215

Inner Child, 5, 189

Inner Dialogue, 94, 140, 190–191

Inner Divinity, 191, 205

Inner Therapist, 87, 191

Innovative Thinking, 137, 139

Inspiration, xvi, 7, 25, 42, 126, 172, 192, 211

Instincts, 4, 162, 205, 209

Integration, 3, 6, 136, 151, 176, 182, 192

Intention, 8, 42, 73, 140–141, 155, 174–175, 177, 182, 185, 189, 195, 212, 214

Interactive Screen Technique, 117, 119–120

Interaction, 36, 44, 88–90, 99, 107, 110, 116–118, 120, 165, 198, 207, 210

International Parapsychology Research Foundation (IPRF), 192

Interpretation, 9, 36, 70, 73, 75, 81, 104, 135, 166, 169, 173, 175, 180–181, 192

Intuition, 45, 66, 84–85, 128–129, 137–138, 178, 180, 192, 207, 213

Intuitive Thinking, 137–139

J

Jewishness, 30

Journal it, 73–74, 93, 116, 121, 156, 160, 175, 180–181, 215

Jungian Psychology, 192

K

Kabbalah, 28, 35–36, 75, 140, 165, 193–194, 201, 212, 217

Kabbalistic correspondences 23, 201

King's Chamber, 9–16, 18–20, 69–70

"Know Thyself," 194

Know Yourself, 79, 94, 109, 111, 121, 125, 129, 131–132, 181, 187, 194
Kundalini, 21, 162

L

Language of the Unconscious, 36, 75, 137–138, 188
Land Speaks, 25–26
Law of attraction, 26
Leaf of Progress, 60–62
Levitation, 101, 135, 194
Life between Lives, 2, 43, 67, 109, 193–194, 201–202
Life-Energy, 68, 108
Life-Journey, 194
Life Purpose, xvi, 6, 37, 67, 82, 132, 186, 194–195, 197, 215–216
"Light of Men," 126, 163, 211
Logical Thinking, 137
Love, xiv, xvii–xviii, 5, 25–26, 92, 131, 140–141, 178–179
Lower Consciousness, 1, 4, 149–150, 161, 163, 166, 170–171, 178, 188, 193, 196, 199, 206, 208, 213, 215–216
Lucid Dream, 195

M

Magic, 12, 28, 105, 140, 167, 193–194, 206, 212, 216–217
Magical Personality, 170, 195
Magick, 86, 106, 139, 166, 173, 186, 190, 193, 205

Magnus Spiritus, 141–143, 149
Major Arcana, 22, 40, 165
Make Conscious the Unconscious, 22, 25, 27–28, 40, 42, 69–70, 74, 84, 177
Manager, xv, 41, 43, 67, 138, 150, 178, 197
Masculine Electrical Energies, 17
Master (the) Process, 72
Mater Libertas, 141–143, 149
Mater Stellarum, 141–143, 149
Matrix, 1, 23, 31, 37, 39–41, 70, 110, 166, 170–171, 183, 195, 199, 206, 210
Matter, xiv, 5, 8, 27, 29–31, 37, 67, 71, 73, 78–79, 81, 108, 110, 127, 130, 136, 164, 174, 178–179, 190, 193, 195, 197, 201, 204, 216
Meaning to Life, xvi, 36, 38, 63, 67, 130, 177, 179, 186, 195–196, 198, 201, 216–217
Meditation, 4, 8, 22, 28, 35, 45, 49, 70, 72–74, 79–80, 89, 93, 105–107, 127, 129, 135–136, 154, 162–163, 166, 174, 187, 194–197, 199–203, 209, 215
Medium, 173–174, 178, 194, 196, 207
Mediumship, 173–174, 196, 200, 207
Memory Bank, 39
Mental Body, 18, 30–31, 52, 83, 150, 162, 167, 170–172, 183,

187–188, 195–197, 199–200, 206–207

Mental Health, 45, 49, 52, 65, 79, 117, 170, 172, 187

Mental Plane, 167, 173, 183, 195–196, 200, 202, 206–207

Mental Telepathy, 58, 84, 101, 196–197, 200, 212

Middle Consciousness, 1, 15, 17–18, 109, 140, 147–150, 173, 176, 188, 190, 199

Middle Pillar, 140–141, 143, 145–148, 150–151, 193

Mind-body connection, 79, 81, 197

Mind's Eye, 61, 140, 145, 147–148

Moon, xv, 10, 21, 31, 43, 65, 71, 141–142, 149, 177–178, 182, 184

Morals, 7, 209

Mythic Images, 4, 75, 162, 208

N

Next Step, 30, 72, 75, 131, 133, 151

New Age Psychology, 67, 138, 197

New Consciousness, xiii, 7–8, 30, 36, 44, 65, 67, 70–72, 83–84, 91, 102, 107, 137–138, 140, 149, 160, 165, 169, 171, 173, 177, 180–182, 184–186, 188–189, 192, 194, 197, 203, 210, 212

New World Order, 70–71

Noosphere, 165, 198

"Not my Will, but Thine," xv

O

Olivine, 59

Operating System, xvii, 4, 162, 171–172, 185, 198–200, 208

"Our Father," 9, 39–40, 92, 106–107, 185–186, 189

Out-of-Body, 49, 86, 93, 101, 112, 115–116, 122, 135, 168, 181, 195

P

Pagan, 30

Pain Management, 80, 199

Paranormal, 67–69, 92, 139, 161, 168, 197, 200

Past-Life Regression, 43, 51–52, 69, 104, 198–199

Personal Consciousness, xv, 1–3, 5–7, 9, 15–19, 21, 23, 26, 28–29, 41–43, 45, 65, 67, 69–71, 75, 89–90, 104–105, 108–110, 135–138, 140, 149–150, 160–161, 163–166, 175–178, 180–182, 184–188, 193–195, 197, 199–200, 203, 206–207, 210–211, 216–217

Personal Fantasy, 1–2, 78, 136–137, 164

Personal Goal, 1–2, 26, 45, 61, 69, 78–79, 93, 116, 120–121, 155–156, 158, 160, 182, 210–211, 217

Personal Unconscious, xv, 1–3, 5–6, 15–17, 19, 21, 23–24, 26–29, 35–36, 39, 41–43, 65, 67, 69–70, 75, 85, 104, 135–136, 138, 150, 160–161, 164, 166, 175–177, 182, 184–185, 188, 193, 197, 206, 211, 216

Personality, 3–4, 18, 23, 39, 125, 161, 169–170, 179, 188–190, 192–193, 195–196, 200, 202, 205–206, 208, 216

Physical Health, 45, 49, 52, 65, 71–72, 79, 81, 99, 170, 183, 187

Physics, 8, 67, 77, 197

Physical/Etheric Body, 30–31, 140, 150, 166–167, 169–170, 183–184, 196, 200, 206, 216

Power, the, xv, 1, 9, 20–21, 26, 32, 45, 47–48, 50, 52–60, 67, 71, 83, 87–89, 92–97, 99, 101–103, 106, 111–112, 116, 118, 120–123, 128, 132, 141–142, 145–146, 148–149, 153, 155, 157–160, 165, 168, 172, 177, 181, 189–192, 197, 204, 206–207, 211

Practical Experience, 8, 31, 73, 85, 168, 174, 199, 203

Prana, 108

Prayer, 4, 8, 73–74, 79–80, 105–107, 129, 194, 199, 206, 209

Precognition, 49, 59, 69, 84, 200

Previous Lives, xiii, 2, 19, 37, 39, 110, 194

Problem Solving, 45, 53, 65, 70–71, 75–76, 135

Projection Screen Technique, 120

Psyche, 2–4, 17–18, 136, 161, 176, 179, 193

Psychic Body, 18, 48, 67, 85–86, 140–143, 166, 170–172, 182, 188, 196, 200, 205, 207, 216

Psychic Center, 53, 140–141, 143, 148, 188

Psychic Empowerment, 18, 44–45, 110, 136, 151, 156, 175, 180, 182, 188, 200–201, 207, 212–213

Psychic Knowledge, 42, 44, 65, 68, 86, 101, 112, 119, 125, 127–128, 156, 192, 196, 200–201, 211

Psychic Potentials, 4, 41, 44, 48, 112, 125, 177, 179, 209, 216

Psychic Powers, 39, 41–42, 44–45, 48, 65, 67–69, 84–85, 101–104, 125, 139, 151, 156, 177, 182, 185, 198, 200–201, 205, 207, 209–211

Psychokinesis (PK), 200–201

Psychological processor, 40

Psychometry, 86, 201, 205

Puer Maris, 141–143, 149

Pyramid, 9–23, 42, 69, 108, 125, 164, 199

Q

Qabala, 193, 201

Qabalistic path-working, 45, 165, 187, 201

Quantum, 8, 60, 67, 71, 77, 100, 102–103, 139, 197

Quartz Crystal, 59–60

Queen's Chamber, 10–16, 18–19, 69

Quit-Smoking, 62

R

Rational Analysis, 41, 66, 86, 177

Reality, 4, 13, 91, 96, 103, 108, 120, 140, 162, 165, 172, 183, 185, 190, 201–202, 208

Recreate a story, 213–214

Recreate an event, 213–214

Recreate an event, 213–214

Recreating your room, 213

Red, 20, 53, 55, 77

Regression, 34, 43, 52, 69, 104, 194, 199, 202

Regression therapy, 34

Reincarnation, 13, 194, 202, 207

Rejuvenation, 45, 55–56, 65, 69, 81–83, 90, 96, 118, 122, 135–136, 157, 183, 202

Relationship, 3, 7, 54, 62–63, 65, 67, 95, 109, 130, 164, 166, 169, 177, 190, 193, 197–198, 209

Remember the day backwards, 214

Repressed Emotions, 19, 85

Rose Quartz, 59

Rules of Conduct, 23

S

Sarcophagus, 20

School of Life, xiii, 6, 109, 120

Self, 3, 13, 37, 82, 90, 126, 130–131, 138, 150, 153, 166, 183, 187–190, 192–194, 202, 204–206, 211, 215, 217

Self-Analysis, 79, 202

Self Centered, 13, 130–131, 192

Self-Development, 45, 61, 122, 131, 186, 188, 202

Self-Dialogue, 95, 183, 204

Self-Direction, xv, 203

Self-Discovery, 49, 57, 79, 111, 116, 180, 194

Self-Empowerment, xiii, xvi, 4, 48–49, 58, 87–91, 93–94, 97, 111–112, 123, 128–129, 131, 136, 153–155, 157, 160, 162, 164, 170, 172–173, 181, 185, 187–188, 191, 199, 203–204, 206, 209–210

Self-Hypnosis, 4, 22, 34, 58, 70, 79, 81–83, 91, 93, 104, 129, 135–136, 153–157, 159–160, 162–163, 170, 175, 182, 187–189, 197, 199–200, 202–204, 209

Self-Imaging, 213

Self-Imposed Barriers, 125–127

Self-Empowerment Cues, 97

Self-Hypnosis, 4, 22, 34, 58, 70, 79, 81–83, 91, 93, 104, 129, 135–136, 153–157, 159–160, 162–163, 170, 175, 182, 187–189, 197, 199–200, 202–204, 209

Self-Improvement, 165, 199, 203–204, 206, 215

Self-Knowledge, 165, 194, 204–205

Self-Programming, 163, 204

Self-Talk, 204

Self-Understanding, 23, 169, 194, 198, 205

Serpent Power, 21

Sexual Dysfunction, 63*

Sexual Relations, 66

Shadow, 4, 162, 193, 205, 208, 213

Skills, xiv, 25, 39, 41–42, 49, 51, 54, 68–69, 84–85, 91, 95, 102, 104, 108, 112, 114–115, 117, 119, 125, 132, 139, 153, 175, 177, 181, 185, 188, 195, 198–200, 205, 210–211, 217

Skrying, 175, 193, 202, 205–206

Skrying in the Spirit Vision, 205–206

Smoking, 61–62, 96–97, 118

Solar System, xv, 22, 71, 159, 182

Sonic pump, 20

Soul, xv, 1–3, 13, 16, 31, 40, 47–48, 69, 88, 108–110, 121, 138, 150, 161, 164, 167, 174, 184, 192, 195–196, 202, 206–207, 210

Source, xiv–xvi, 9, 21, 26, 39, 45, 57, 68–69, 79, 81, 88, 99, 126, 128, 150, 162, 165, 186, 199, 211, 216

Source of Human Knowledge, xiv–xv, 21, 39, 126, 128

Space/Time, 26, 31, 69, 168, 175, 216

Spark of Divinity, 191, 206

Spirit, 7, 25, 29–31, 44, 49, 69, 81–82, 84, 87–88, 92, 99–101, 107–110, 112, 120–123, 135, 142, 149, 156, 162, 173–174, 178, 181, 194, 196, 200, 205–207, 211, 216

Spirit Being, 99–100, 120–121, 123, 142, 162, 206–207

Spirit Body, 29–31, 49, 81, 99, 135, 142, 149, 162, 196, 205–207, 216

Spirit Communication, 69, 84, 101, 109–110, 135, 173–174, 181, 196, 200, 205–207, 211

Spirit Guide, 88, 120–122, 156, 196, 200, 205–207

Spirit Helper, 207

Spirit Realm, 44, 49, 81, 87–88, 92, 99, 107, 109–110, 120–123, 206–207

Spirit World, 25, 29, 31, 87, 92, 99–100, 107–108, 110, 122–123, 135, 200, 206–207

Spiritual Attainment, 6, 45

Spiritual Body, 18, 29–30, 52, 83, 86, 99, 139–140, 150, 167, 170–172, 194, 196, 200–201, 206–208

Spiritual Enlightenment, 6, 44, 47–48, 53, 55–56, 118, 120–121

Spiritual Genotype, 47, 207

Spiritual Growth, 23, 44–45, 47–48, 53, 86, 91–92, 109–110, 112, 120–121, 139, 150, 173–174, 186, 194, 203

Spiritual Interaction, 44, 90, 99, 109, 207

Spiritual Plane, 30, 167, 196, 200–201, 206–207

Spiritual Realities, 44, 99

Spiritualism, 7, 175, 192, 196, 207–208

Spiritualist, 208

Spirituality, 7, 52, 99–100, 107, 123, 208

Storehouse of Knowledge, xvi, 43, 91, 203

Storehouse of Personal Experience, 29, 91, 135

Stress, 2, 12, 61, 90, 96–97, 118, 156, 159, 187, 216

Sub-Atomic, 8, 71, 85

Subconscious Check-in Program, 48–52, 55–56

Sub-Conscious powers, 135

Subconscious Memories, xv–xvi, 1–5, 16–17, 19, 21–25, 27–28, 32–35, 37, 39–41, 43–44, 65–68, 91, 110, 135, 161–162, 171, 176, 181, 185, 187–188, 195, 197–199, 201, 208–209, 215–216

Subconscious Mind, xiii–xvi, 1–7, 9, 14, 16–17, 19, 21–29, 32–33, 37, 39–45, 47–48, 50–51, 55–56, 61, 65–70, 72, 74–75, 77–85, 94, 100–105, 107, 110–111, 115, 117–118, 120, 125, 127–130, 132, 135–138, 148–151, 155, 161–164, 166–167, 171, 173–174, 176–177, 180–182, 187–188, 191, 193, 195, 197–199, 201, 203, 205, 208–211, 215–217

Subconsciousness, xiv, xv, 17, 18, 21, 23, 34, 36, 42, 65, 68, 137, 177, 208, 209

Subconscious Resources, xvi, 3–4, 7, 24–25, 40–42, 47–48, 61, 66–68, 70, 72, 80, 83, 87, 95–97, 102–103, 110–111, 118, 120–122, 176–177, 180, 187–188, 191, 197–198, 203, 209–211

Subterranean Chamber, 13, 15–17, 19–20, 22, 69

Success, 5, 22, 45, 47–49, 53–54, 60–61, 63, 70, 84, 87, 90, 93–97, 112, 118, 121–122, 131–132, 136, 156, 158, 170–171, 183, 185, 217

Sun, 22, 30–31, 43, 65, 102, 141, 163, 169, 177–178, 184

Super Conscious Mind, 208

Super Heroes, 126

Superman, 211

Symbolic Thinking, 137

Symbols, 21, 36, 70, 75, 80–81, 96, 108, 137, 142–143, 149, 166, 171, 180, 183, 189–190, 211

T

Table-Tilting, Table-Lifting, Table-Turning, 212

Tarot, 4, 22, 28, 35–36, 40, 70, 74–75, 78, 135, 165–166, 180, 192–193, 212

Telekinesis, 178, 200, 212

Telepathy, 49, 59, 69, 84, 101, 197, 200, 212

Teleportation, 200, 212

Therapeutic Applications, 92–93

Therapeutic Power, 45, 52, 87–89, 92–93, 203

Thinking, 42, 53, 65, 68, 81, 100, 103, 127, 129, 137–139, 163, 166, 177, 196, 208

Thought, xiii, 22, 41, 50, 66, 69, 76, 85, 94, 106, 137, 149, 163, 166–167, 170, 173, 177, 184, 187, 191, 196, 198–199, 212–213

Thought Form, 76, 149, 166, 170, 173, 184, 212

Three Levels of Consciousness, 13, 16, 136, 149, 178, 213

Time, 7, 10, 12, 21, 26, 28–35, 50, 54, 56, 65, 67, 69, 73–74, 76–78, 80, 82, 84–85, 93–94, 100–101, 106, 111, 113, 115, 117, 120, 128–129, 131, 133, 137, 142, 145–146, 151, 156–157, 162, 168–169, 175, 178, 180–181, 185–186, 191, 194–195, 197, 200, 202, 207–209, 213, 216

Tools of Nature, 58

Trained Mind, 27, 69, 205

Training Programs, 213

Trance, 58, 155–158, 162–163, 166, 171, 174, 180, 187–188, 196, 204, 212, 215, 217

Transmittal, 73–74, 175

Transmuted, 215

Transpersonal Psychology, 139

Tree of Life, 62, 92, 165–167, 172, 187, 193–194, 201–202, 206, 212, 215–217

Trees, 58, 60, 92

Trinity, 29, 136, 178

U

Ultimate meaning to your life, xvi, 186, 216

Unconscious, xv–xvi, 2–3, 6, 14–15, 17, 19–24, 26–29, 32, 35–37, 40, 42–43, 65–67, 70, 75, 84–85, 104, 125, 127–128,

135–136, 138, 150, 161–162, 164, 166, 176–177, 182, 185, 188, 193, 198, 203, 206, 208, 211–212, 216

Universal Consciousness, xiv–xv, 1–3, 6, 9, 14–17, 21–24, 26, 38, 40–41, 66–67, 75, 84, 101, 103, 105–107, 110, 123, 125, 136–137, 150, 164–166, 176–177, 182, 193, 195, 197–199, 206, 208, 210–211, 216

Universal Field of Consciousness, 21–22, 103, 110, 166, 195

Universal Memories, xv, 1–3, 6, 16–17, 19, 21–23, 38, 40–41, 66–67, 110, 176, 182, 195, 197–199, 208

V

Vibration, 141–142, 216

Victim of Fate, xiv

Violet, 54, 56, 143, 145

Visualization, 56, 61, 79, 106, 157, 176, 187, 199, 216–217

Visualizing scenes, 148, 217

Vital Body, 9, 162, 167, 217

W

Waking Trance, 163, 217

Whole Person, xv–xvi, 3, 6, 43–44, 69–70, 86, 108–109, 126, 130, 151, 153–154, 171,

176, 184, 186, 192–193, 195, 200, 203, 210–211, 217

Wholeness, 43, 67, 90, 104, 178, 191, 198, 217

Will, xiv–xv, xvii–xviii, 1–6, 8–9, 15, 21, 23–24, 26, 28–29, 31–34, 36–37, 39, 41, 43–44, 49, 51, 57, 61, 63, 73–82, 84–88, 92, 94–95, 99, 102–103, 106–107, 109–110, 116–120, 122–123, 126, 130, 132, 136, 142, 146–150, 154–160, 165–166, 171, 174–176, 178, 180–181, 184–185, 187, 191, 195, 202, 204–207, 210–212, 214–215, 217

Wisdom, xvi, 5–6, 8, 22, 40, 47, 110, 130, 138, 163, 180, 199, 207

Word, The, xiv, xvi, 13, 29, 31–32, 49, 69, 81, 96, 100, 107–108, 118–119, 138, 142, 164, 185, 198, 201, 216–217

World Peace, 71, 99

World Problems, 54, 57, 102–105, 109, 111, 131, 198

World Trade Center, 35

Y

Yellow, 53, 118, 143, 145

"Your Destiny is in Your Own Hands!", xiii, 156–157

TO WRITE TO THE AUTHORS

If you wish to contact the authors or would like more information about this book, please write to the authors in care of Llewellyn Worldwide Ltd., and we will forward your request. Both the authors and publisher appreciate hearing from you and learning of your enjoyment of this book and how it has helped you. Llewellyn Worldwide Ltd. cannot guarantee that every letter written to the authors can be answered, but all will be forwarded. Please write to:

Carl Llewellyn Weschcke and Joe Slate, Ph.D.
% Llewellyn Worldwide
2143 Wooddale Drive
Woodbury, MN 55125-2989

Please enclose a self-addressed stamped envelope for reply, or $1.00 to cover costs. If outside the USA, enclose an international postal reply coupon.

PRIVATE LESSONS IN SELF-EMPOWERMENT!

Imagine an original set of lessons in self-empowerment, complete by themselves, delivered to you by the authors of *Self-Empowerment Through Self-Hypnosis*. Now you can listen to these amazing private lessons with the *Self-Empowerment Through Self-Hypnosis* **CD Companion!**

This is *not* a book reading. These are *additional* and completely independent teachings shared live by Dr. Joe H. Slate. By themselves they're incredible. Combined with the book you'll have an amazing system for spiritual development. On the CD you'll learn:

- The true nature of the conscious and subconscious minds
- The facts about hypnosis and trance: what they are and are not
- How to enhance sensitivity by retraining your imagination
- Simple ways to improve your memory
- Astounding tricks to increase mind power
- How to make use of normal sleep to access your subconscious mind
- Ways to use Western mystical technologies—Kabbalah, Tarot, astrology—for inner and outer development

These exclusive lessons are *only* available on this CD. You'll also receive an original booklet written by Carl Llewellyn Weschcke that reveals everything you need to use this CD effectively, including a convenient glossary of terms. This set discloses induction techniques and scripts that will empower you to realize your potential both spiritually and practically.

The *Self-Empowerment Through Self-Hypnosis* **CD Companion** will help you on your path of spiritual evolution, vibrant health, and potentially unlimited wealth. Order and use it to improve your life!

Self-Empowerment Through Self-Hypnosis CD Companion
Carl Llewellyn Weschcke and Joe H. Slate, Ph.D.
9780738726724   CD and booklet
$16.95

Psychic Empowerment for Everyone

You Have the Power, Learn How to Use It

CARL LLEWELLYN WESCHCKE
JOE H. SLATE PhD

Surging within us all is a limitless wellspring of psychic power. Open yourself to spiritual enlightenment, personal enrichment, and lifelong empowerment by tapping into this incredible resource.

Llewellyn's own Carl Llewellyn Weschcke has teamed up with parapsychologist Joe H. Slate to write this comprehensive guide to the psychic realm. Exploring the link between psychic phenomena and the paranormal, they map inner and outer psychic dimensions and explain how to access them. Easy techniques in self-hypnosis and dream work demonstrate how to expand your consciousness, navigate psychic planes, and communicate with the spirit realm and your higher self. Featuring a seven-day psychic empowerment plan, this exciting path to self-discovery will help you develop vast psychic skills to enrich your relationships, enhance your career, grow spiritually, fulfill your life purpose, and prepare for 2012.

978-0-7387-1893-4, 264 pp., 6 x 9 $15.95

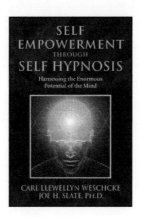

Self-Empowerment through Self-Hypnosis
Harnessing the Enormous Potential of the Mind
Carl Llewellyn Weschcke
Joe H. Slate, Ph.D.

Take charge of your life. Realize your full potential. Discover the limitless opportunities of self-hypnosis.

Carl Llewellyn Weschcke, chairman of Llewellyn Worldwide, and Joe H. Slate, a licensed psychologist and experienced hypnotist, can help you tap into the unlimited power of your subconscious. Follow helpful scripts and practice easy techniques—involving trance, meditation, and sleep—to transform into the empowered person you're meant to be. Once you've learned how to access your subconscious, anything is possible: changing your appearance, quitting bad habits, elevating your consciousness, and evolving into your higher self.

978-0-7387-1928-3, 264 pp., 6 x 9 $15.95

Connecting to the Power of Nature
Joe H. Slate PhD

From the calming grace of a garden to the stabilizing strength of a tree, nature holds a magnificent power—one that awakens human potential.

Connecting to the Power of Nature opens a gateway to self-discovery, helping you achieve an attuned, balanced, and empowered state of mind, body, and spirit. This unique book offers an extensive collection of enjoyable and inspiring step-by-step activities and meditations, using rocks, trees, flowers, leaves, and other natural elements. Cope with grief, manage stress, get insight into problems, discover new power in yourself, and accomplish your goals by tapping into nature's power. The possibilities for creating a richer and more rewarding life are endless.

978-0-7387-1566-7, 216 pp., 5³⁄₁₆ x 8 $14.95

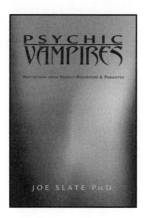

Psychic Vampires
Protection from Energy Predators & Parasites
JOE H. SLATE, PH.D.

Is somebody sucking your life-force energy?

Consuming energy instead of blood, psychic vampires come in a variety of unsuspecting guises. In this unique approach to the subject, you will be introduced to a trio of new thieves: (1) group vampires—organized efforts of predator corporations and institutions; (2) parasitic vampires—an inner vampire state that feeds on your internal energy resources; and (3) global vampirism—widespread conditions that erode the human potential for growth and progress.

Exploring environmental, developmental, and past-life factors, *Psychic Vampires* incorporates practical, step-by-step empowerment procedures that anyone can use to protect themselves and replenish their own energy reserves.

978-0-7387-0191-2, 264 pp., 6 x 9 $15.95